# My Journey Home

## REPORTING ON THE FINAL DAYS OF MY CANCER BATTLE

### Don McCall
as told to
### Karen I. Westphalen

Windtree
Press

Copyright © 2021 by Karen I. Westphalen

All rights reserved.

No part of this book may be reproduced in any form or by any electronic or mechanical means, including information storage and retrieval systems, without written permission from the author, except for the use of brief quotations in a book review.

Published by Windtree Press

https://windtreepress.com

Cover Design by Christie Caughie

PRINT ISBN: 978-1-952447-84-6

EBOOK ISBN: 978-1-952447-83-9

BISAC Categories

RELIGION / Christian Living / Personal Memoirs

RELIGION / Christian Living / Death, Grief, Bereavement

RELIGION / Inspirational

BIOGRAPHY & AUTOBIOGRAPHY / Personal Memoirs

MEDICAL / Diseases / Cancer

## CONTENTS

Foreword     v

**Section1: The Big C**     1
1. Diagnosis     3
2. Whipple Surgery     11
3. Living through Treatment     21
4. Life Gets an Expiration Date     29

**Section 2: The Journey Begins**     35
5. Day One     37
6. Making Plans and Letting Go     45
7. Things I'll Probably Never Do Again     55
8. Connections and Purpose     67
9. The Inconsistent Energy Curve     75
10. Rejection, Recycling, Remembering     89
11. Leaving the Job     97

**Section 3: Reconnecting Past, Present, And Future**     109
12. Seeing My Son's Family     111
13. Finding Peace in the Inevitable     121
14. Visiting the Oregon Coast     129
15. Introduction to Hospice     137
16. How People Respond to Sad News     147
17. Running out of Marbles     157

**Section 4: Hospice Care Begins**     165
18. Mother Teresa, Billy Joel, and Faith in Action     167
19. Starting to Lose Ground     177
20. John and Johnnie     185
21. Confusion and Compassion     195
22. Meeting the Hospice Team     205
23. Inspired by Nature     213
24. Facing Reduced Mobility     223

| | |
|---|---|
| 25. Birthday, Bills, Bath Water | 231 |
| 26. Setbacks and Exhaustion | 239 |
| 27. Portland, Oregon | 245 |

**Section 5: Daily Routines and Worsening Symptoms** — 253

| | |
|---|---|
| 28. A Need to Re-Build Bridges | 255 |
| 29. Bounce-backs, Bears and Barbershops | 263 |
| 30. More Reactions to Sad News | 271 |
| 31. No Roadmap for What Lies Ahead | 281 |
| 32. Fear, Friends, Fatigue, FAITH | 289 |
| 33. Seeking and Accepting Help | 295 |

**Section 6: To Die in The Summertime** — 303

| | |
|---|---|
| 34. Memories: One Joy that Cancer Hasn't Stolen | 305 |
| 35. Finding Ways to Stay Positive | 317 |
| 36. The New Normal: Aides and Brain Episodes | 329 |
| 37. A Reliable, Competent Healthcare Team | 339 |
| 38. Youth, Choices, Maturity, Appreciation | 351 |
| 39. Mobility Throughout a Lifetime | 363 |
| 40. Planning for the End and Beyond | 371 |
| 41. The Handwriting on the Wall | 383 |// 
| Epilogue | 397 |

| | |
|---|---|
| *Acknowledgments in Alphabetical Order* | 403 |
| *Author Photo* | 405 |

# FOREWORD

In March 2012 Don McCall was diagnosed with cholangiocarcinoma, cancer of the bile duct. This is his story from diagnosis through treatment and death. For me, it's a story seen through filters of love, friendship, and ultimately having to say goodbye. Don was hugely important in my life. Recording, transcribing, and sharing his story is my final gift to him.

My hope is that anyone reading this story may find some blessings for themselves as well. Don was not perfect. He was not a saint. But, to me, he was a good man.

I'll start off with a quick explanation of how this project went from a series of recordings to the book that follows, and then I'll talk about Don and how we met. Then we'll let Don's words take you through his journey. In case anyone's wondering, all the names have been changed except for Don's and mine.

**From a No-Brainer to a Non-Starter**

In March of 2013 I was 44 years old and living near Portland, Oregon. I had a temporary job which involved visiting truck stops throughout the U.S. to inspect electric plug-in stations for tractor-trailers. My best friend, Don, had been diagnosed with and treated for

## FOREWORD

cancer in 2012, but a year later the cancer was back and it was terminal. He was 75 years old and only had a few months to live. We were romantically involved when we first met in 2010, but by 2013 we were mostly focused on dealing with his illness.

Once Don had his prognosis, it wasn't long 'til we decided to make daily audio recordings for as long as he was capable of telling me about each of his last days, to document his experiences as he faced the end of his life. For several years, I had enthusiastically been making audio recordings of people telling their life stories, and editing those recordings into listenable narratives. Don liked to talk about his life. I liked to record stories; and facing death seemed like one of the most significant stories a person could tell. So, making daily recordings every day for five months was a no-brainer. We'd either record in the living room of his downtown Portland apartment, or I'd record the conversation in a phone call, putting him on speaker phone. Sometimes I was six miles away, where I rented a room in a beautiful, peaceful home in Beaverton, Oregon. Other times I was up to three time zones away, wherever I was doing truck stop inspections.

By the time Don died on September 13, 2013, he and I had made recordings on 171 days. Day One was the day after his primary care doctor confirmed that his cancer had returned and there was no cure. He died on Day 175. For over two years after his death, the recording files resided on my computer and in cloud storage. I had no idea what to do with them. I thought about editing the audio into listenable chunks to create a podcast, but with that much material, and the low audio quality I had recorded coming through my cell phone, plus the full-time job I started in April 2014, the project had gone from a no-brainer to a non-starter.

One rainy weekend in November 2015, I rented a yurt at an Oregon coast campground. In November in Oregon, daylight does not stick around for dinner. Rather than cook by myself, at my campsite in the dark and the rain, I went to a restaurant in nearby Manzanita. I sat at the bar where it wouldn't be so obvious that I was the only person dining alone. A man soon took the seat next to me and we had a fun conversation, during which we discovered we were the same age and he was single too. We made plans to meet up there the following evening to watch the Oregon Ducks football game. I was absolutely stoked – in town only a couple hours and I already had a date lined up for Saturday night!

Saturday evening I arrived at the bar at the agreed-upon time. My date didn't. Instead, about a half hour went by and a different man asked if the seat next to me was available, and I figured that by then it *was*. Instead of watching the Ducks, I had an even more entertaining and enjoyable conversation that evening, and the gentleman even bought me dinner. We discussed the fact that I'd been stood up, and devised a variety of ridiculous scenarios to explain how or why that might've happened. He asked, "If Romeo made such a great impression on you, why didn't you ask for his phone number?" Well, yeah, good point. This man was (*is*) an award-winning, best-selling author, and he gave me his business card when I eventually left for the campground later that evening.

I ended up keeping in touch with that author, and in February of 2016, I told him about my recordings of Don. He strongly recommended transcribing them, and explained that if it seemed like a daunting task – transcribing a speech recording takes about three to four times as long as the actual recording, and I had a lot of them – I should simply commit to spending a couple hours a week on the project. Assuming the recordings were that important to me, I had to do *something*, even if I didn't yet know what the end result would be. I took his advice and for the next two and a half years I spent two hours nearly every week transcribing Don's recordings, until – in August of 2018 – I had finished with all 171 of them.

In February of 2019 I began editing the transcriptions. By then I was living with my boyfriend whom I'd met in 2017, and my employer had agreed to let me work a four-day week, so I had Fridays available and could spend more than two hours a week on the project.

That's how over 171 audio recordings became a book. Now, who was Don McCall?

FOREWORD

**Older Man, (Somewhat) Younger Woman**

Don first approached me in Pioneer Courthouse Square in downtown Portland, Oregon in June of 2010. I was wearing a big yellow sign with red lettering, asking passers-by to answer the Question of the Week. I had my c. 2005 Marantz portable digital recorder and an Audio-Technica shotgun microphone. To the best of my abilities, I convinced people to let me record them answering the question I had come up with. Don showed up with his first, brand-new, digital SLR camera, to see whether he'd find enough going on in the Square to start a blog about the one-block public space, nicknamed Portland's living room. Later on he told me that finding me there, gathering random recordings, confirmed for him that yes, the Square would provide enough material to start a fun blog.

Why would a 41-year-old woman with degrees in civil engineering and music, plus a professional engineer's license, born and raised in Massachusetts, be hanging around downtown Portland, Oregon on a weekday morning soliciting audio recordings from complete strangers, for zero financial benefit? I guess it's because I still didn't know what I wanted to be when I grew up.

Why, several months later, would that same woman start dating a mostly retired blog/photography-hobbyist 31 years older? That's probably because I was a child when my father died of brain cancer, and I had some issues to resolve. I'm not going to spend much time discussing that relationship choice. But I will say that I've *always* wondered if there are other women out there who lost their father at a young age and have sought out relationships with guys who were considerably older. I can't imagine that I'm the only one. Our first outing that I'd call a date was on Sept. 13, 2010, exactly three years before Don died.

**Don As I Knew Him**

Don was handsome, even over the age of 70. His hair was totally white, his eyes a cheerful medium-blue. He was over six feet tall. Something in his smile made him look decades younger sometimes, somehow. When we met, he had a part-time janitorial job at an apart-

FOREWORD

ment building that he used to live in. His professional life had been in the publishing industry in Los Angeles from the 1960's through the 1980's. Sometime in the 1980's he moved to San Diego, and then in the 1990's he moved to Portland, Oregon. In Portland he held various jobs such as self-storage facility attendant, computer and software salesperson, and driver for the Portland Auto Auction. When we met, he talked about starting a non-profit focused on providing portrait photography to seniors and others who wouldn't typically be able to afford a photographer's services.

Don had a great sense of humor and creativity he'd often conjure up hilarious scenarios. One September evening we went to see the Vaux's Swifts (thousands of birds flying into the chimney of an elementary school) in NW Portland. It was a free event. Don said, "Hey, look at all these spectators. Imagine if we hung out in Pioneer Square and sold $10 tickets to this event. How many people would fall for it? It'd be 100% profit!" He often saw humor in other people's behavior. One time we saw a guy at one end of Pioneer Square taking pictures with a huge zoom lens. He said he was getting great candid shots of people all the way across the Square. Later Don said, "Wow, at least I have the guts to go right up to people and they *know* I'm getting their picture; I'm not hiding a hundred yards away like *that* guy was! Do ya think maybe he was doing surveillance instead of art photos?"

Don had at least a dozen T-shirts with different baseball team logos. He wore them intentionally during baseball season to spark conversations with anyone he passed on the street who had an opinion about the team whose logo he had on that day. One time he was wearing a Yankees shirt and a woman said, "You're too cute to be a Yankees fan!" Naturally I bought him a Red Sox t-shirt on one of my visits back to the east coast.

Even as he faced one loss of ability or new strange physical symptom after another, Don didn't dwell on those things or complain a lot. Well, he did often talk about being exhausted, but it was more a statement of fact than a complaint. He acknowledged that his situation could be worse, and he often expressed gratitude for the blessings in his life. (I set many of these apart as they came up in his story, as numbered blessings.) One of his home health aides told me that she really admired Don for the dignity with which he faced the end of his life.

Don thought and talked about how he felt. If a phone conversation ended on an angry note, he'd call me back within a few minutes. "Baby, we can't end our day with this bad feeling between us…" If he was edgy and distant one day, the next day he'd identify what had weighed on his mind so much to make him act that way.

Don and I were quite different in terms of spiritual beliefs. He was a Christian and he believed that acceptance of Jesus as his savior would lead to spiritual salvation. He didn't specifically talk about going to heaven after death, but he believed he was going to be with Jesus and with God the father, even though he said that no one truly knows what happens to us when we die. As an agnostic who would prefer to have deities representing both (I should probably say "all") genders, if there even *are* any deities, and would prefer that a female entity doesn't have to be "pure" or a virgin to be considered worthy of worship, I did my best to respect Don's beliefs in editing his words for this book. However I chose not to capitalize male pronouns (he, him, etc.) when referring to Jesus and God.

I knew Don for a little over three years. Others in his life knew him for *much* longer. To me, he was a conscientious, kind-hearted, supportive, non-judgmental friend. From what I've heard, not everyone who knew him always thought as well of him through all the chapters of his life. Obviously I can't argue with what I didn't experience personally; in this book I've just presented the story as he told it, and presented him as I knew him.

**A Few Transcription Notes**
In this book, Don refers to me in the third person, i.e., "Later, Karen came by…" In the recordings, he was talking to me directly, and actually would've said "Later, you came by…" I wanted to avoid having his story sound like a conversation that was limited to him and me only, because I believe he truly wanted and expected others to

hear his words someday. So I changed his references, from second to third person. That may make his story sound as though I wasn't there listening, but I was.

There were a lot of things to "research" as I edited the transcriptions. When did the Dodgers leave Brooklyn? In which L.A. bar did Billy Joel "hide out" during a contract dispute in the 70's, inspiring his big hit *Piano Man*? Where is the road, a few miles north of Eugene, Oregon, that connects Route 99 with River Road, where Don and a friend raced an oncoming train to the railroad crossing? It was fun to seek answers to those questions online, although I know that not everything you find on the internet is the absolute truth. If I got any historical data wrong, I apologize – my main focus was, after all, what I experienced personally, my conversations with Don.

There was a striking difference between the first recordings and the later ones, that I obviously can't convey since the reader can't hear the recordings. A few months into transcribing, one day I skipped ahead to Day 171. I thought if I knocked out a few of the shorter transcriptions, I'd feel like I was farther along in the process than I actually was. I was shocked by how exhausted and beaten-down Don sounded at the end, compared to his energetic tone at the beginning of the five months. Yet he still sounded like he cared about living, and sincerely wanted to share something about his day. That was one of the few times I really felt sad while transcribing; I could hear how much the cancer had drained him to the point where simply getting out of bed in the morning was a monumental achievement.

Here's one instance where I was irked about Don's choice of language. On Day 142, he tells the funny story of how he met his first wife. He mentions that he and a male friend were "talking about girls." I'd lose my credibility as a transcriber if I'd changed "girls" to "young women" in this book. Ah well, I chose to leave it the way he said it, having never felt any gender-based negative judgments from Don.

A coworker once asked if it was sad to hear Don's voice, long after losing him. I truly didn't feel sad. Throughout working on this book, from transcribing through editing, I looked forward to the hours I spent on this project. I laughed as I heard many of Don's stories again.

FOREWORD

I felt honored to work on this project for him or maybe *with* him, whichever way you look at it. Don often laughed as he talked about his day – I conveyed this by writing "Ha!" wherever I had noted "[laughter]" in my transcriptions. I was also impressed with how he chose to speak openly about times when he was upset, scared, hurt, humiliated or confused. He told me once, "I was in sales. I can just keep talking and talking. If you make an objection, I'll find some other angle and continue talking." Well, that talking was what made this narrative possible. Please enjoy!

# SECTION 1: THE BIG C

There was a big whiteboard in the hospital room, and someone had already written the name of the cancer on it: Cholangiocarcinoma. Those white boards are for the nurses – they come in and say, "What's wrong with this guy?" Well, just look at the white board!

# 1
# DIAGNOSIS

**MARCH 2012**

My name is Don McCall and I'm sitting here this afternoon with my very best friend in the world, Karen Westphalen. We're discussing the beginning of the journey that I'll be on now for the rest of my life. It started about a year and a half ago when I began having some medical problems.

I turned jaundiced. I had some jaundice in my face and I didn't know what it was. People kept saying, "It looks like you've been getting a lot of sun," but I didn't really pay much attention. I thought, *No, I haven't really been getting out in the sun; I don't know what that's all about.* I wasn't convinced that it was a problem.

Then one day I got into an elevator with someone whom I barely know, and he said, "Wow, your skin really looks yellow; are you okay?" And I thought *Wait a minute, maybe there is something wrong with me; I better check this out.* That was on a Sunday night.

I was having a little bit of stomach trouble at that time, indigestion. I had taken to using Tums here and there. I had a big bottle of multi-colored Tums, the large ones. I started eating more and more of them but it wasn't helping my stomach all that much. So when this person whom I didn't know very well said that to me, it was kind of a wake-up call. I thought, *Maybe I better look into this.* At eight o'clock the very next morning when the medical office opened, I called my primary care doctor and I said, "I have a problem. I'm looking jaundiced and I really need to get checked out." He said, "Come on in this afternoon. I don't like the sound of that." So I went to his office on Monday afternoon.

He confirmed that I definitely *was* jaundiced, and he was pretty sure it was hepatitis. I thought *Oh no, I don't want hepatitis; that's a horrible disease. It's hard to get rid of and it's with you for life!* But I went down to the lab to be tested for hepatitis A, B, C, D – any and all forms of hepatitis. They took a blood sample and said it would be ready the next day.

I went home and immediately jumped on Google and WebMD to get the scoop on hepatitis, because I didn't like the sound of it. How could I have gotten it? The doctor asked if I'd been to any strange restaurants lately.

The blood test came back the following day. My doctor called and said, "You do not have any form of hepatitis. I want you to see our specialist, a gastroenterologist. There could be something wrong with your gallbladder; it could be fouled up, maybe you have a gallstone."

So the gastroenterologist examined me and he thought it could be a gallstone. Several things can cause bile to back up into your liver and then spill into your bloodstream and make you turn yellow. The gastroenterologist said, "You need to come to the hospital. There's a blockage. We can see it on the scan but we don't know what it is. It could be a gallstone that slipped down into the bile duct. I'll go in with a probe and try to break it up so the bile can start flowing properly into your intestine again." He said it would be an outpatient appointment. "You'll be in the hospital for an hour for prep, then I'll come in and do my thing, put a tube down and break this thing up. Then you'll rest and recover and go home."

That Friday, I took the bus from downtown Portland to Providence St. Vincent's Hospital, and I made arrangements with Karen to pick me up afterwards since I'm currently not driving. I got prepped and did the thing with all the nurses, got my name right and all that sort of thing. I told them not to call me Donald; I want to be called *Don*. Just call me Don. We got all that straightened out. Then they had me take a couple of tranquilizers. Everything was going great and I went in and I could hear the doctor come in. I was knocked out by the time he did his thing.

Then I woke up in the recovery room. The gastroenterologist came in and said, "Well, I tell you, there is a blockage but it's not a gallstone. It's a mass. We really need to find out what it is. You'll need to stay in the hospital overnight."

I said, "I don't want to do that; I've never been in a hospital. I've made it this far without ever staying in the hospital. Can't I just come back tomorrow?"

He said, "No, you can't go home because I want to be sure you don't get any food or fluids. I want to be in full control of your situation so you don't do something stupid. The first thing we have to do is take the bile out of your liver because it's blocked. The bile isn't getting through to your intestine where it's supposed to go. You're going to continue to get more and more jaundiced from that bile because the gallbladder can't do its job."

I said, "I still don't understand why I have to stay here all night!"

And he said, "You just have to stay here, so we can find out what's going on."

I reluctantly agreed to spend that Friday night in the hospital. It was a nightmare.

I was barely settled in my room when people started coming in, taking tests. Every hour somebody was in the room waking me up to do something. That's when I met Mary Margaret, the stereotypical Catholic nurse from a 1950's Catholic hospital. An older lady, working part time. She was mostly retired, only working certain days. She was very stern. She reminded me of the nurses that I had known as a child. She was tough and she wanted to let people know that she was in charge: *you* weren't dictating the terms of your care, *she* was. We had a real battle of wills all night long. She kept coming in and trying to do things, and I said, "No I don't want to do that; I don't need to do that," and she said, "Yes you do." All night long, taking blood samples and vital signs. She didn't need sleep – she was working – but I needed sleep.

Hospitals have all of their procedural stuff. You're in *their* hospital and they don't want you to die from something that they did wrong. But I don't like people doing that type of thing, probing and needles and all that. We had a tough night, Mary Margaret and I. We battled each other all night long. And I wasn't allowed to eat or drink *anything* until my next procedure on Saturday morning.

The next procedure involved inserting a tube under my rib cage and pushing it through my body and down into the liver. It was a plastic tube about an eighth of an inch in diameter that went all the way down through the liver and into the bile duct. By gravity it would pull out all of the bile that was supposed to go to the intestine but couldn't get there. By gravity it would feed into a plastic bag attached to my body and then every so often the bag would have to be emptied. So they inserted the tube and they couldn't use an anesthetic – they couldn't knock me out – because I needed to be awake in case they had a question for me. They gave me morphine to deaden the pain, but there was no deadening *this* pain. It was absolutely excruciating, the most excruciating pain I've ever endured in my whole life. It was unbelievable. I'm sure people have endured far worse than that, but as far as I was concerned it was the most excruciating pain *I've* ever experienced. Overall it was successful; they got the tube exactly where it was supposed to go, and it immediately started draining out to the bag. The bag was about ten inches long and four inches wide. And you could see the bile as it drained into the bag; it was yellowish-brown.

Then they told me the good news, that I would be spending Saturday night in the hospital as well, *and* Mary Margaret was going to be on duty again that night. I don't think Mary Margaret had ever seen this particular type of tube and bag before. She was supposed to monitor it, but while I was trying to sleep, the tube got crunched up and nothing drained into the bag all night long. The tube was folded up under my body so the bile couldn't get into it. Mary Margaret was just doing her job; she was checking it, but it just wasn't working. We had the same battle that we'd had the night before, conflict all night long. She would say, "I want to do this," and I'd reply, "No, leave me alone, I want to sleep." I liked her and respected her but we didn't get along very well.

On Sunday morning I was told that I would be having my third procedure of the weekend. This would be done by another specialist, and it involved putting a probe down my throat, through my stomach and around to the bile duct. This probe was a little more sophisticated. It had a sonar device on it, and the ability to get a biopsy sample of the mass, now that they knew exactly where to look.

The bile duct starts at your liver and goes to your intestine. It's kind of y-shaped: it comes down a certain way and then there's another little tube that goes off to the side with the gallbladder on top. The whole object of the bile duct is that the bile drains through it and goes into your intestine. The excess bile is pulled off to the side and stored in your gallbladder. When you eat, the partly-digested food passes through and squeezes the gall bladder which then releases bile to help you digest. My bile duct was all fouled up; it was full. The tube they inserted was now starting the process of draining the bile out of the gallbladder.

This next doctor's job was to find out what the mass in the bile duct was. I was very comforted by the fact that as soon as I was assigned that doctor, a nurse came in and gave me his complete credentials and explained what an incredible doctor he was.

The doctor came in and talked with me before the procedure, and said that he was going to take a sample of the mass. He said that by the time I came out of recovery he would have a result. At that point I still figured it was a gallstone.

The doctor was absolutely true to his word. When I woke up after the procedure, he was right there in the room and the first two words out of his mouth were, "It's cancer." That was the first time I'd heard the word *cancer* concerning my situation.

It was cholangiocarcinoma, cancer of the bile duct. He said, "Your gastroenterologist will give you all the information you need, but I have definitely confirmed it." So I was wheeled back to my room.

There was a big whiteboard in the room, and someone had already written the name of the cancer on it. Those white boards are for the nurses – they come in and say, "What's wrong with this guy?" Well, just look at the white board!

I was in shock. They tell you you've got cancer... all of a sudden your mind just spins out of control, like, *What does that mean?* We all *know* about cancer, what a serious disease it is. My first questions were, how serious is it and what can be done about it?

Later in the afternoon, the doctor who had made the diagnosis came to the room and said, "I'm in contact with a clinic at Providence Hospital, where they have one of the best bile duct cancer surgeons in the United States. Dr. Andrew Lawrence. I'm going to try to get you an appointment with him. I don't know if I'll be able to because he's very busy and difficult to pin down. If I can't get *him*, I'll get one of the associates on his staff. They're all fantastic but he's the best."

I had no idea at that point what might happen in terms of treatment. I figured I'd have the cancer removed and that would be it; then I'd be OK. No problem! It was a shock to find out I had cancer because, for the past 20 years or more, I had really tried to take good care of myself. I hiked all the time. I got all kinds of exercise. I went to the gym three times a week. I tried to eat good food. I rode my bicycle. I consumed a lot of antioxidants. I never thought I was the kind of person who would get cancer; I thought I was really strong. I didn't believe I could get it; I thought I might get something else, maybe, but not that!

I was told that I'd be going home on Monday with my bile bag attached. A nurse showed me how the bag worked and how to empty it. They told me I'd be fine but I wouldn't be able to go to work. The bag would probably get in the way when I tried to bend over or do anything active. So I went home on Monday, with the bag strapped to my waist. I couldn't take a shower at that point because of that bag.

On Tuesday I had an appointment for a scan to check whether the cancer had migrated to my lungs or any other part of my body. On Thursday I was scheduled to go to the surgeon's office at the Oregon Clinic. I didn't know which doctor I was going to see but I wanted Dr. Lawrence because of what I'd learned and heard about his expertise.

2

## WHIPPLE SURGERY

The appointment on Thursday was late in the afternoon. I filled out paperwork and I was taken to the exam room. Three or four doctors came in and talked with me briefly. Finally Dr. Lawrence came in. He told me about the procedure and how it worked. He said, "You may be a candidate for Whipple surgery." I had never heard that term so I had no idea what it meant. I said, "Oh, a *candidate*, that must mean something special because not everybody gets it." Maybe it was really a good thing – something special? Everybody *else* gets regular surgery but I might get *Whipple* surgery. Dr. Lawrence explained that it took three weeks to recover in the hospital after Whipple surgery. I thought, *Oh. That doesn't sound as good; now I'm not sure I want to be a candidate.*

He went on to explain everything that he could possibly explain. He answered every question before I could even ask it! He had it all laid out for me. Finally I got up enough nerve to ask, "So... who's actually going to do the surgery?" and he said, "*I'm going to do it.*" I said, "Oh thank you, I appreciate that so much!" I'd had such a big build-up about him and his qualifications; I wanted *the best*. He pulled out his calendar and said, "The soonest I can do this will be April the 2nd." Monday, April 2nd, 2012.

That meant I had roughly two weeks to wait for the prized Whipple surgery that was planned for me. Dr. Lawrence said they would *prepare* to do the Whipple procedure, and then make the final decision on whether to do it once the surgery was underway. First they would send a robotic probe to look at the tumor, to determine the best way forward. Then they would make the decision. It could turn out to be a very simple procedure if it was just a small tumor.

The next two weeks became the Battle of the Bile Bag. I couldn't go to work but I had my computer so I kept pretty busy during the day. A Providence home health nurse came by twice a week to help me with the bile bag. She did some cleaning and changed my dressing where the tube went into my body. I almost suspected she was flirting with me; she asked a lot of personal questions and said, "You look good for your age," and that kind of thing.

I became interested in how much bile the human body produces in one day. I set up a spreadsheet. Several times a day I would empty the bile bag into a measuring cup and record the number of ounces in my spreadsheet. Soon I saw how many ounces I was producing daily. It was amazing – I learned that I produced roughly one quart per day. Thirty-two ounces of bile every single, solitary day! I had daily and weekly totals in my spreadsheet. I was preoccupied with this research. I showed it to the nurse when she came and she was impressed.

I went online and read about Whipple surgery. I thought, *Wait a minute, this is worse than I thought!* It turns out Whipple surgery is one of the most complicated surgical procedures in modern medicine. It's right up there with heart transplants. They take out the bile duct completely. They take out the gallbladder which is attached to the bile duct. They remove portions of your stomach and pancreas. They remove a portion of your large intestine and then they miraculously tie it all back together with stitches, so that everything functions somehow with all those parts missing. It's one of the most difficult surgical procedures! Plus I wasn't too pleased thinking about the three-week recovery in the hospital.

. . .

## Blessing #1

*But I was really thankful – incredibly thankful – to have a doctor with the credentials that Dr. Lawrence has. In parts of our country – and in much of the world – you probably couldn't get that surgery. I was one of the chosen few, to live in a place where you can get it, and from someone so competent at it. I also thought about the millions of people who have died around the world from not being able to get any of this type of care because it's simply not available to them. I really started to appreciate the medical care system that we have. The system is goofed up in many, many different ways, but it still is amazing, the things that can be done in this country and other countries around the world. I was very thankful that I could have this surgery.*

For the two weeks prior to surgery, I was pretty much in training. I kept exercising, and taking my bile out and measuring it, and waiting for the nurse to come, and giving her my full report on everything. I was doing my best to prepare. The surgery sounded so complicated to me that I wasn't sure I'd survive it, so I put together a list of what to do and whom to contact just in case Karen and I made out an Advance Directive, and we were clear on that.

## APRIL 2, 2012

My son Allen came from Atlanta, Georgia to be with me during the surgery. Allen and Karen and I went for dinner the night before, Sunday April 1st. Karen and Allen hadn't met before. Between that and the fact that the next day I would be having a huge medical surgical procedure, the dinner felt really strange.

My friend Emma wanted to take me to the hospital on April 2nd, which meant she had to pick me up at 5:30 a.m. Emma is one of my dearest friends. She has also had surgery for cancer – not just once, but twice because her cancer reoccurred after the first surgery. In addition to two major cancer surgeries, she has had chemo as a follow-up. So I was happy to have her take me to the hospital because I felt like on some level we were soulmates based on that shared experience.

Walking through the corridors of the hospital early in the morning, there was almost nobody around. It was eerie and I almost felt like I was headed to the gallows. I arrived at the preparation area and was assigned to a private room, where I put on the hospital gown. Karen arrived around 7:30, and then my son arrived, and then one of my favorite pastors, Pastor Phillip, also came to see me. I felt really blessed at that moment; just before major surgery I had already seen four of the most wonderful people in my life.

Dr. Lawrence came in and talked with us for a while too. He lived a ways from the hospital but he had jogged to work. I thought, *Wow, that's impressive – he certainly has his blood flowing and he's ready to get started!* I liked this doctor a lot; he's an amazing person. He had called me the day before the surgery to ask how I was doing, and to give me some last-minute encouragement.

Finally I was ready to go into the operating room. Surgery is an amazing experience. You go in there and the voices start to fade out. You see the light and all that scrambling and bustling around the room: the doctor and his assistants, nurses and the anesthesiologist. It's a beehive of activity, like being in an alien spaceship. Then they start the IV, and you start to phase out and then *boom* you're out and you don't know anything for hours, however long it takes. The lights and the noises go down, and the next thing you hear is, "You're awake now, you're out of surgery. You're in recovery." It feels like it's been a minute, but for me, it was fourteen and a half hours later.

I remember waking up. Karen was there. I was really groggy and my hands kept floating up as though they were filled with helium. Later the nurse told me that typically happens to people right after that type of surgery. Karen leaned in to talk to me, and my hand rose up, unintentionally, and I touched the top of her head. Later I placed my hand on top of my own head and said, "Clean head." Karen had helped me wash my hair the day before surgery, so I had gone into the hospital with a clean head. This was important because it had been difficult to bathe during the prior two weeks, with the bile bag and tube attached to my body.

At some point I mentioned to Karen that I didn't have my Chevron credit card with me to pay for the surgery. They had put all these tubes into my body: the bile bag, a painkiller bulb with wires going to my stomach, and another thing that was draining blood from the site of the surgery. I saw the tubes and bulbs and bags and for some reason I thought it was like being at a service station, where you get your oil and other fluid levels checked. So I thought I should have my Chevron card to pay for it!

The nurses added a new procedure for this hospital stay. Because they took out part of my pancreas, they were concerned about my blood sugar level. They had to prick my finger with a pin every two hours to test my blood sugar because if it was over a certain level, they had to give me insulin. Every two hours, there they were. A hospital is no place to get any rest; the nurses come in so frequently.

I was pretty groggy for a while. Initially I didn't realize that Karen had stayed, to spend the night in the hospital room with me. I became aware of that when things quieted down. She was lying on a fold-out couch and she must've rolled over or something. All of a sudden I realized she was in the room. It was the sweetest thing I could possibly imagine, knowing that there was someone else there with me. I couldn't turn my head and I could barely talk, and I needed water so badly. I tapped on the tray to try to get Karen's attention. Finally she heard me and came over, and fed me some ice chips. I wasn't allowed to have water. It was so amazing to have her there; I'd had no idea that a visitor could spend the night in the hospital room.

I got through the first night and I started feeling better. I heard that I'd been in the operating room for fourteen and a half hours, yet now I was coherent and should be able to walk and talk. Knowing what I'd been through, and that at least some things might return to normal, I began to feel more comfortable. I thought, *Well, if I can get through that, I must be doing pretty well.*

My son came to visit me that morning. He had stopped by the

Oregon Ducks shop on the way and gotten me an Oregon polo shirt. Allen graduated from the University of Oregon and I grew up in Eugene and attended the U of O briefly, so we're great Duck fans and we talk about the Ducks sports teams all the time. So I really liked the Ducks shirt.

**Blessing #2**

*Later Dr. Lawrence came in and said the all-important words: "My team and I were extremely pleased with the way that surgery went." He said, "I biopsied twenty-eight lymph nodes and we only found cancer cells in one lymph node, meaning that you'll probably undergo chemo and maybe radiation. I would be very concerned if I had found six, or eight or ten, something like that. But finding cancer cells in only one node, I feel really good. The surgery went beautifully and I'm really pleased."*

An hour later, one of Dr. Lawrence's associates came in. He had been in the operating room during the surgery, and wanted to see my abdomen. I had a seven-inch scar, all stapled together. This doctor looked at the surgery and checked me over, pushing around here and there. Then he stood back and shook his head. I asked, "What's the matter?" He replied, "Well, I'll tell ya. Dr. Lawrence is so damn good at what he does. I just can't believe it." I thought, *Oh wow, that's great! That's really wonderful to hear.* He was literally looking at the whole thing like, *Wow, that's a masterpiece!*

Then he said, "The first thing you gotta do today is get up. You gotta walk. You can't stay in bed. You gotta get up and do some exercise."

I said, "I don't know, I'm not sure about doing that. It sounds like a bit much after what I've been through, you know?"

But he said, "No, you can do it. You *can* get out of bed."

## WALKING TO RECOVERY– APRIL 2012

The nurses helped me put my feet down on the floor. I'd never been so shaky in all my life. I did not believe that I'd be able to get up on my feet, never mind walk somewhere. They gave me a pole with four wheels, with a little tray around the outside to carry all my accessories: the little thing that was collecting the excess blood, my pain-killer bulb, my bile bag and all that.

The nurses had told me, "This little bulb is a pain-killer. It has a little button. If you start having pain, hit that button and painkiller will be injected directly into the surgical area. So you don't have to worry about pills and all that kind of stuff." I called it the "Punch in the Gut" button. And it really worked! If I had a little bit of pain and I pushed that button, *boom!* It would go away immediately.

Anyway I loaded all my stuff – bags, bulbs, bottles and so forth – onto this rolling pole, and I was able to get up and stand up. I realized that I needed two gowns: one in front and one in the back so I wasn't walking around with my bare bottom hanging out I got out the door of my room and took a short walk down the hall, dragging all this paraphernalia along with me. An aide helped me at first. Initially they don't trust you to go it alone. I had non-skid socks on, but they kept falling off. Those socks were more dangerous than no socks at all! At any rate, I managed my first walk. I thought, *Wow, that was really amazing. I don't know how on earth I did that, I really don't.*

The aides said, "That was fabulous! That was great! Take another walk whenever you feel like it." Later another doctor came by and said, "I saw you walking in the hall; that was great!" Later the nurse came in and said the same thing. It started to dawn on me: they *really* like it when you walk. They think that everything's great when they see you walking around. So I decided that I was gonna walk my way out of that hospital.

At first I wasn't allowed any solid food, only ice chips. I wasn't allowed to drink anything either, only the sponge on a stick, dipped in a glass of water. That was driving me crazy; I wanted water so badly. Dr. Lawrence had said that everybody who has this surgery loses at least twenty pounds. I thought, *I can see why; they starve you. You can't eat.* It was a "no food and water" situation for three days.

But I like exercise so I started making a game out of exercising and walking. Whenever I had enough energy, I would take a walk. I'd get out of bed, load all my bulbs and things onto this pole, and head off down the hall. It was a long hallway where you could do a lap: go down to the end, turn, go down to the corner, come back up the other hall. It took me quite a while 'til I could make my *first* lap: I'd go down the end and come back, and then go a little bit farther and come back, so on and so forth.

As I walked by the other rooms, I saw people just lying on their beds. They weren't moving or doing anything. I'd hear the nurses say, "Come on now, you've got to get up, you've got to get up." And they'd say, "No, no, I'm not getting up," and all that. That confirmed my feeling that walking was key; that really was the way out! So I got better and better and better at it. I walked more and more. I'd walk by the doctor's station and notice the doctors who were on Dr. Lawrence's staff. They knew me, and I noticed them kinda looking at me out of the corner of their eye, thinking, *There he goes again!* Like the Duracell rabbit. Or maybe it's the Energizer bunny? Anyway I really enjoyed the walking because I felt that that was gonna help me get out of there faster.

On the third day they told me I could have juice. I asked for grape juice. I honestly think that that eight-ounce glass of grape juice was the most wonderful, delightful nourishment that I'd ever had in my entire *life*. It was un*belie*vable sipping that grape juice and getting a taste of something other than ice chips.

As the week progressed, I got used to the routine. I became more savvy as to how the nurses worked, and I became a much, much better patient than I had been with Mary Margaret. They even started *telling* me that I was a good patient! So I thought, *I'm making progress here.* Of course my goal was to get *out*.

Around the fifth day, Dr. Lawrence came in and asked, "How long do you wanna stay here?" I said, "I wanna go home!" He asked, "How does Monday sound?" I said, "Fantastic!" He said, "OK, we'll shoot for

Monday," which would make one week in the hospital instead of the minimum of three that he had originally talked about. I realized I must've been winning the battle! In order to be released, I needed to be stronger. So I increased my walking even more. When people came to visit, I'd say, "Hey, you wanna go for a walk? We'll do a lap around the hall." It was more enjoyable to have people walking with me. I just had to get out of there, and walking was the answer.

*Blessing #3*

> *One time I walked down to the other end of the hallway and sat on a seat by the window there, looking out at Mt. Hood. The sun was shining in on me, nice and warm and bright. It was absolutely amazing. I felt like I was starting a new life. I'd been through a really incredible ordeal, but now I was able to sit and relax in the sunshine, and enjoy it. Later they confirmed that I could go home on Monday and I was delighted. I had only been in the hospital for one week.*

Dr. Lawrence told me that if everything went beautifully, it would take a year to recover from the surgery. Whipple surgery was that intensive on the body. He said, "Don't worry if you have problems such as fatigue or you don't wanna eat. That's normal." A side effect of surgery was that I got free lap-band surgery thrown in. The size of my stomach had been decreased so I didn't want to eat as much. I started losing weight right away.

Dr. Lawrence told me that I needed to see an oncologist right away for treatment, to try to prevent any cancer cells from spreading, and to get my body completely clear of cancer. I was determined to do what I was told, to do everything I could to make sure I did my part in battling this disease. So much money and so many resources had been put into the fight already; it was *my* obligation to do everything I could to make it work. I decided, *Yes, I'll do the chemo.* I was also told that I might have to have radiation as well. Dr. Lawrence recommended two or three oncologists to get me started.

### Blessing #4

*At that time I'd had a part time job, 20 hours a week, for close to four years. Between the bile bag and recovering from surgery, I ended up taking close to two months off from work. I had never been paid for vacation or sick days because the company had said I didn't work enough hours to be eligible. But at a weekly meeting about a month before my first time in the hospital, our new part-time assistant manager had complained that she hadn't been paid for one of her sick days. I was perplexed because I didn't think she could be eligible for sick days, given her schedule. A couple weeks later, I finally asked my boss about it. She checked, and found out that I too should've had that benefit all along. In the end, I got a check for a big jackpot of days; they made the payment retroactive back to when I started working there. It was amazing that as a result of one ten-minute discussion with my boss, all of my time off for cancer surgery and recovery ended up being covered. That took a lot of pressure off of me because I didn't have to worry about missing work.*

3

LIVING THROUGH TREATMENT

## CHEMOTHERAPY – SUMMER OF 2012

*I* decided to go to Oregon Health & Sciences University (OHSU) because it was easy for me to get there. I could get on a streetcar a block from my house and get to the main office in a matter of fifteen to twenty minutes. I picked the closest oncologist that Dr. Lawrence had recommended, who happened to be one of his neighbors, Dr. Sara Benito. That was kind of an amazing coincidence.

Dr. Benito laid out the plan for me: first, a weekly dose of Gemzar, which is a chemo infusion into your bloodstream, that takes about an hour. Second, a pill called Xeloda; multiple pills, several times a day. I had no idea how it would work out. You hear horror stories about chemo.

Karen and I went to a seminar about it. The seminar scared the bejeebers out of me, with all the things that come with chemo. I felt like, *Wait a minute, do I really wanna do this? I mean, listen to what these people are saying can happen to you!* I had second thoughts but I knew I needed to do it and get it done. At least they told me that my hair would probably *not* fall out with this particular combination of drugs. So I started chemotherapy, and it went on for three months.

Chemo was two weeks on and one week off. I learned that the week off is not really a week off. You feel better, obviously, since you don't have to take the stuff. But you don't recover enough during that week to really feel like you're taking the week "off."

Chemo is designed to kill cancer cells but it also kills white blood cells. White blood cells are where you get your energy to perform during the day; they're your energy source. Your blood is sampled every time you go in for treatment. If the white blood cell count drops below a certain point, they don't administer chemo. That happened once in the three months.

I often wanted to throw the Xeloda away, rather than take it. With pills, it's kind of an honor system. I mean, you could go home and dump 'em all out if you wanted to, and nobody would know the difference. You could just say that you took your pills. But I did actually take my pills. Well, OK, I did cheat a couple of times. I think there were two or three days where I skipped one dose. I confess that right here. There were about nine pills out of the whole 240 that I didn't take. On the record, I didn't take *every single one*.

In the end, I got through chemo with minimal difficulty. I had a list of what *could* happen, but very few things on that list happened to me. Mostly I experienced a lot of fatigue and some forgetfulness, some "chemo brain." By the end, I felt that I had done my job; I had done what the doctors had told me to do.

## THE RADIATION SKY TRAM – OCTOBER 2012

Once chemo was done, I had some time off from treatment and I started to feel really good. I sensed that my energy level was going to surge at that point. But I had one more obstacle: radiation was strongly recommended. I was very, very skeptical about it. I thought, *This is dangerous stuff.* The radiation schedule would be every day, five days a week, for four weeks. A total of twenty sessions in one month, which seemed to me to be excessive. It felt like I was doing so well; I felt good! I thought, *Why should I do this?*

But I also thought, *There again, I've committed to this.* So many people had put so much effort into getting me healthy, and so many resources had been used, that I needed to go through and finish the program to the end. Otherwise I would've always had the thought that I didn't do everything that I could have. I never wanted to think that I had turned down treatment that might have made the difference. So, reluctantly I decided to do the radiation.

The only enjoyable thing about the radiation appointments was the transportation. OHSU has offices down along Portland's southwest waterfront – by the Willamette River – and at the top of the hill in that part of town. A tram runs all day taking people up and down between the two campuses. The streetcar around the corner from me goes to the OHSU offices at the bottom of the hill. Since my appointments were up top, I got to ride the tram every day, up and back. Riding the tram was a lot of fun.

The radiation thing was an unusual experience. There was this giant machine with all these funny lights, and lasers shooting all over the place. The technicians tattooed a pattern on my stomach so they could get the radiation machine perfectly aligned each time. They wanted to radiate all the organs in my stomach area *except* my liver. They had a mapping procedure for shooting the radiation only within a specific area; it went all the way around the liver and got to all the other organs. Obviously it was complicated.

I didn't miss any radiation treatments. I even pushed them on a couple, three occasions to get it done, when they were running behind. I said, "I will stay here until midnight if you need me to, because I want it done today. I don't want any extra days tacked on at the end; I want to stick to my one-month plan and be done with it." So we had some friction there. But I got it done on time and didn't miss a day. In fact, one of the nurses said, "You are an exemplary patient," and I said, "Thank you."

## LIVING FROM ONE CANCER SCREEN TO THE NEXT – NOVEMBER 2012 TO JANUARY 2013

Radiation was done, and I had completed all of my treatment: a massive surgery, chemo, radiation. End of story. Treatment was done. The last day was the 6th of November.

I'd had my first scan right after chemo, as a benchmark. I learned quickly that in a cancer patient's life, you live from scan to scan. Because if you have a scan and it's clear, that's fantastic news – but just for a moment.

*When's the next scan?* Six months from now. But you don't really have six months to relax. By the end of the fifth month you start thinking, *I'm coming up on my next scan.* Throughout that last month, you're wondering if anything has changed. The anxiety starts to build. After a while, that's what you live for – the next scan.

My first scan had shown a little mass of some kind of tissue in my stomach, and my doctors had agreed, "That's just soft tissue as a result of the operation, and it will eventually clear up." So the first scan was clear, from their point of view. The oncologist who ordered that scan, Dr. Benito, told me I didn't have to be scanned again for six months. That was great! I had six months! But after completing radiation, the radiologist wanted to do a scan in two months, which was a lot sooner than I was expecting. I wasn't thrilled but he insisted that it was necessary. I started to get nervous about it. My stomach acted up and I felt edgy.

I had my next scan on January 11th, 2013. In hindsight, I should've made my follow-up appointment for the very next day instead of waiting for the results. You do not wanna wait a week after a test like that. But I didn't think of it when I scheduled the appointment. I had the scan and then I just sat there wondering, knowing that *someone* had extremely important information about my health that I couldn't access.

Finally I went in to see the radiologist.

"We found two spots on your liver. They're suspect, although they *could* be something else," he said.

"What are the chances that they're something else?"

"I would say it's a 50-50 chance that they're something else."

*That's* not the greatest statistic in the world! As I saw it, I had a 50%

chance that there was cancer in my liver, not a 50% chance that I *didn't*. That was very upsetting. He said he wanted me to return in two months for another scan. He didn't offer to show me the report, so I asked the receptionist to print out a copy for me as I left the office.

## THINGS ARE NOT WHAT THEY SEEM – FEBRUARY TO MARCH 2013

I have this favorite place at OHSU where you sit in a wonderful chair and look out through the windows over all of Portland, with the sun shining on you. It's a great place to relax. I headed over there and sat down in that chair and read the report, which the radiologist hadn't given me. The doctor who actually performed the scan wrote that the two spots were "liver metastasis."

*What's liver metastasis?* The report didn't say they *might* be, or they *could* be; she said they *were*. Right away I had a red flag go up. Why would the radiologist just say the two spots were "suspect" in some way, yet the report said "metastasis"? That didn't make sense to me.

I called Karen right then and there, and she came to pick me up. Instead of heading to my apartment, we drove over to Mt. Tabor, another one of my favorite places in Portland. We sat in the car to talk things over. I told her that I was highly suspicious, and things didn't make sense to me. There was this huge red flag.

We discussed the ramifications of "liver metastasis," so on and so forth. I wasn't feeling nearly as comfortable anymore about the outcome of my treatment. I also admitted that I hadn't been progressing quite as well as I'd hoped. In the weeks between chemo and radiation, I'd felt stronger and stronger every day; I'd felt better and better and better. Since radiation had ended, I realized that things felt different.

Karen suggested, "It's probably just left over from the radiation," because one big side effect of that treatment is fatigue. Radiation leaves you feeling tired, constantly. Also I tend to feel kinda depressed in the winter anyway, with the lack of sunlight. But I felt like it was a lot more than that. Otherwise, why would the radiologist have told me to come in for another scan only two months later, instead of six?

I scheduled my next scan for March 11th. In February I began to feel like that would be too soon. If I was gonna get bad news, I wanted more time to prepare. I consulted with my primary care doctor, rescheduled the scan for April 11th, and then tried to put it out of my mind. My apartment had been completely renovated in January, and I wanted to enjoy getting settled again and redecorating it a little bit. I had a couple of creative projects that I wanted to make some headway on. We'd had a few days here and there where I'd been able to go for a nice bike ride. I just wasn't ready to deal with that next scan just yet.

But then in March I started to notice a little jaundice around my eyes. I figured, *Well, I have been in the sun quite a bit, riding my bike and sitting in the little bit of sun that we've had, for half an hour a day.* My face has a tendency to get color pretty fast, so that's probably what it is.

Then one afternoon I had coffee with a friend, and she said, "You look a little yellow around the eyes. Have you noticed that? Why is that?"

I agreed. This lady knew all about my condition, so I couldn't completely ignore her observation.

"I think there's probably some bile that's not getting through." I hoped that explanation would be enough, but I thought to myself, *Well, if she noticed it, now I really do think something's wrong with my liver!*

The next day I called my primary care doctor again and told him about the yellow, the jaundice. I said that now I did want to have the scan sooner instead of waiting that extra month, and he agreed that that was a good idea.

"Can I see you a day or so afterwards?" I asked. Although he's my primary care physician and not an oncologist or radiologist, he certainly knows how to read reports! I wanted to get the results *immediately* this time, rather than waiting a week.

I went for the scan on Wednesday, March 20th, at about four o'clock in the afternoon. In addition to the scan, they took four vials of blood to get an indication of liver function. The follow-up appointment with my primary care doctor was scheduled for four o'clock on

Thursday afternoon, so I only had to wait 24 hours to find out what was happening. I wasn't that shaken up about it. At that point I already honestly believed that things had gone haywire, because turning yellow is not normal. Fortunately this time I had enough sense to schedule the follow-up appointment immediately, rather than sitting around for a week and getting all anxious.

4

LIFE GETS AN EXPIRATION DATE

**THURSDAY, MARCH 21, 2013**

*I* went in for the follow-up on Thursday at four o'clock. The doctor was a little bit late; he came in about a half hour after I got there. The nurse had been in to do all the usual stuff: blood pressure, temperature, oxygen reading, all the things they do before you see the doctor. Everything was perfect: good blood pressure, a hundred percent oxygen, good heart rate, everything. Vital signs – all great. Then she left me waiting for the doctor. A few more minutes went by, then all of a sudden there was a knock on the door. Doctors always knock a little bit before coming in. I thought *OK, that's it, the time is here, the time has come.*

The door opened. He came in and said, "Well Don, it looks like you really nailed it, you were a hundred percent right. The first two spots that they found in your prior scan have doubled in size. Plus several more spots have emerged. There's only one thing that this could be. The cancer has reoccurred in your liver and it's basically untreatable."

I had already decided that I didn't want long-term chemotherapy if my cancer had come back. I wanted to have a clear head and be able to do as much as I could for as long as I could. I didn't want to be knocked out by chemo, where I couldn't eat, couldn't taste my food, and my head wasn't working right.

My primary care doctor agreed with me one hundred percent. "You need to do what you feel good about. And to be honest, the chemo wouldn't help that much anyway. It can't cure the cancer at this point. Your plan to do as much as you can for as long as you can, is right on,"

And I asked the all-time big question – which you have to ask. I distinctly remember asking, "In your very best opinion – I'm not pinning you down, I'm not asking you for something that you don't know – how much time do you think it will take for this to end my life?"

"I would say between six months and a year."

Other than hearing that you *have* cancer in the first place, having someone tell you that the disease will in fact kill you, and it's not preventable, *that's* The Biggie. That's when – all of a sudden – your life changes forever. Before my appointment, I had already been expecting to hear that news, but now I had this final confirmation.

There's no way to explain how it feels when you're told that you're gonna die within a certain period of time. Everybody knows that each day we live, we're dying one more day. We all know that at some point death will happen. But very few people are given the specific times and dates involved in that. I mean, it's just something that most people never hear. So when you hear that news, it's an incredible shock, like, *Can this really be happening?* Is somebody really *telling* me that I'm going to die within a certain period of time? Of course it's not an exact science: it could be three months, six months, nine months – or it could reverse itself! Some miracle could just *stop* its progression; it *has* happened before. But you have to take this kind of information seriously and believe that that's what's happening. The liver will eventually shut down, in a fairly short period of time.

Two things occurred to me right away. First, this kind of information forever changes everything about your life: you're no longer thinking in terms of things that you might wanna do or places you might wanna go. You realize that now it's all about immediate priorities, things that you *really* need to get done as quickly as possible.

**Blessing #5**

*The other thing that occurred to me was that I'm a Christian, and I believe in the Lord Jesus Christ, and I believe in eternity. Jesus says that my faith will get me into heaven. Heaven is a very special place that none of us really know how to define. We just know that Jesus makes that promise. He's gone to prepare a place for us; that's what he says in the book of John. As a Christian with that belief, I've always thought that the earth is not my home; it's an intermediate place – not a destination. The destination is being with the Lord, with Jesus. That's the destination.*

When you hear that you only have a certain amount of time left to live, you've begun a new journey. A whole new journey. Before getting that news, it's like you've thought about planning a trip for a really long time but you're not exactly sure what day you're gonna leave 'cause you haven't bought a ticket yet, to wherever you're going.

Then you pick a date and you go to the ticket counter and give 'em the money. They push a few buttons on the computer and the ticket prints out, and it says when you're leaving. The ticket shows the date and time when your trip will start; it's there in black and white. Right away, you've got a lot of things to do before the plane leaves: for example, making a list, buying snacks for the plane ride and packing your bag. You've got to get certain things done before you travel; that's a finality. For me to get to the other side and be with Jesus in heaven, I have to start *my* journey; I have to get a ticket and get it punched the way the conductor comes around and punches your ticket when you get on a train.

The doctor punched the ticket for me when he told me I had six to twelve months to live. Now I'm on the journey to my destination. It's like I've boarded the plane and it's gonna take off. So I have things that

I need to accomplish, if at all possible. That goes back to the chemo thing. I don't want to do it because I know that all my senses would be dulled and I wouldn't have an opportunity to do anything between now and my final days.

The doctor was fabulous; he was comforting. He said, "I'll arrange for you to get hooked up with a hospice doctor as soon as possible. I'll touch base with your oncologist to see if we've left any stone unturned here. But I think what we've talked about is the reality of the situation." He said, "I'll make these calls and get the ball rolling for you."

I couldn't be more thankful that I have this guy in my life right now because he's a tremendous, compassionate and caring person. I can tell just by talking with him. Anyway, we shook hands and he wished me the absolute very best and left the examination room.

That's when it really hit me; I felt like I was in a state of shock. I walked out of the doctor's office and went the wrong way. I couldn't find the exit! I bumbled around in there for five minutes trying to get out because I'd had the last appointment of the day and almost everyone else in the office had gone home. So I wandered around in a daze, literally trying to figure out what was going on.

The first thing that comes to mind in that situation is, who do you call and who do you talk to? What's the progression and how does all of that work? Because now you have a reality that you're dealing with. That afternoon before my appointment I had spoken with my ex-wife, Ellen. She knew about the appointment so she had been all over me to call her as soon as possible. She had said, "I want that information as *soon* as you get out of there," and so on and so forth. So I thought, *Well, I better fulfill my first obligation*, which was to call Ellen, because she had made me promise to call her two minutes after I heard the news.

I've known Ellen since she was fifteen years old, and now she's 72. A long time. She was my high school sweetheart. We fell in love and got married, and we were married for approximately twelve years. We have one son, Allen, who was out here for my operation.

Allen had also called just before my appointment, and of course he had asked me to call him as *soon* as I got the results of my scan. Both Ellen and Allen knew the whole story about the spots on my liver.

Ellen's response when I called was, "Ohhhh shit. This is terrible news." I don't remember exactly what I said to her, probably something like, "Well, it is what it is, and I had to call and tell you." She was very upset. I don't remember the whole conversation because I was still in shock at that point. She said, "You can count on me to help you in any way I can," and so on and so forth – and I know that that's true; she is someone whom I can count on. It was very comforting to hear her say that. Ironically, the person whom I've known the longest was the first one to receive the news.

Then I had to call my son.

"Well Dad, what happened? What'd the doctor say?"

"It's not good news. The two spots on the liver have grown to two or three times their size, and there are six or seven *new* spots. It can only mean one thing."

"It's not fair! It's just not fair. You worked so hard. You tried so hard. You did everything they told you to do. And before that, you took the very best care that you could take of yourself. It's just not fair."

As far as I know, my son doesn't believe in Jesus. Allen is a good person and he loves his family, and I have nothing but the highest respect for him. But he's not a believer, so I can't share with him in that way. He reacted by focusing on fairness, but I didn't see fairness or unfairness as an issue. I wasn't thinking along those lines, so I didn't really respond to him.

Then he said, "We've *got* to get you out here as soon as possible. Come visit us in Atlanta. I'll start the arrangements; when can you do it?"

"I don't know," I said. "I only just received the news, and I don't know what days – I've got my work, I have to figure out, I got the... I don't know."

"You've gotta tell me as soon as possible when you can come out here. We've *got* to get you out here."

"I will. I'll work out the details tomorrow and we'll pick a time."

After I hung up with my son, it dawned on me that I was leaning up against a dumpster, making my phone calls. I was still in the medical office building, and somehow I had wandered down a corridor and turned in through a door to the trash room.

*I'm standing in the trash room here!* It was comfortable because I could put my arms up on the dumpster while talking on the phone. I'd felt like I needed to prop myself up anyway. But – in the trash room! I looked around – there was a lot of junk, and this big dumpster. Well, it was a quiet place, not a bad spot to make telephone calls.

Then I had the dreaded call to make... my next call would be to my closest friend, Karen.

That was the call that I least wanted to make. Karen has been through this with me every day since the very first encounter with the very first doctor, and we talk daily. She was the *last* person that I'd want to call with this kind of news. I actually stood there for a few minutes, working up the courage. Finally I called. I told her that the news wasn't good, that the cancer had spread and it was basically untreatable. She said, "I'll come over right away." We spent the evening together, and it was incredibly helpful to me that she was available to just hang out and talk right then.

After Karen's visit on Thursday evening, I made up my mind that I wouldn't go to work the next day. I typically work on Fridays for about five hours. I felt that the news of my prognosis was too overwhelming. Instead of working, I would just sit at home and absorb the shock. So I went to bed with that intention and didn't set the alarm. I planned to call in at about 8:30 or 9 a.m. to say that I wasn't coming in that day.

That night I thought I would have a very difficult time getting to sleep. But I took a shower and went to bed, and I went to sleep like a *baby*. I just went right to sleep. I don't think my head was on the pillow for more than a minute, then I was *out*, like a light.

# SECTION 2: THE JOURNEY BEGINS

On that first day, I realized that this final journey is the most incredible experience that anybody could ever have. Especially the interactions with people who either love you or barely know you. I hope to make a recording every day until it's no longer possible for me, and make note of everything that transpires. I wanna let people know what this process is like at the end.

5

# DAY ONE

**FRIDAY, MARCH 22, 2013**

Around 6:45 Friday morning, I got a call from Josh, one of my coworkers. I was shocked to hear from him that early and I had no idea *why* he would even call. My first thought was to tell him, "I'm not coming in today and we don't need to talk about whatever it is you're calling about."

But he wasn't calling about that day's *work*; this was about a situation which had evolved over the past week, which he thought would likely blow up today.

We have a new manager who started five or six months ago. Last week Josh and I had had a discussion about her, where we both concluded that she wasn't doing a very good job. Among other things, the building has a lot of low-income residents, and Josh suspected she was keeping the rent money instead of depositing it. Earlier this week, Josh had gone over her head and spoken about these problems with the woman who used to be our manager, Allison, who's now the portfolio manager of the building.

After a five-minute telephone conversation with Josh, I decided, *Well, I better get out of bed and go to work. I'm awake now, and we've got this intrigue going on. This is the first day that I have to deal with this information about my health, and maybe work will take my mind off it.*

I got dressed and went to work. Later that morning Allison showed up and confronted our current manager regarding the issues that Josh and I had discussed, and the manager quit and stormed out.

After that, Allison and I talked, and I felt that I had to let her know right away what was going on with my health. We'd grown close after working together for five years, even though I don't see her as often since her promotion. She sincerely wanted to know how I was feeling.

"Well, I seem compelled to tell the truth," I said. I could easily have told her that I was doing great. But when somebody tells me I'm gonna die in a few months, I'm *not* really doing great! So I explained that the cancer has returned and nothing can be done about it.

Allison stopped dead in her tracks, and said, "Oh Don, I am so sorry to hear that." She hugged me and said, "I love you Don." I thought, *That's sweet, that's really nice!* Then she said, "Don, I'm an atheist. I don't believe in God, I don't believe in eternity, I don't believe in any of that. But I *do* know that you're not supposed to steal from poor people!"

She had started off being compassionate and sympathetic about my situation, but then she returned her focus to the departed manager; and she felt obligated to tell me that she believes *none* of what I believe, except that you're not supposed to steal from poor people.

Later Josh heard the whole story about the manager, and he was shocked. He saw himself as the instigator, the guy who had set the whole thing in motion by talking with Allison earlier this week. Now that he knew that the new manager had left, he started laying out the future of the building for me, saying, "It's gonna be fantastic and it's a whole new world now. We're gonna be back with a leader and we're gonna have the building back the way it used to be."

"Well, you know, Josh," I said. "It doesn't really matter that much to me right now. I got some news yesterday which really shook me up, and I'm not going to be working here much longer."

"What happened?"

"I found out my cancer has progressed seriously. It's a terminal situation."

I could tell he was still thinking about the manager and all that, and wasn't paying a hundred percent attention to what I was saying.

"Well, after you leave here I really wanna keep in touch."

I thought, *Well! That may be harder than you think!* But I said, "Yeah, definitely, we will keep in touch." That was the end of it. What I told him just sorta went over his head and he didn't really focus on it.

That's kinda how my first day started off. I had told two people, one who understood it immediately and felt sympathy, but then completely shifted gears to remind me of our spiritual differences; and the other, my co-worker, for whom it just went over his head.

I'm starting to get my first glimpse of what this is gonna be like, going through the progression of meeting people whom I know, having this subject come up and having to tell them what's really happening. I figure I'll get a lot of different reactions. I pictured a conversation like this with a friend.

"Why don't we get together at such-and-such a time?"

"I don't know whether I'll be able to. I might not be well enough anymore by then."

"Why wouldn't you be well enough?"

Then I'll have to explain. It's gonna be a long road here, talking to people and sorting it all out.

Soon my cell phone rang. I didn't recognize the number but I sensed that I should answer, given all that's going on. It was my primary care doctor, who had given me the news the day before. He called to see how I was feeling and whether there was anything he could do to help. I told him I didn't need anything but I appreciated the call very, very much.

"I'm here for you," he said. "And I will help in any way that I can. I've called your oncologist, and she agreed with me that there really isn't any treatment available at this point. She said you might consider having a biopsy to see whether the cancer in the liver is the same cancer that originated in the bile duct a year ago. There's a chance that if this is a *new* cancer, it could be treated in some other way and might possibly be eradicated. But the chances of that are very slim."

"Well how do *you* feel about that biopsy?" I asked.

"I'm 50-50. I don't think it's really worth it, but there is that incredible possibility that it might be. It's *your* decision."

I figured I should do it, so that I'd know I hadn't missed something critical that could've been done. Just to make sure. So he said he'd email me the telephone number to make the appointment. It would be a minor thing: they'd knock me out, then go in with a needle to pull a biopsy. I wouldn't feel a thing. I'd have the procedure, then go home; no staying overnight.

My doctor also said that he'd contacted the hospice unit at OHSU. We needed to have a consultation with the hospice people so they could get me into their system and prepare for the down-the-road eventuality of hospice care. They would contact me to set up the appointment. I thanked him; I really appreciated his help.

About an hour later I got a call from the hospice unit to set up the appointment. That'll be on April the 29th.

I finished work, came home, and realized that I had a lot of other things to do. On my first day, I wanted to start planning. I wanted to think about what I could do in the time I had left. I felt energized because I had gotten through that first morning.

**Blessing #6**

*The strange thing is that if Josh hadn't called me at 6:45, I probably would've been lying in bed until noon! Seriously. I was in a depressed state that would've kept me in bed for several hours. But instead, because of this crazy situation at work, I got out of bed and went to work. I realized that that's what I have to do. I have to get up in the morning and do everything that I can do, even if my days are numbered now.*

I called Ellen to reply to an email she sent me that morning. She was planning a trip to Mexico with several friends and she suggested that I join them. She figured it was something I'd enjoy, spending five days in Mazatlán. Actually, I *didn't* wanna do that. She also commented, "You're going to go see your son, *our* son, and I would like to accompany you and help you on the trip." And so on and so forth.

**SETTING BOUNDARIES**

I realized that Ellen wanted to be helpful and caring but that she would get very involved if I didn't set some boundaries and tell her what I wanted and didn't want. People suddenly think, *Given your prognosis, we need to do this or we need to do that.* Well no, we don't! We need to do what *I* feel like I need to do, not what other people think I should be doing, with my remaining days. It's like: "Wait a minute, whose days *are* these? Who needs to make these decisions?"

I called Ellen and told her politely that I don't wanna go to Mexico.

"I have too many things to do," I explained. "I gotta get a lot of balls in the air here, and I wouldn't enjoy a vacation just two weeks from today when I have so many unanswered questions."

"No problem, don't worry about it," she said. "What about the trip to to Atlanta?"

"Well, I'm not sure of the exact dates yet. Allen and I haven't sorted that out yet. And I – I don't know. I don't think that... I don't know."

I just kinda got out of it and that's where the conversation ended.

Next I called Allen so we could pick dates for my visit. He said, "I talked to my mother an hour ago. She wants to come out here with you. She thinks it's really important."

I told him I didn't want that, and *he* needed to find a way to tell her. He said he'd take care of it. We worked out a timeframe which corresponded with a week when he could work out of his home office. That way we could spend time together throughout my visit.

I also decided that day that I would give my two-week notice at my job. I have bigger fish to fry! A number of things are critically important to me right now, and working at that building is not one of them. I called my boss, Allison, to explain, and told her that I'd report back to her with the date of my last work day. She's gonna be in the building now for three or four weeks while she breaks in a new manager. That's a great blessing because I know her so well; I don't have to work with someone I don't know. Today she said, "You have carte blanche; do what you need to do and I'll sign off on it." I called her after speaking with my son, and said that my last work day will be Saturday the 13th of April. Then I'll leave for Atlanta on the 14th.

By two o'clock in the afternoon, I had given notice at my job, planned a trip to Atlanta, and gotten out of a couple trips that I didn't wanna take. I thought my day was going pretty well at that point! I got to thinking, *This is such an amazing journey; it's really going to be worth keeping track of and talking about it.* Especially people's reactions when I tell them what's happening to me. An interesting thing came up in conversation with Ellen, a story I had never told her, about life and death.

## Blessing #7

*The beginning and ending of life are so closely related. My birth mother died of cancer when I was in my fifties. In her last few weeks, we knew she was dying. The circumstances were unusual in that I could only see her a couple of times a week. She was at home in a hospice situation. It was incredibly difficult to go and visit her, twice a week, and see her failing more and more each time. Dying. Right before my eyes. Every week a little bit closer. It got to the point where I had a lot of anxiety before each visit. But we had wonderful conversations, beautiful conversations.*
*At that time I was dating someone who had a brand-new grandson, about six or seven months old. I've never understood why, but this baby just loved me. The baby's father was out of the picture so the only people in his life were his half-brother, his mother and his grandmother. From the moment I met him, he just gravitated toward me. I would hold him and he'd put his arms around my neck and sob until*

*he went to sleep. He cried a lot. But any time I picked him up he would put his arms around me and sob himself to sleep and lie there for like an hour. I'd just sit there holding him, and he was so content. I would visit my mother and go through this really painful process of watching her die. Then I always made a point of going to visit the baby as soon as I left my mother. The baby was always so excited; he'd giggle and laugh and so on. Every visit, I'd spend time holding that baby. It became the most amazing experience: facing death, visible death right before my eyes, and then holding brand-new life. It was so powerful that I can't explain it. It was an incredible blessing, to have that vivid contrast.*

One other thing happened Friday night. I'm very competitive; I always need to have a benchmark to relate to. I decided that my benchmark would be an exercise that I've done, to show me where I am physically and how I'm deteriorating as I go through this. What I do is walk ten flights of stairs, up to the top floor of my apartment building. Then I walk crossways and down the stairs on each floor all the way to the bottom. Ten flights up, then walk each floor, back and forth, all the way to the bottom. Right now, I can start on the first floor and walk fairly briskly without stopping, ten flights up, with just a modest increase in heart-rate. As I come back down, my heart-rate decreases in a very natural and healthy way until it's back to normal. That will be my daily benchmark. Not many people my age can do that: walk up and down ten flights plus all the hallways, and get to the bottom feeling good. Not feeling stressed. As I get worse, that will cut down. There will be a time when I can only do nine flights, then eight, then six. It will tell me, physically, how my body is doing. It's a simple, little thing to keep track, like logging data in a spreadsheet.

On that first day, I realized that this final journey is the most incredible experience that anybody could ever have. Especially the interactions with people who either love you or barely know you. I called Karen that evening and we talked about doing our daily recordings. Some days my report will be very short, and other days will be longer depending on what happens.

I have a lot of activities and projects that I wanna do in my remaining time. I'll have more hours for those things after I leave my job. Depending on how long I'm healthy, I'll be able to work on projects. I have a beautiful work arrangement right here: my computer, and all the things I'll need for what I would like to do. My apartment is set up kinda like a disability apartment: it has grab bars in the bathroom and in the shower. It's very comfortable here and I hope that I can be here 'til the very end of this whole process.

6

# MAKING PLANS AND LETTING GO

**SATURDAY, MARCH 23, 2013**

The second day was not as eventful as the first. I felt much better about getting up Saturday morning because I had accomplished so much on Friday. I knew I was going to leave my job and take a trip to Atlanta, and Karen and I had decided to do daily recordings. I went to work and then came home and relaxed a little bit.

***Blessing #8***

*My big realization on day two was that instead of having anxiety go sky-high because of a terminal prognosis, you lose many layers of things that you'd normally worry about. Anxiety actually comes down a bit. For example, not worrying about having a heart attack. Not worrying about riding my bike and getting hit by a bus. I have a detached retina in one eye, and I've always worried about the other eye. I'm not worried about that anymore. Because of this sentence of time, I've just peeled away layer after layer of things that people normally worry about. I don't care what kind of car I get or whether I ever even get another car. I used to be concerned about these things and now I'm not! They're not even important anymore.*

I saw two friends on Saturday morning. At the building where I work, people always leave stuff when they move out. Every two weeks my friends—two brothers, Frank and Chuck Anderson—come by and pick up the stuff and take it to the Union Gospel Mission, where it gets sold in the thrift shop. They've been taking stuff there for four or five years now. I told them what's happening with me. Their reactions were really very interesting. One of them said, "Well, it's sad, but we're three Christians and we're all gonna die *some*day, and then we'll all be together again, so that's all it is – it's just sad." I thought, *Yeah, I guess that's true. It's just sad.*

The other one made a very strange comment. I said that I'm gonna make it to 76 years old, and that I think that's pretty good in today's world. Seventy-six is a good number. He said, "Yeah, 76 *is* a good number! It represents freedom!" I asked, "What? What do you mean?" And he said, "Well, you know, 1776! You know, freedom." I replied, "You're right. 76 *is* kind of a freedom number." So that was *his* unique take on it.

## DAY THREE – SUNDAY, MARCH 24, 2013

Today, the third day of my journey, was very important. It was my first time going to church after hearing the news about my health.

For the last several months I've been unsure of which church I want to attend. I've been going to two or three and I like all of them, but I haven't made up my mind on which one to make my permanent home. They're all close to where I live, and I have very specific reasons for liking each of them. They're different in doctrine and standpoint, but they're all based on Jesus and that's the key thing anyway.

Today I thought, *I have to make a choice about a church.* For the last months of my life, I can't continue bouncing around from one church to another. I need one that I can go to every week and do the best I can for *that* church. So I settled on the Presbyterian church that's only three blocks away, where technically I'm still a member. That will be my home church.

I went there this morning with the idea of telling only two couples in church about my situation. One couple is the pastor and his wife, Jared and Alisha. They have four kids. Another couple there whom I love is Christina and Aaron Lee. They have one child, still a baby. My goals were to go to church and to inform these people. Before the service started, I told each of them that I wanted to speak with them afterwards. Then I sat down to listen to the service, which was about Palm Sunday.

**Blessing #9**

*Today is Palm Sunday and next Sunday is Easter, and I thought, how incredible! The first time I'm in church after hearing that my life will end soon, the topic is the crucifixion of Jesus, and next week it'll be about the resurrection. Could the timing be more opportune? I sat there in church feeling awe-struck. Hearing a sermon about Palm Sunday and the death of Jesus deeply impacted my thoughts today. It was incredible timing, learning about my prognosis just three days before Palm Sunday and one week from Easter, the two most important days, for me, in the Christian year. I was astounded.*

After the service, Alisha and Jared came over to me. I shared the news with them, and they were visibly shaken. I told them, "It's OK because I'm going home; this is my journey now. Today is the third day of that journey." I thanked Jared for the sermon because it was totally spot-on for me today; it couldn't have been more incredible. I told him I wanted to make that my church home for the remaining time that I have.

I've already gotten a lot of different reactions from people when I tell them the news about my health. Sometimes it's a from-the-heart reaction and sometimes it's just a matter-of-fact reaction.

With some people, I'm sure they care, but they have so much going on in their lives that they don't react from the heart. Sometimes I hear that someone in radio or television has died, someone I don't know personally but I've felt a connection with all my life, and I get tears in my eyes. Because it's about my heart! Somewhere along the line I've grown to love this person and it's sad to lose them. It's an automatic reaction.

But then I hear about other people who have died, sports personalities or whoever, and I think nothing of it. It goes right over my head. Even though they're just as famous as the other person, they don't matter to me as much. There's definitely a difference. When you hear that somebody is dying, or you tell somebody that *you're* going to die, that from-the-heart reaction is powerful. It's not scientific stuff; it's just a feeling.

As I go through this, telling people about my situation, I'll have to see and respond to their reactions without being negative or judgmental or anything like that. It'll just give me an indication of what our commitment toward one another has been.

This afternoon, Karen and I got together for our daily recording session. That pretty much wraps up Day Three of my journey. I hope to make a recording every day until it's no longer possible for me, and make note of everything that transpires, day four, day five and so on. There's a number here; no one knows what it'll be. It might be 150, it might be 180; it might be a lot less. But I wanna share my experiences and let people know what this process is like at the end.

## DAY 4 – MONDAY, MARCH 25

Today is Day Four of my journey home. I really felt the Monday morning blues today. Everybody experiences that: the weekend is over; you get up on Monday morning and go to work and it's like, "Oh no, not another week." You gotta start all over from scratch and go through the whole week until it's the weekend again.

Having somebody tell you the previous week that you're approaching the end of your life really adds a new dimension to the Monday morning letdown. I woke up thinking, *I don't want to get out of bed; this is crazy! I could just lie here and sleep, and let Monday go away somewhere.* That feeling just made Monday morning seem absolutely unbearable. Finally I figured I had to get going, to get over to the building by a certain time and get my work done. So I got up, had my breakfast, and headed out.

I wanted to call a few people today, whom I really care deeply about, to explain my situation. Already it's getting more difficult to share this news with people. Then there are those whom I know casually, folks with whom our conversations are at least somewhat more meaningful than just discussing the weather. Today I bumped into half a dozen of those people. They always ask how I'm doing. Ha! *How am I doing?* I just say, "I'm doing OK." I don't know how to start the conversation about what's really happening. Today I ran into a young woman in the elevator, who lives in the building where I work. She asked how I was doing, and I said, "I'm OK." She replied, "I think about you often, about your health." It felt a bit strange because I hadn't spoken with her in a long time. Of course it was the perfect opportunity for me to say, "Well, by the way...," but I didn't. I just thanked her.

The residents in the building where I work know that I was out for two months last year for cancer surgery. When I returned to work after the surgery, it was obvious I had been through an ordeal, because I looked pretty bad. I'd lost twenty pounds. But now, because I'm still there a year later, I think they just assume that I'm fine. They figure, *He's back, he's OK; the crisis has passed.* Now when they ask casually how I'm doing, I haven't learned how to deal with it because I don't like deceiving people. But I also don't feel like telling the whole story to every person I run into.

With a lot of people you don't really have that kind of time either.

The "how are you?" is a quick, passing conversation, so you're not gonna say, "Hey, wait a minute, let me tell you about everything that's happened to me this past week."

In all of life's circumstances – it might be work, or church, or anywhere else – there are two or three people who, if you just tell *them* some news, everyone else will know within a very short period of time. If you've been around an apartment building or a workplace long enough, you know who these people are. If you don't want to literally broadcast your circumstances to everyone, you just avoid conversation with those particular people. I know who those people are, at work and where I live.

One reason I'm *reluctant* to have everyone know about my circumstances is that I know I won't like some of their reactions. Many will treat me differently, and I don't want that. They may just stop talking to me because they don't wanna confront the situation. In other words, if they see me coming down the street and they have an opportunity to go in a different direction, they will – because they don't know what to say or how to react. I don't want people thinking, "Uh-oh, I have to treat him differently now; I can't joke or have fun with him."

---

## INSIGHTS ON FAIRNESS AND EQUITY

**Is life fair? Should it be?**

At my job over the past few years, I always had a lot of time to think. Today I started thinking about the word *fairness*. What's fair and what isn't? My son had brought it up, along with a couple of other people, since this all started. Some people look at my situation and think that it's not fair that this happens to people. Many people don't believe in God because they think, *What kind of God would allow this to happen to people?*

I thought about it. Is this unfair to *me*? How does my situation compare with some of the other people that I know personally?

I know people in much worse situations; their lives have really been shattered and incomplete. For instance my friend Carl, who lives a couple blocks from me. When he finished college, he got a job in Hawaii where he had to sign a two-year contract. He thought Hawaii would be great, but then after awhile he didn't like it because he missed his family. Toward the end of the two years, he started looking for another job. A company in Los Angeles thought he was perfect for their situation, so they made arrangements to fly him there for a day of interviews. And at the end of that day, they told him he was definitely a top candidate for the job and they'd get back to him very soon. He thought it was a great opportunity.

A gal who worked at the company was assigned to drive him back to the airport for his return to Hawaii. They got in the car and on the way to the airport, she careened off the road and ran right into a big telephone pole. Carl was thrown through the windshield of the car and sustained a really serious spinal injury which made him quadriplegic. His career plans were shattered at that point, only two years out of college. The gal driving had been at fault, so he won a settlement which has provided for his lifelong care.

Today I thought, *Well, wait a minute. That's really not fair.* Carl has spent much of his life in a wheelchair so far, and he'll spend the rest of it in a wheelchair. Today was a sunny day and I saw him across the street, the first time I've seen him outside in a very long time. And I thought *that's not fair*, to have to go through all of that.

Then there was Eddie, a guy whom I volunteered with at church. I used to go to this huge church that had a huge parking lot; hundreds of parking spaces. Eddie organized a parking lot ministry. On Sunday mornings we'd greet people way out in the parking lot where it was a long walk to the church. We'd greet them and give them umbrellas and help them find a parking space, and it was a really fun thing to do. Eddie was a dynamo. He absolutely loved being in charge of that ministry, and everybody really enjoyed working with him. If it was raining, snowing – whatever! – out there, we loved the parking lot ministry because of his leadership. He was a great guy.

A few years after I met him, he developed Alzheimer's and he couldn't do it anymore because he couldn't remember anything. He just wasn't capable. He was probably in his late sixties by then. He disappeared from church and I hadn't seen him for a really long time. Then one day his wife brought him to church, something like five years later. I was really happy to see him so I went over and said, "Eddie, how are you?" We started shaking hands, and he had a big smile on his face. He looked just like he always had, a tremendous person full of life.

We started talking and I thought, *Wow, this is really cool.* It seemed like a totally rational conversation, as if we had a connection and he remembered me. Then, after about two or three minutes, his face went blank and he stared at me and he asked, "Do I know you?" I was shocked beyond belief! I thought he knew who he was talking with, based on how he reacted to me. But a look of confusion came over his face. He had no clue who I was or how we had gotten into a conversation.

His wife was standing off to the side and she realized that things had fallen apart, so she came over and reassured him, saying, "We've got to go now." He shook hands with me and said he didn't know who I was. I saw him several times at church after that, but he didn't remember me. About five years later he died from the complications of Alzheimer's.

I got to thinking – that was about ten years of living a life of not really connecting with the world around him. Not knowing anybody – even his wife! To me, *that* is unfair. And the wife had to go through all of that with him, but he was in total oblivion. I talked with her after he died and she described how unbelievably difficult it was to be around him. In the final days he was cared for 24/7 by somebody else because she couldn't handle it anymore. Imagine spending all those years in a nursing facility, not knowing anyone, not really being able to experience life at all. *That's* not fair!

When I got home from work, I got on my computer and the first story that popped up on Yahoo News was about an Iraq vet who was wounded five days after arriving in Iraq in 2003 or 2004. Wounded severely. Over the past ten years he has had countless operations and suffered incredible pain, and his life has been completely ripped away from him but he's still living. He's still living!

Now he has decided to cancel all medication and all food and drink, and he's going into hospice and he just wants to die. He has had enough and he can't do it anymore. I got the distinct impression from the story that he's not necessarily a person of faith. He just wants to leave; he wants out because he can't take it anymore. The story went viral and now he's got all kinds of people telling him, "Don't do it, keep fighting, don't give up!" But he feels he just doesn't have a life. He's been living for 10 years but has no life, just pain and suffering every single, solitary day. I thought, *Well, that's certainly not fair.*

What if somebody my age gets bile duct cancer in another part of the world, and can't even find a doctor to help? *That's* really not fair either! So this issue of fairness and unfairness and so forth – I can't answer that question. I just thought about these other people. In my opinion *their* situations are unfair, these horrible ordeals – living all those years just suffering.

### Blessing #10

*By the end of the day, I figured out that the question of fairness does not apply to me in my current situation. Fairness doesn't play a role in any of this. Until just a little over a year ago, I lived an entirely pain-free life. I was able to go hiking any time, I was able to go anywhere I wanted to go, be with anyone I wanted to be with and understand what they were saying, and practice my faith. I really had the opportunity to live life to the fullest. I didn't always do that, and I wish I had lived life more fully than I did, but I can tell you one thing: the question of fairness does not apply to me. I've been blessed with opportunities throughout my entire life.*

Whatever I have to go through in the coming months doesn't hold a candle to spending ten years in an Alzheimer's facility or ten years in bed wracked with pain because of war injuries, or any of the other things I mentioned. I have my faith and I have my friends, and I have so many blessings. I don't know what the future holds for me, other than knowing that things will go downhill from here. But even if I experience pain and that sort of thing, it still doesn't compare to the experiences of millions of people in this world in much worse circumstances.

# 7
# THINGS I'LL PROBABLY NEVER DO AGAIN

### DAY FIVE – TUESDAY, MARCH 26, 2013

I'm really tired tonight because I had a strange and interesting day. The big thing this morning was my dental appointment at eleven o'clock.

Before I knew that the cancer had metastasized into my liver, I had planned to have my teeth worked on. Some of the crowns I've had are 25 – 30 years old and they have to be replaced. I also have four cavities, which I've known about since before the cancer. Let's face it, I didn't pay any attention to my teeth last year! They didn't hurt so it didn't bother me. But then I had a dental examination a couple, three months ago when I thought I was in the clear. I made plans to have a number of things done – you know, expensive work, two crowns, a bridge, and then like four cavities.

Of course now I obviously don't need to do all of that; it'd be a huge waste of time. So the plan today was to have a consultation with the dentist and see how far he thought I could go without doing any of the work. I know my dentist through my ex-wife, so we have a personal connection and he had already heard about my condition.

I headed over, checked in, and got in the chair. The nurse wanted to know, "How are you doing, Don?" So on and so forth. She asked, "What can we do for you today?" I go, "Hopefully nothing! I'll have to talk to the dentist and see." Then the dentist came in and asked what I wanted to do. I said that I wanted him to look at my teeth and tell me what we absolutely *have* to do to prevent pain. He pulled up the x-rays and started probing around and checking all four of the cavities very thoroughly.

For the first one he said, "That one's OK, it won't materialize." He looked at the second one and said, "No, that's gonna be OK too, it won't materialize." In other words, he was thinking in terms of months or a year. He looked at the third one and said, "You know, that one's a little bit on the edge but it's not gonna give you that much trouble." On the last one, the most serious one, there's decay in the anchor tooth for my bridge, so working on that tooth would mean that I could lose that bridge. But he looked at it, and he probed it, and he picked at it, and finally he said, "Well, I tell ya, I think you can make it."

You can't imagine how that felt. Great, we'll just let these cavities go, but I can probably make it through 'til the end. Probably one of the strangest dental exams that he's ever given. It was certainly the strangest dental exam *I'd* ever had! I asked, "I can keep these areas as clean as possible, but is there anything else I can do that would help to forestall the decay and prevent pain?"

He asked whether I have a Waterpik. I don't, so he sent his assistant to get me one. She returned with this nice big box, this Ultra Waterpik floss thing. It was a *big* box. He showed me which teeth to keep an eye on, and said to Waterpik those areas, really hit 'em with high force every day to help keep them clean. That would maybe postpone more decay, and avoid pain.

I decided to schedule a cleaning as well. They'd had a cancellation at three o'clock. It was noon by then, so I realized that this was just gonna take my whole day because I had to go back home on the bus, have lunch, and then come back on the bus.

I walked the two blocks to the bus stop to head back home. There was a trash and recycling bin right by the bus stop, and I stuck the

Waterpik box on top of it because I didn't have anywhere else to set it until the bus came. As I was looking down the street for the bus, I heard this guy come up and start rustling around in the garbage can. I turned to look, and he was pulling out pop bottles and putting them in his bag. He was being pretty thorough so he found quite a few bottles, and he seemed really happy about that. He was saying stuff like, "Wow, this guy didn't drink half his Coke," and making all these comments to himself. I turned back to look for the bus, and a moment later he stopped talking to himself. I turned around again to see what he was doing now, and he was reading the Waterpik box. It has a picture on it, with an explanation and a description.

The guy asked me, "Is this yours?" I replied, "Yeah, it *is* mine." And he said, "I sure wish I had gotten one of those while I still had my teeth!" Then he walked away. I thought, *Wow, there's another one of those times where someone should've done something while they had the opportunity!* It was kinda funny; maybe if he'd gotten one of those, he wouldn't have lost his teeth. I wasn't laughing at his plight in particular, but I laughed about circumstances and people, you know – how often in life do you say, "Well, I sure wish I had done that when I still had the chance!" It was just ironic.

After lunch and some telephone calls, I returned on the bus and saw the hygienist, a guy who only works there on Tuesdays so he doesn't know all the people who come and go there. So of course his first question was, "How are you doing?" He seemed a little confused about cleaning my teeth when it looked like a lot more work should've been done on them. I said, "I haven't been taking extremely good care of my teeth this last year because I've been battling cancer." He asked, "How's that going?" Uh-oh, I got myself into that one. I told him, "It's not going well. The cancer's spread and it now looks like a terminal situation." He replied, "Oh I'm sorry to hear that, I really am." Then he went through the whole procedure and cleaned my teeth up really, really nice; they feel great now. Then I got back on the bus and came back home. By then it was 5 o'clock, so my whole day was caught up in this battle to save the teeth so that they don't cause me big trouble in the next few months. I think it worked out pretty well; I don't anticipate a lot of pain and suffering now.

Other than all that dental stuff, one person called me today, my friend Geraldine. I've known her for years; we used to work together and we're really good friends. Typically we end up playing phone tag, and that's been going on for about four or five days. She called when I got home from the dentist. She was all concerned. I had told her about a month ago that I was having a scan, and I never got back to her with the results. So today she was calling to find out what happened with that scan. What was the outcome?

I hadn't planned to talk to anybody today about my condition; I wanted a day off. So I didn't really wanna talk about it tonight when she called. But I didn't have a choice because at that point, you know, she had asked me a direct question. I couldn't tell her, "I'm doing good," and then call her back tomorrow and tell her the real truth.

I've discovered that these conversations tend to be long and tiring. There's a lot of emotion involved in telling somebody that you only have a short time to live. I was exhausted when I finished talking with her. Absolutely exhausted! I have a lot of people to talk to, and I'm gonna have to space these things out. Geraldine got all choked up and very upset. She started saying, "I need to drive out to Portland and see you." She lives a long ways away! I haven't seen her for like two years, maybe three.

So that was my day. It's funny what sticks with you at the end of the day. I'm beginning to see this: at the end of each day, there's something that just stands out. Today it was that guy telling me that he should've gotten a Waterpik before losing his teeth.

---

### A LAST TIME FOR EVERYTHING

*Also, another thing occurred to me. As the guy was cleaning my teeth, I thought,* Wow, this is probably the last time I'll ever get my teeth cleaned. *I had the urge to tell him, "It's my last time; do a really thorough job!" He was probably thinking, Well, I really don't have to do such a great job here because this guy's on his way out soon anyway. So here I am hoping for an extra-special, super-deep cleaning, and he's probably thinking it really doesn't matter all that much.* I wonder what was really on his mind.

---

## DAY SIX – WEDNESDAY, MARCH 27, 2013

I went to work today. I felt really good when I got up, and I was anxious to get my work done so I could come home and do some other things. I'd been at work for about half an hour when I bumped into a resident, a guy that I talk baseball with all the time. He's a big San Francisco Giants fan. He said, "Oh wow, baseball is starting in a couple days; what do you think of the Dodgers?" And I thought, *Well, I don't think anything about the Dodgers!* I haven't given them any thought at all, and baseball season is only two days away.

That felt really strange; he caught me completely flat-footed. He expected me to come back with all kinds of stats in anticipation of the season, but I didn't have anything for him at all! He had a very strange look on his face, like, *What's going on with you?* It dawned on me that March is always spring training month, with the baseball season starting on April 1st or 2nd. I realized that I had paid absolutely no attention to the ramp-up to the baseball season this year, none whatsoever. That's incredibly unusual for me.

Every year, throughout the month of March, I've always studied the Dodgers' rosters. The Dodgers are my favorite baseball team so I'd wanna know who they got, who their new guys were, and what their potential was. Plus I'm a really big baseball stats person; I know the stats and I really love the sport. I've always been all excited for the beginning of baseball season. But I realized that *this* year I hadn't even thought about it.

So the guy at work goes, "Well what do you think of the Dodgers' chances?" I didn't know! I don't know what their chances are. I asked him what *he* thought. So he started to tell me about the Dodgers. I felt bad. I thought, *Wow, how could I completely forget about the Dodgers?*

Then I remembered yesterday's theme that started with the dental hygienist, when I realized it was the last time I'll ever have my teeth cleaned. Suddenly I realized that I might not even be here for the World Series! That'll be in October. It felt strange – first of all I haven't even thought about baseball, and now I realize that I might not even see the end of the season. And here's this guy telling me all about the Dodgers, the first time I had thought about them this year!

I've been a baseball fan since the age of eight, around the mid-1940's. The first team that I followed was the New York Yankees. Growing up in Eugene, Oregon, we had no professional baseball teams. The Portland Beavers were about two hours north of Eugene, so I didn't have the opportunity to see their games. My first experience with professional baseball was listening to the New York Yankees on the radio. At that time they were the only baseball team with their own radio network, and one station in Eugene subscribed to it. I automatically became a Yankee fan, simply because I could listen to their games. And I *did* become a fan. Joe DiMaggio, Phil Rizzuto, and all the guys that played with the Yankees at that time.

So, for the first six or seven years that I was involved with any kind of baseball, it was all listening to the Yankees; that was all I knew about. During that time they won about four World Championships, which further engraved them in my mind as being the greatest thing that ever happened in baseball. Which they were! They've got the best record in baseball throughout the whole history of the sport. I followed them from the time I was about eight until I was 18 or 19 years old.

At age 20 I left Eugene and moved to Los Angeles. Around that time, the Brooklyn Dodgers announced that *they* were moving there too. I thought, *Oh no! Not the Brooklyn Dodgers! That's the worst possible team!* They were the Yankees' nemesis. I mean, when the Dodgers played in the World Series, I *hated* them. I didn't want to have anything to do with them, but all of a sudden they were coming to the city which I chose to be my home! What a confusing situation that was.

The Dodgers were called the Brooklyn bums, and that's what I thought they were, a bunch of bums. I was going to have to associate with these bums if I ever wanted to see a Major League Baseball game. Either that or get on a plane, but I didn't have that kind of money; I was broke. So I had no choice. If I ever wanted to *see* professional baseball instead of just listening to the radio, I was gonna have to go to a Dodgers game.

I started going to their games and I fell in love with them. Soon I thought they were the greatest thing that ever happened. Dodger blue. I didn't forget about the Yankees, but the Dodgers rapidly became my team because I was actually able to go see them play. I've been following them ever since!

So that's why I was so shocked today when I realized that I hadn't given them a thought throughout spring training. Not one single, solitary thought. Chances are really good that I'll never see them play baseball again; I would have to get to Los Angeles. Kinda sad, you know? But it doesn't really make any difference in the grand scheme of things. I mean, I'm going home to the Lord. What's baseball got in comparison with that?

When I got home from work, I checked the results of the Grapefruit League, the pre-season games down in Arizona and Florida. They play 30 games during that period of time, and report the standings at the end. The Dodgers were the worst team in the Grapefruit League! But that doesn't mean anything; in the pre-season they're just trying players out. A team might lose most of their games in the Grapefruit League, and then win ten in a row when the real season starts. You follow it if you're a fan, but I hadn't even looked at it. My priorities have obviously changed; it's really not important now.

---

## A LAST TIME FOR EVERYTHING

*There's this theme of "The Last of Things". Meaning the last time you're going to do something, whatever it is. In the general scheme of things, some of those things don't mean anything on their own. But you like a lot of the things you've done during your time on this earth. I took my son to Dodgers games when he was little. Six, seven, eight years old, going to games, getting hot dogs. I bought him all those silly things that they sell, like miniature baseball bats and cheap hats. So it was just sad to think that I'll never see another Dodgers game.*

*Then there's the Oregon Ducks football team. The past four years have been the greatest in the history of Ducks football; it's been incredible. Oregon football has been going on since 1888 or something like that, so I had the opportunity to see the four best years in the history of the program in over a hundred years. I felt pretty good about that. They're supposed to have another great team this year, but the outcome of the 2013 season won't be known until the end of December. There's a really good chance that I won't make it that far.*

*I thought about Easter coming up this Sunday, my favorite religious holiday of the year. This Easter will very likely be my last one on this earth. That made me sad. But wait a minute, Easter is a beautiful day to think about Jesus and the resurrection. Jesus promised us that we'll participate in resurrection and we'll be going home to be with him. It's a Catch-22 situation, where it's so sad to give up things of our lives here on earth. Nobody really wants to die, yet there's a glorious future for us beyond death. Right now I'm in between the two places.*

---

I had a burst of anger today, for the first time since I got the news about my cancer being terminal. I didn't realize I was angry! I opened the bottom drawer of my filing cabinet in the living room, and left it open. I put down whatever I'd taken out of there, and all of a sudden I walked back over and just kicked the drawer closed as hard as I could. With all my might. Boom! Slammed it shut. I thought, *Wow, where did that anger come from?* I have no idea, but it sure felt good! It was harmless. I guess I just had to take out my day's frustrations on *something* and it happened to be that drawer.

I'm actually looking forward to tomorrow, to seeing what will attract my attention and catch my eye. What am I gonna focus on tomorrow?

## DAY SEVEN – THURSDAY, MARCH 28, 2013

Today was a day off from work. The first thing I needed to do was to write a letter of resignation from my job, to make it official. Leaving this job is emotional because I've worked there a long time. It was a simple job that didn't require much brain work, so it was kinda therapeutic in a way.

I really spent some time at my computer thinking about my resignation letter, but in the end it was only two short little paragraphs. I didn't explain why I'm leaving. Basically I said that I'd be leaving on such-and-such a date, and I complimented my manager as a person whom I'd enjoyed working with. I was always impressed with her commitment to excellence. So I wrote the letter, made copies, and delivered it to the building.

I had to go over there anyway to put together one of my recycling projects. A big frustration over the past year has been that the cancer and surgery and recovery interrupted a huge entrepreneurial project that I wanted to do. I call it the Micro-Recycling Network. Prior to working at that building, I didn't much care about recycling; it was like, *Well, so what!* A lot of people have the opinion that it costs too much and it's just not worth the effort. But then I got involved with that building's recycling process.

In the beginning, it was a mess – recycling was being done, but it was done poorly. Many things were put into the bin that shouldn't have been. Multi-family buildings don't do a good job of recycling because the residents don't know how to do it: they try to recycle but they throw in the wrong things and it becomes a huge mess. And no one knows which residents are putting the wrong stuff in the bin, so management can't educate them. After I'd worked there awhile, I recognized these problems and I thought there could be a business opportunity there. I could design and print posters to put in recycling rooms to inform residents about little ways they could become better recyclers. For example, a nice poster with a photograph of a half-full jar of peanut butter. Don't put that in the recycling bin; clean out the jar first! It happens all the time. Or they put the eggshell carton in, with eggshells in the carton. It goes on and on. They wanna be recyclers but they don't understand what it takes. If you're gonna be a recycler, be responsible about it! So I decided that I would design a series of posters to educate people. Things like breaking down cardboard: don't stuff it in as a whole box, and don't try to stuff it down the trash chute.

After being frustrated with all of that for a while, I designed several posters, 8½ by 11, nothing complicated, and started posting them, one at a time. It helped! People stopped doing some of the things that we asked them not to do. So that was the first part, putting up simple posters. The city and county provide large posters, but they're so complicated and hard to read that the residents don't bother. They're not interested in the fine print. But a single poster with a single idea is very effective.

I've been an entrepreneurial person all my life, involved in many kinds of start-ups, so this looked like a great end-of-the-road entrepreneurial project for me: producing and selling recycling posters, and a recycling newsletter and blog. It would've been marketable and filled a need, because multi-family buildings don't have those materials available to them. My new enterprise, the Micro-Recycling Network, was going to be my big retirement money-maker. I planned to help the environment and line my pockets with riches, all at the same time, a win-win for the planet and for me. Ha! Seriously, I didn't actually expect to get wealthy, I just wanted to replace my discretionary income with a worthwhile project.

But then I found out about the cancer. For a whole year I didn't have a chance to work on this project; I couldn't focus, couldn't do the photography or think clearly enough to write copy. So now, even though I know that my life is going to be cut short, I decided, *So what!*

I can still try to start it. Perhaps I can get enough done in the remaining months, that somebody else can take it over and take it forward. I think about a quote that I really like, from Martin Luther, something like, "If I knew the world was going to end tomorrow, I would still plant my cherry tree today." This project probably can't be done in three, four, six or eight months, so working on it may seem like a waste of time. On the other hand, it's worth doing if somebody else can take it over. Plus it would keep my mind occupied and it'd be fun.

Another one of my projects in the building was a Styrofoam recycling area. Residents could bring block foam from shipping containers and boxes down to a designated area in the parking garage. I had put up a simple sign: Recycle Block Styrofoam. And people started coming. I accumulated a huge mountain of this stuff several times. Dealing with the current mountain of Styrofoam was gonna be my big, ambitious project for the day.

My friend Frank picked me up and we headed to the building. I gave my letter of resignation to the manager, and we had a brief chat. Then Frank and I worked on reorganizing the Styrofoam. We broke it all down, put it in plastic bags, and drove to a company called Far West Fibers here in Portland. They have bins for all sorts of things that people can't put in the normal recycling, stuff that usually ends up in a landfill. Block Styrofoam takes up an enormous amount of space in landfills. It resists moisture, so it doesn't break down – it just sits out there for eternity. Imagine how much of that type of packing material is generated in the United States every day, and I've heard that only like 20% of it gets recycled.

By late afternoon I was tired and worn out. Then I ran into the only person whom I told about my illness today. She lives in my building and I'd been reluctant to tell her about it because I know she will start putting articles under my door: what foods to eat or avoid, plus all sorts of other information that would just give me a headache. I like her; she's a nice person. But I've decided that my policy, basically, will be that I won't talk to people about the terminal cancer part of my situation unless they ask me a direct question. If the question is very direct and they have enough interest to ask me point-blank, "How's your cancer doing?," I'm not going to say, "Well, it's coming along, it'll be OK." I'm gonna tell 'em the truth at that point.

So I had evaded talking with this lady about it, but I happened to run into her in the hall. She asked point-blank, "Didn't you have a scan recently? What were the results?" I didn't have much of a choice. I had to tell her that the cancer has spread dramatically in my liver in a period of two and a half months and that theoretically there isn't anything they can do for me. They can't do any more radiation, and although they could do chemo, it wouldn't really do me any good.

"So you're not going to get any treatment?" she asked.

"No, because it won't help. It would just make me sick in the meantime."

"When my mother had cancer, she was in the Kaiser health insurance plan. And Kaiser won't let you commit suicide on their plan."

I really didn't know what to say to that! I assumed she meant that they wouldn't let you refuse chemo if there was any possibility whatsoever that it might help; you'd have to do it or they'd kick you off the plan. I guess that's what she was saying but I didn't bother to follow up on it; I just said, "Well that's interesting." I'm contemplating asking her what she really meant.

8

# CONNECTIONS AND PURPOSE

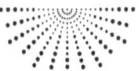

### DAY EIGHT – FRIDAY, MARCH 29, 2013

Today was all about Jesus. It's Good Friday, the day that he was crucified, the day that he suffered unbelievable punishment and went to the cross. It has always been a sad and difficult day for me, thinking of how our Lord suffered. In Portland, Good Friday is usually a rainy, dark, cloudy, overcast day, which brings home the sadness even more. When I woke up this morning, I thought about the incredible timing, for me to be looking ahead to my death, and have Good Friday and Easter weekend right at the beginning of this period of time. No other time of the year could've been more incredible to coincide with my prognosis, than the same week that Jesus suffered and died on the cross. To me, it's incredibly powerful.

I thought about people who know in advance that they're going to die at a certain time. I mean, that's not the norm. I've been given this news: I have about six months to live. Who else experiences that?

A convicted killer does, if given the death penalty; there's a date attached to that. I'm sure their lives take a drastic turn at that point, as they start to think about their own death. Of course we don't see much of that now because many executions are stayed for years and years and years. But when I was a little kid, nearly every state had the death penalty so people died weekly as a result of it. People were electrocuted on a regular basis, so you read and heard about it all the time.

All of those people were told that they would die on a certain day, and they had time to think about it. But that's unusual; only people with terminal illnesses, and people who have been condemned to die, know in advance. So I'm in a unique position, and I have to deal with it and get used to it.

Jesus knew that he was going to die, and that it was gonna be a horrible death. He even knew that one of his close friends would betray him, and that betrayal would lead to his death. But Jesus handled his final days with great courage, and showed his concern for people right up 'til the time of his death. I am extremely humbled by that.

Considering what Jesus went through, and what other people who are sentenced to die have to go through, why should I be so concerned about what I have to deal with? It was uplifting to think about Jesus and his trials and tribulations during the last week of his life, knowing what the outcome would be. It renewed my faith and made me feel closer to him. It gave me great comfort and courage today because if Jesus could go through something that horrible, I certainly can face what's ahead for me.

From an earthly point of view, I still had to get through the day, thinking my own thoughts, doing what I had to do to. Today was a work day. The manager of the building called a staff meeting so that I could tell them about my intentions to leave, and tell them – if I wanted to – why I was leaving. I decided to tell them that I was leaving because my cancer had recurred with a vengeance. My coworker Josh already knew, and he had supposedly not told anybody else. But when the meeting started, only one other person in the room didn't know, and that's the former assistant manager who's now been promoted to manager. She got all upset and told me how sorry she was to hear that news. I could see in her eyes and her face that she was very sincere; she was shaken by the information.

Later in the day I encountered Josh in the hallway. He told me about a documentary that he really wanted me to watch. I agreed to check it out on Netflix and report back to him; then I asked, "What you would watch if you were dying and only had so much time left?"

Think about those people who used to tape everything on VHS, and now they have a basement full of stuff that they'll never watch again. I never taped any shows; I didn't even have time to watch everything that interested me when it first aired. But now I have to be even more discretionary in what I watch. I have a very short list on television.

I've been watching *Breaking Bad*. The big attraction there is that I discovered the show around the same time as when I found out I had cancer. In *Breaking Bad,* a chemistry teacher named Walt gets cancer and rationalizes that if he makes methamphetamine and sells it, he'll be able to provide a giant amount of money to take care of his family after his death.

I was intrigued because of the cancer – where would *his* mind go with it, and where would *my* mind go? I think I'd like to take a big trip but I don't have the money so it's crazy to even think about it. But couldn't I just rob a bank? I mean, what could they do to me if I held up a bank? Chase Bank *loses* more money in a month than I could ever take from them! They've lost hundreds of millions since the 2008 crash, trying to manipulate the markets and make money off bad times. So if I held up a Chase Bank, who would really get hurt in any of that?

Well, that's crazy. I'm not gonna hold up any bank. But I could see how Walt from *Breaking Bad* could think that way. "People are gonna buy meth, whether or not I'm the one who makes it." He thought that making really great meth for people who would be buying meth *anyway* was sort of a public service, at the same time that he'd be saving his family. Even if he got caught, it wouldn't mean anything because he was gonna die anyway. I've identified with him through this whole thing.

I don't like Walt because he really is a bad guy, but I could absolutely understand where he was coming from. If I had a family with children, I know I'd be like, *What can I do to save my family?*

So that conversation with Josh about television just drove home the point that when you know your life is ending, everything changes about how you look at things. Walt on *Breaking Bad* is the perfect example of that, and that's why I love the series; it's so true, so incredibly real.

After work every day, I'm pretty tired. I come home and take a nap for an hour to recharge my batteries for the rest of the day. After that I like to go to Pioneer Courthouse Square in downtown Portland to take pictures for my Square People blog. This afternoon after my nap, I rode my bike down to the Square. It's close to a mile bike ride, all downhill; just coast all the way.

For close to three years, I've been going to Pioneer Courthouse Square in downtown Portland on occasion to shoot photographs, and then put them on a photo blog. I've got eleven hundred photographs of the Square on the internet, in 276 individual posts. The blog has had about 12,800 hits. In a couple, three months it'll be up to 13,000 views.

My other reason for going to the Square was to get a cup of coffee. After my surgery, the doctors recommended avoiding coffee and caffeine because they're so acidic. With part of my intestine removed, my stomach is now hooked up differently and acid is a bad thing.

I stopped drinking coffee for several months, but then I kept thinking about how much I really enjoy it. I've consumed coffee since the age of eight, when I had a paper route. I thought maybe I could go back to it if I limited it to two cups a day. One in the morning around ten, to get me through 'til noon and make my head function a little bit better, and one in the afternoon to get me through the evening. Perhaps it would help me accomplish more and feel better.

And guess what, it works! I have a clear head because of coffee. My stomach gets a little funny but not enough to really bother me. I have absolutely faithfully stuck to the two cup a day limit, and I'm very proud of myself. Going to the Square, hanging out and shooting pictures – having my cup of coffee thrown into that is a huge treat.

So today I sat in the sunshine, in my favorite place where you can see the whole Square and look for photo opportunities; it was amazing. I was sitting there looking around, and then I heard a street preacher behind me. He was talking about Jesus and the crucifixion – all the events leading up to Jesus' death, and *why* Jesus died for us. I finally turned around and realized I had photographed him before but hadn't used his photograph in a blog post.

As I listened, I realized he had an amazing grasp of the Bible. I agreed with everything he said; every statement he made was right on spot. Sometimes I'm really amazed by people who can stand on the street and preach really well, even with people just walking by not paying one bit of attention to them. I started listening because he was talking about what I'd already been thinking about: Jesus' death on the cross. I decided to go and say hello to him. I walked up at a moment when he had stopped and there wasn't anybody around.

I said, "I just wanted to thank you for what you're doing here today. I really enjoyed your sermon. You did a great job representing the Lord. I have terminal cancer, and this Good Friday and Easter may be my last."

"That's not true!" he said.

"What do you mean, it's not true?"

"It's not true that you're going to die. How do *you* know?"

I explained that I have metastasized liver cancer

"Don't you think God has something to say about that?" he asked.

"Well of course he does. It's his will that I'm living by; I either live or die and I have to accept that."

"Well how do you know it's his will that you won't be here next Easter?"

"I don't *know* that it's his will. I'm going by the medical information that I have."

He persisted, "I still say to you, how do you know it's his will? Have you asked him to let you live longer than that period of time?"

"No, " I admitted.

"Well why don't you *ask* him?"

"I understand what you're saying, and I understand the will of the Lord. God didn't cause my cancer, but he'll work with it and use it to his means. I don't know what the outcome's gonna be, I just know what the doctors are telling me."

"Well, you'll be here next year if I'm here next year," the preacher said.

"You can't say that."

"Have you *asked* the Lord to give you more time?"

"I told you before: no, I haven't."

"Well, why not?"

"I'm not sure I deserve it."

"Well then find out!"

"OK, I will. I'll do it."

What had started out as just walking up to a man whom I admired and simply trying to pay him a compliment, ended up in this confrontational situation. I actually felt somewhat guilty because I've never asked God if he would give me more time on this earth. It was just a very, very strange conversation. He certainly gave me food for thought, and confronted me on my faith!

It's a conflicting thing, and I'm wrestling with it. I've always known that this is the will of God, one way or the other. Just before I went in for my operation last year, I was in that room all by myself for a period of time and I said the same prayer I always say. I say, *God, I will accept your will. Whatever happens during this surgery, I understand. Your will be done.* That's how I approach illness. That's how I approach everything. I understand the concept of God's will. If God wanted to save my life, he could do it in an instant. Cancer has been known to go into remission even when it's in a very bad state. It just stops growing. That would be a huge miracle, right? For me to be saved would be a huge miracle because right now the cancer is growing rapidly.

But the Lord says, "I'm not gonna have mercy on *everyone*. I will have mercy upon whom I will have mercy." Somehow it's difficult to think that I deserve any more time than anyone else, so I am willing to accept the will of God. God didn't cause this cancer but he can use it in a variety of ways in the overall scheme of the universe.

After that conversation, I started walking back to my bike, where I had it locked up. I saw another guy that I see at the Square all the time. He comes down with a sign that says, "Israel – they already control the U.S. Congress," and some other stuff. I've walked by him maybe twenty times when he's out holding that sign. I've even photographed him but I've never talked to him. Today I thought, *I need to find out exactly what this guy wants*. He's down here all the time with that sign, all by himself.

I stopped and said to him, "I'm not here to argue or be confrontational. I just wanna know. I can read your sign, but what do you want?"

"Israel has way too much control over the U.S. government," he said. "They get over 50% of our foreign aid. Just that one country! That's way too much! They have control of the U.S. Congress."

"OK, what do you want to do about that? What are you saying?"

"We have to stop doing it. We have to stop listening to all of their lobbying."

He pretty well explained what he wanted and how to do it. We had a really nice conversation and I finally understood the guy. He did have some facts, like how much foreign aid, and this and that. I assume they were facts; I didn't look them up to confirm anything. But I walked away with a much different understanding as to why he was there and what he wanted.

That second conversation brought home another thing about having what you consider to be a short amount of time. You need to tie up loose ends. You can't just keep walking by people whom you wonder about all the time, without stopping to ask, "What are you doing?"

It happens all the time, in everything you do. You just walk by people: the same person standing on the street corner, week after week, with a sign or some kind of newspaper or whatever. You have questions, but you walk right by instead of asking, "What do you want? What are you here for?" It's fascinating to get those answers! So I promised myself I was gonna do more of that: when I see somebody with a sign, I'll stop and ask nicely about it. You know, just out of curiosity.

We really don't live in the here and now during much of the day, or focus on the things that are going on around us. We spend way too much time worrying about what's gonna happen tomorrow, what happened in the past, or something else, and we're not really focusing on what's in front of our eyes this very moment. That's something that people need to do a lot more of, just focusing.

Like, I've been sitting next to this person at work for 20 years and I don't know anything about them or what their problems are. Why not strike up a dialog and try to find out a little more about them? That's just an off-the-wall example, but you know what I mean. This has come home very sharply to me in this first week, that I don't pay enough attention to what's right in front of my face – *today*. I've begun paying attention more, this first week, than I've ever done before, and I find it really interesting and fascinating.

This evening I went to a Good Friday church service. After coming home from the Square, my mind was whirring from the conversations that I'd had down there. I had a quick bite to eat, and went to the service. It was a little different: they had tables, each one with a couple loaves of bread and wine glasses, set up sort of family-style. The pastor came around to each table. He poured wine or grape juice into each glass, and started a dialog about Good Friday with everyone at the table. We broke the bread and talked with each other individually around the table, rather than sitting in the usual congregational seating arrangement. It was very nice.

I had a lot to think about. Today I learned things that I wouldn't have learned if I hadn't had this news about my diagnosis. Everything has changed. I've started to approach everything somewhat differently than ever before. It's like having a new feeling of *What's going on, what do I need to do here?* rather than automatically going through the day and not paying attention.

9

# THE INCONSISTENT ENERGY CURVE

## DAY NINE – SATURDAY, MARCH 30, 2013

Today I felt like I was just kinda drifting along. It was a work day, and the thing that I like about working Saturday mornings is that there's no one there except me. The office is closed and the residents aren't up yet. Many would've been out on Friday night hitting Portland's downtown night life, so they're still resting and the building is very quiet. I go around and do my job, get things done, and don't run into anyone. The day didn't seem to have any central theme; I didn't have any specific ideas or thoughts running through my head. I was taking a mental vacation.

I've talked a little bit about drinking coffee. The building has a coffee shop at street level, where the donuts are absolutely delicious. I mean, they're amazing, some of the best donuts in Portland. The shop is owned by a young family who moved up here from California. Big-time donut-makers in California, with a chain of stores. They gave their daughter the donut recipes and said, "Go someplace where you wanna live, and start a donut chain." She picked Portland and rented space in this building. She's very knowledgeable about donuts; she grew up in a donut family. Not that I've ever known anybody from a donut family before…

**Blessing #11**

*Having that donut shop ties in perfectly with my routine of having a cup of coffee at ten a.m. I look forward to it: I get away from the job, I have one of these great donuts, and enjoy a cup of coffee. Yesterday they were sold out of my favorite donuts, and my favorite leather chair in the shop was already occupied, so I got my second-favorite type of donut and a coffee to go, and went across the street to the light-rail station to sit on a bench. Normally it's cold and raining in Portland this time of year and you can't do that, but today was special because the sun was shining brightly and it was warm and really nice. I missed sitting in my favorite chair, but the sunshine pretty much made up for that, so I enjoyed it tremendously. I felt really blessed that I was able to be there, still feeling good, just having a cup of coffee and a delicious donut.*

That was pretty much my work day. I realize I'm not gonna have an intense day every day; I certainly hope not! After work I took my nap. Karen picked me up about 4:30 in the afternoon and we went to Starbucks where I had my second cup of coffee for the day. So my day was pretty much made up of two cups of coffee, one donut, and a nice conversation with a dear friend!

## DAY TEN – SUNDAY, MARCH 31, 2013

**Blessing #12**

*This has always been my favorite time of the year in my faith: the day of Jesus' resurrection. I woke up this morning filled with anticipation about going to church. I know I've said this before but I feel really blessed to have gotten this medical news right around Easter. It's exciting to think about the future, based on what happens during Easter weekend. Easter is the most joyous day of the Christian year; it is the good news of the Christian faith: after a horrible death, Jesus is resurrected.*

Church has become very casual, everybody knows that. People wear jeans and t-shirts and nobody notices anymore. Come to church as you are. I'm not saying that's wrong, but when I was a child and went to church, it was very formal. Women wore beautiful dresses and hats, and men wore suits and ties. Little girls wore pretty dresses, and little boys had little suits. I really miss that; it was beautiful to see. It was everyone's way of honoring the Lord by putting on their finest clothing and going to church. Clothing has nothing to do with faith; but on Easter, it seems appropriate to me to dress up and go to church and honor the Lord. That's my take on it.

I planned to put on a jacket and a tie to go to church. I turned on the classical radio station where they tend to play music on Sunday mornings that's more of a religious genre. I enjoyed getting dressed and getting ready to go.

In downtown Portland on Sunday morning, the people out on the sidewalk are really a mixed bag. You see all sorts of people – some have been up all night, some are homeless. You *don't* really expect to see anyone with a jacket and a tie. If you *do* see someone on Easter morning with a jacket and tie, you *know* where they're going; they're going to church somewhere. These days that can be good or bad depending on who you run into. I decided it was time to go and I strolled out onto the street, started walking down the sidewalk, and these two guys came walking toward me. They were a little on the scruffy side. As we got closer, one of them said, "Hey, man, you're really looking *good* today! That's pretty cool!" I thought, *Well that was very nice.*

Portland is a very strange city, as far as dress is concerned. Probably the most casual city in the United States. When I lived in Los Angeles, I had jobs where it was really important to be dressed properly because I was in sales. I felt that it helped me in selling things if I looked a certain way. I read a book called *Dress for Success*. It specifically laid out what you should wear to be successful in business, because dress is about first impressions, especially in sales. It said, "The *only* city in the United states of America where it's OK to wear a sport coat in business is Portland, Oregon." In other words, wearing a sport coat instead of a suit. That was back in the 70's, but that's the kind of place this is. Nordstrom's and Macy's in Portland have all these really trendy clothes for sale, racks of them. They must sell but I never see them on the street.

## A LAST TIME FOR EVERYTHING

*I got to church and I was really excited to be there and hear the message about Jesus. I was also feeling good about the way I looked. It's not a pride thing; I was there to honor the Lord. A few people said, "You look really nice today, Don." I sat down and thought,* If this diagnosis is correct, this will be my last Easter on this earth. *That gave the service a more special meaning. It's a joyous day in my faith, an incredible feeling of exhilaration about Jesus and his resurrection, but still, nobody wants to give up the things they've enjoyed here on earth. It's hard to let go of these things – nice clothing included!*

I chose a seat, and started reading my bulletin and anticipating the service. The musical prelude was beautiful. Normally babies go to the nursery during church services there. But suddenly I realized that there were a lot of babies in the pews, in the congregation. Furthermore it seemed as though I was sitting in the designated baby section. Not long into the service, a baby right behind me started talking baby talk in a pretty loud voice. My first impulse was to move to another seat so I could hear the service and focus on it. I thought the baby was actually mimicking the pastor!

But then I thought about the baby. I could tell this child was less than a year old without turning around to look. I realized, *It's my last Easter in church, and it's that baby's first Easter in church.* I wondered, *What will this child's life be like?* What if this child lives to be my age and is sitting in church someday and hears a baby right behind them, chattering away? It was a moving thing for me. It really was. From that moment on, the baby didn't bother me at all. I was happy about that baby being there on its very first Easter.

The pastor's message really inspired me and I thoroughly enjoyed the service. The last song was my second-favorite hymn, *How Great Thou Art*. My favorite hymn is *Amazing Grace*. I usually get a little teary-eyed when I hear either of those hymns.

Afterward I stopped to talk with a few people. I've always been someone who walks up to people and says, "How are you doing, I haven't seen you in a while, how have you been?"—that kind of thing. Given my situation, now I don't want people asking *me* those questions. Rather than just deceiving them, I could simply say, "Well, I'm blessed" or something. But I don't want to be drawn in and have to talk about my situation and then have to deal with people's reactions. I just get uncomfortable.

## DAY 11 – MONDAY, APRIL 1, 2013

Today is April Fools' Day. It was an excellent day. When I woke up this morning, my breakfast tasted great, it was warm outside and I was looking forward to going to work. I only have eight days left on that job. I'm looking forward to the end of the job so I can get on with other projects.

I went to work and everything went well. I just felt good. I did something that I'm trying to do more of: reaching out to people that I've seen and talked to many, many times but really don't know very much about. Today I ran into a guy whom I've seen many times: a caregiver for one of the residents. He's a pleasant guy and we always say "Hi" to each other. Today he told me he was pretty tired because he works seven days a week.

"On weekends I work for an organization that owns a hospice facility," he said.

"Is it a difficult job?"

"Physically, I'm fine, it's no problem."

"I didn't mean difficult physically, is it difficult emotionally?"

His demeanor really changed., "Oh yeah, it's really difficult emotionally. It takes a real toll."

I didn't mention my situation. We didn't talk for that long. But it was a nice conversation. It just goes back to that point about taking a couple minutes to reach out to somebody. You find out a lot about them and it's really interesting. I've seen this guy so many times, and it turns out he's a hospice caregiver.

Later I was having my coffee and donut break. The donut shop manager and I haven't had a particularly warm relationship. The same waste removal company picks up recycling from the apartment building and the donut shop, and we've had some conflicts regarding the recycling. Little problems from time to time. But we've never really talked.

Today he happened to be hanging around the donut shop, so I asked a couple questions and we started talking about recycling because that's where we've had conflicts. It was a really interesting conversation!

He's from Japan, and there they make a major recycling effort all the time. So he has a real problem with recycling efforts in the U.S. because he thinks we do things wrong; we don't do as much as we could, and we don't educate people. That was kinda strange to hear because I think he doesn't know what *he's* doing either when it comes to recycling. In the end we didn't really come to a consensus, but it seemed like a start toward better communication.

Anyway I just wanted to keep that little thing going about being more attentive to people, reaching out a little bit more than I have before. Especially with people who have been kinda difficult, whom I usually just blew off with a "Hey, how you doing?"

I had a pretty physical day. I felt strong. That made me think about how this cancer is invading my body and destroying it. Aside from cancer, my body functions really well. It's amazing to me how suddenly an insidious disease can attack what is otherwise a strong, healthy body.

## DAY 12 – TUESDAY, APRIL 2, 2013

This morning I got up feeling really tired. I overdid it yesterday, as I've done many times in the past when I've felt great. So the day didn't start off too well. I had to work on all my finances. I pay my bills on the first or second of the month so the first thing I did was get all of that out of the way.

I have a lot of people to call and tell about my situation. So far only a few people know. I haven't returned some phone calls because I know the subject will come up. Then I remembered the email from my friend Ronald Beale, early 2012, when he told me that he had cancer. He was one of my very best friends.

He'd said, "Hi Don. Bad news to pass on. I'm being treated for cancer. It was caught too late, and I only have a few months left. I declined chemo, but I'm taking radiation treatment. I can still walk with a walker and cane, bathe, dress and eat. My wife is a perfect companion through it all, and I get daily strength and guidance from the Lord. Spending most days getting things in order. We plan on home hospice soon. Give me a holler on the phone when you get a chance."

I remember how devastated I felt when I got that email. Today I thought, *That's pretty much what I'll have to tell people when I call them.* Ronald died within 30 days after that email; he didn't have a few months.

In the end, I decided *not* to call anybody today. I couldn't visualize calling people I haven't talked to for a while, and giving them this kind of news. But I will definitely have to! While I'm still healthy and walking around I wanna see anybody that I can see. I know that as I start to feel worse I won't wanna see them.

In the afternoon I went for a walk. I ran into a guy from the neighborhood whom I talk to once in a while. I asked him, "What have you been up to?" He said, "I had a busy day yesterday! I watched a Three Stooges Film Festival. It started at eight o'clock in the morning and went until nine at night." I thought, *Well, I haven't had a great day, but I certainly had a better day than watching a Three Stooges Film Festival for thirteen hours!* I could last about twenty minutes with the Three Stooges. The idea of watching them for thirteen hours is mind-blowing. So I felt pretty good after that conversation; it wasn't such a bad day after all.

## DAY 13 – WEDNESDAY, APRIL 3, 2013

Today was a workday so I got up at 6:45 a.m. after a good night's sleep. I was looking forward to getting to work and getting through the day. I felt physically better today than yesterday. It felt good to go to work and get the job done. Now I have only six work days left. I found out that they hired a replacement for me and I'll be meeting that person and working with them next week.

After work I went to the grocery store on my bicycle. I started to lock up my bike when I saw a guy loading bins into a truck. The truck door had the name of an organization, *Store to Door*. I forgot to lock my bike because I walked over and started talking with the truck driver, who told me that it's exactly what I thought it was: a nonprofit organization that shops for people who can't get to the store.

I'm already having an awfully hard time telling people that I'm sick, so I asked the guy, "I know someone who may be needing food delivery in a month or so; how does this thing work?" Of course it *is* true, I *do* know someone! I just didn't tell him it was me.

He said, "You sign up and become a client. We call you every Wednesday to take your food order, then we shop and deliver your groceries on Thursdays and Fridays, depending where you are in the city. We shop here at Fred Meyer's."

They only shop at that one store, that one big Fred Meyer. It's 99% volunteer people. Volunteers do the shopping, they put it all in the truck, and then the truck brings it to your door and you give them either a check or cash. They request a ten percent surcharge on the order. So for a fifty-dollar order, you pay a five-buck delivery fee, which is really, really reasonable. That's really cool if you think about it!

There will be a point, down the road somewhere, where I won't be able to go to the store any time I want to. If I can use something like this, that'll be great. Bring the groceries to me. Safeway, the grocery store a couple blocks from me, has home delivery too, but they charge a lot more for it. So I got the guy's card with all the information. It was fortuitous to run into him, and I felt good about making that connection.

Then I came home and worked on my Square People blog. There are thousands of red bricks throughout the Square. The whole surface, the walls, everything, is red brick. They sell the bricks: you can have your name engraved on a brick for a donation of a hundred dollars. So I was walking around the other day and I saw a brick with "Elvis Presley" on it. I decided to take a picture of it. I got a close-up shot. I thought I'd do a post on that: "Elvis Presley...question-mark."

In the post, I said that I assumed somebody donated it for Elvis. It might have been someone whose name really was Elvis Presley, but I decided to go with the idea that somebody donated a brick to the King. That's pretty cool, that the King has his own brick out here. The post turned out pretty good. I included a few other random pictures as well. (See http://squarepeople.blogspot.com/2013/04/elvis-presley.html)

During the last part of the day I had some papers to photocopy, so I walked down the street to a copy shop. I've known the shop owner a long time, at least 13 years. I thought I'd start a conversation, kinda like what I've been doing, trying to have longer conversations and connect with people. I went in and said, "I know you've been here a long time. How long has your shop been here?"

He said it's been 27 years. We started talking about the old copy machines that were around 27 years ago, and the brick cell phones that Motorola made, and the original fax machines which came out around that time. It turned out to be a fun conversation, reminiscing about all these things that kids today can't even fathom. All that old electronic stuff. Meanwhile he still only charges ten cents a copy. But he does so much more: posters, booklets, printing on poster board and foam core stuff, and so on. I really liked the guy – he's older but he's kept up with all the technology.

He knew that I'd had an operation last year. Not long after the operation, I was sitting on the bench out in front of his store and he came out and said, "Oh, I see you've lost a lot of weight." I looked terrible at the time, and I had to stop and rest on my way to the store *and* on my way home. Karen and I were calling those excursions "Store Trek" at the time.

Anyway, the guy from the copy shop would see me out there on the bench, and he'd come out and ask if I was OK. So *today* he said, "Wow, you've really made a good recovery, you look really good." I thought, *Well, I'm not gonna go there and spoil his day!* I said, "I feel pretty good, too," which wasn't lying because I did feel good today.

I feel like I'm deceiving people but, by the same token, I don't wanna take the time to explain; and I don't wanna ruin their day with a sad story, you know? But I think any time you deceive someone by not telling the whole story, you're basically lying to them. You're not lying to them directly, but you're not telling the truth either – it's complicated!

All in all it was a good day; I would have to give it high marks. I didn't overdo it but I'm ready to get to sleep. Today I picked up some good information about the food delivery service, and I got to sit out in the sun a little bit. I know that if I'd had a chemo infusion a couple days ago, it wouldn't have been a good day.

## DAY 14 – THURSDAY, APRIL 4, 2013

Tonight I feel really tired. I don't know why, because I didn't do that much today and it wasn't a work day. It seems every time I have a high-energy day, I have a lower-energy day the next day. But I can also feel that my energy level is going down a bit overall.

I was excited when I got up this morning because I had a project to work on today. I decided to do a blog post for my micro-recycling blog. In two buildings, I've been conducting a lid recovery program for over a year now. Plastic lids, like on Coke bottles and juice bottles and any plastic bottle that has a screw-top lid. They can't be recycled in the normal flow of recycling because when the bottles are crushed, the lids explode and fly all over the place and get caught in the machinery.

Lids can actually be cooked and made into motor oil. I decided that today was the day to gather them up from both buildings, take pictures and get them to the recycling plant. So my friend Frank, who's been helping me with this project, picked me up. We took six large plastic bags full of lids over to Far West Fibers, where they have a special bin for lids. It was a yucky, rainy day, but we got 'em out there. Along the way I took pictures to illustrate the process so I could put it on my recycling blog.

Along with educating people, the idea behind my recycling blog, the Micro-Recycling Network, is to promote diverting things from the trash collection and the landfill – things that aren't picked up by the major recyclers – and finding ways to get those to separate recycling facilities. For example, in Oregon it's against the law to put any kind of broken electronics in the garbage: televisions, cell phones, CD players, computers, electric razors, anything like that. You can be fined for that.

The problem is, those items don't get picked up by the recycling companies either. You have to literally separate them out and take them to a special place where they'll be broken down and handled properly. There's a lot of material inside all of those appliances that can be used in various ways, but they have to be broken down and handled by someone who's specially-trained. So I wanted the blog to explain those things and help people in apartment buildings find better ways to dispose of those types of items. I had high hopes for the blog. But I didn't post anything the entire time I was recovering, a whole year. Now I've got the Styrofoam post from a few days ago and the lids post that I got done today. I've discovered that recycling really makes me feel good.

The other thing I had to do today was rearrange a couple of medical appointments. That kind of thing is getting really annoying for me. Now that my condition has been deemed as terminal, dealing with medical people on just run-of-the-mill stuff can easily make me angry.

For example, today I called to cancel an appointment. The intake person wanted to review all my medical information – *again*. I've given this hospital all the information they could ever possibly want about me! It's in their computer, and each department uses the same computer system, but whenever I call, they can't seem to find my info.

The woman said, "OK, let me just verify your address." She had the wrong apartment number. Right there I started to get a little bit upset. Then she said, "I have Karen listed as your emergency contact; what is her last name?"

"Wait a minute. You have my emergency contact as Karen, but you don't have her last name?"

"No. What is Karen's telephone number?"

"Wait a minute. Please explain something. Do you think that when your organization first asked for my emergency contact information, all I said was, 'In case of an emergency, call Karen'? No last name or phone number? Is that what you think I did?"

I was getting angry. I shouldn't have been angry, but it seemed absolutely ridiculous that they didn't have Karen's telephone number or last name! We got into a little bit of a tussle.

"Just follow me on this," I insisted. "You come in, they ask you for your emergency contact, and you give 'em the person's first name, and that's it. Does that make any sense to you at all?"

"Well, I don't have it here," she said.

"Then I'm not gonna give it to you. If you don't have it, forget it. I'll call back another time; I don't wanna deal with it right now."

"OK, *have a nice day!*"

Ha! Obviously the phone call didn't go well. But anyone can see how frustrating that would be. For somebody in my condition, you would think that these people would have the information at their finger-tips 'cause it's really, really, *really* important.

I've been going to that medical facility for years. So I was very frustrated. These are the people whom I expect to see me through to the end of my life. Yet they can't keep track of who my emergency contact is? Maybe I better find another provider!

I was very shaken by the whole experience; I lost my confidence and trust in them because of that conversation. Karen is the executor of my Advance Directive, so it's really important to me to make sure that the people I'm dealing with have the right information. It was kinda scary.

There's something else I want to say about today. I have a friend whom I've known for over 20 years, who does some things that really frustrate me. He's roughly 60 pounds overweight, and he keeps talking about getting on his bike and riding the extra weight off. He hasn't said anything about changing his diet or other habits. We recently got into a discussion about how ridiculous that is.

You would have to ride 60 miles a day to burn enough calories to lose 60 pounds. The real trick in losing weight is a combination of diet and exercise, good sleep, drinking lots of water, all of those kinds of things. I can go to the gym, get on a recumbent bicycle, knock myself out for a half an hour, and burn 250 calories. That isn't even a milk-shake in the course of a day. So burning 250 calories on an exer-cycle isn't gonna get you very far in weight loss; you have to exercise *and* diet at the same time. His real problem is his diet – what and how much he eats. He put his extra weight on by e*a*ting, *not* just by not exercising.

Now he's signed up for a 60-mile bike-a-thon. He tried to do it last year, but halfway through he started having severe dizziness and fatigue and muscle cramps, and he had to quit. This year he's in worse shape and he's gonna attempt it again. I get frustrated by that. I told him he has to train for it, get on his bike 15-20 miles a day for a long period of time before the bike-a-thon. Of course he's not doing that. So in a few weeks he'll get on his bike and try it again. He could die of a heart attack before I die!

One thing that works in my favor, regarding what I'm going through, is my state of mind. I have my faith and that's huge, but aside from my faith, I'm comforted by the fact that I have really tried to take good care of myself in recent years. I exercised, I rode my bicycle, I went to the gym, I really tried to eat right, I took vitamins and supplements. I did everything in my power to prevent disease in my body. None of that prevented my cancer, but I can look myself in the mirror and say, "I didn't get cancer because of some stupid thing that I did." My surgeon even told me there was *nothing* I could've done to prevent it. In his opinion this particular cancer is about 99% environmental. And he has seen hundreds of cases.

You look at these things differently when you hear that you have a short time to live. I've noticed obesity more than I used to. Recently I was in a restaurant and I saw half a dozen people – we're not talking about 50 pounds overweight, we're talking about a *hundred* and fifty pounds overweight. When you see so many people in that state, you go, "Wow, what's going on? Why are people doing this to themselves?" I've noticed so many things that people do to themselves. For instance, smoking. I think about these people: they don't know if there's a tumor forming in their lung as a result of the cigarettes they're smoking all day long. And I have news for them – they do *not* want that tumor in their lung. But you can't go up to them and say, "Stop doing this immediately, it could kill you." I can't be the policeman of the world, going around telling everybody that they're on a slippery slope, and they *don't want* to have to have chemo someday, and they *don't want* to have to experience radiation.

Anyway, I wanna close it there. It was a bittersweet day. Some really good stuff and some bad stuff. Hopefully I'll have a little more energy tomorrow, a little less frustration, and a more positive day.

# 10

# REJECTION, RECYCLING, REMEMBERING

### DAY 15 – FRIDAY, APRIL 5, 2013

*Blessing #13*

*I woke up this morning feeling pretty good. I felt rested and ready to go. Today was a workday. Counting today, I have six workdays left. I had breakfast, got dressed, and hopped on my bike. It was a really nice ride over, except that there was a really strong headwind. I've come to view every day as a huge blessing if I get up in the morning feeling good, with a good appetite and no pain. It's really great to start off the day that way, considering my current medical condition.*

When I got to work, none of my coworkers were there so I was roaming the building alone for a while. Then my work cohort Josh the maintenance guy showed up. He was all excited. He said, "Lemme tell ya what we're gonna do. We're gonna have a smudging." A *what*? I asked, "What are you talking about?" He took me into the office, where he had a pan with a rolled-up bunch of dried leaves tied with rope, about a foot long. That didn't answer my question!

There's a woman who has lived in the building for just over two years, Penelope. She has been unbelievably disruptive to me and the rest of the staff in the building. She didn't like the way I do my job and for a while, she complained constantly about it. She was the only person that I ever had an issue with, really, in that whole building, and she just kept at it, kept at it, and kept at it. She got the rest of the staff involved and was causing a lot of problems. But she moved out on the first of this month. I had become so used to her negative attitude towards everything, that it was stressful to do any work on her floor. I had a huge sense of relief when she moved. But Josh told me they were gonna take it one step further and smudge the apartment.

I didn't get what he was talking about except that he had this pie pan with the rolled leaves in it. The building manager came in, and although she didn't seem too enthusiastic, she was willing to go along with it. I was actually really reluctant; I don't know why. It just seemed like a silly thing to do. But Josh kept at it. He got everybody to commit to a time to meet at Penelope's apartment.

It was all empty and cleaned out and they were getting it ready for the next tenant. Josh contended that in addition to cleaning the place, we had to get rid of the spirits too, the disruptive spirits. Now it was starting to make sense. Josh brought his smudging stick and the pan, and Allison came up with a video camera to tape the event. Josh put on a hoodie sweatshirt and lit the end of the stick with a match. It started to smoke. He went around, under the sink, all around the outside, in the bathroom, and the closet. You go through the whole apartment with the smudge stick and try to get the smoke in all these different places where the evil spirits are, you know?

I was just standing there; I didn't know what to think! It seemed like an occult type of thing. It was kinda creepy, to tell the truth. But everybody else was really having a good time with it. I started thinking about Penelope. I thought: *Wouldn't that be terrible, to have somebody do that when you move out of an apartment?* You've caused such a ruckus, and so much chaos, that people would want to do that? It's really sad in a way. Spiritually, from my own belief, I didn't really wanna participate in it. And I didn't really; I just watched. From everyone else's perspective, it was funny, nothing more. They didn't give Penelope a second thought.

But from my perspective, it was more serious. There's no question that this woman had been my enemy. On several occasions she had really tried to single me out and cause trouble for me. But as a person who believes in Christ, smudging her wasn't the answer. You're supposed to pray for your enemies! Pray for her that she's gonna have a better life wherever she's gone, that she matures and becomes a person who can get along better with others. That pulled at me throughout the whole thing, the idea of forgiveness. After she moved out, it was time to forget and forgive. But the others wanted to go through this ritual.

After I came home, I turned to my most favorite thing of all, Google, and looked up smudge stick. Sure enough, there's a Wikipedia page about it. Sometimes it's used as a cleansing technique by New Age or Neo-Pagan religious practitioners, to get rid of evil spirits. I didn't really like it and I didn't really wanna participate. The smudging is gonna *stick* in my mind for a while...


## DAY 16 – SATURDAY, APRIL 6, 2013

Today was a pretty non-descript day, another workday.

Frank and Chuck came by the building where I work, to pick up usable things that people have left behind, and take them to the Union Gospel Mission thrift shop. The items are sold there and the money goes directly to the Mission, which helps the homeless in downtown Portland. There was a sizable load of stuff at the building and I've also been giving away my *own* stuff, clothes I can't wear anymore because they're too big after all the weight I've lost.

I have four more days on the job. I think next week would've been about the last week that I'd have the energy to do it anyway. Even *this* week was a stretch. I found myself taking longer naps every day after work. My energy is slowly but surely going downhill.

I'm feeling a little anxious about my trip to Atlanta, Georgia, which starts on Sunday the 14th. I'm going to be so far from home and my little routine here. Three thousand miles away from the Safeway grocery store that I go to every day! Getting on an airplane and flying that far will take me out of my comfort zone. I certainly wanna go and spend the time with my son and his family. But I feel anxious. Then again I also feel excited about the trip, so I guess overall the excitement is outweighing the anxiety.

For quite a few years I've used a football game analogy for life. I reflected on that today. My goal has always been to live 80 years; that would be a really good life. I'd reach 80 and just go to sleep or something. 80 years is four segments of 20 years each, which is like the four quarters of a football game. I love football. Just like a football game, the first 20 years of your life – or the first quarter – you're trying to figure out your opponent and what's going on around you, what it's all about. You're kinda bumbling around, trying to get your life going. The second 20 years, just like a football game, you start to really put it together. You start to figure out your strategy, based on what the opponent is like. And in life at that point you've decided on a career and you're just starting out. Like a football game, you've got a better idea what you're doing but you don't know for sure what it'll take to win the game.

By 40 years old, let's say half-time in a football game, you pretty well know what the opponent's all about, and you pretty well know what your life is all about. You're either on a career track or you're not, but you know what you're doing and where you're going. Just like in a football game, you start to make progress in that direction, real progress toward winning the game, or else your opponent is stronger than you and you start to fall back a bit. I know people who have gone in both directions at that point. So the third quarter is a little more difficult – you're either cruising along and winning the game or else you're starting to get beat up a little bit.

Then you get to the 4th quarter, which is like 60 years old. At that point, it's pretty clear how this game's gonna go; you're either winning or losing. By 'losing' I mean you're just not accomplishing everything you wanna accomplish and you aren't able to get everything done. Then you reach the 80-year mark, the end of the 4th quarter.

Today I also thought about the people who either die earlier or make it past 80. If you get to 80 and you still have years left in your life, that's bonus overtime. You've done a lot of things well, to get to that point, and hopefully now you have time to do other things. Like a football game, you do different things to win it. But if you *don't* make it to that point in the game, that means you got knocked out of the game somehow, which happens all the time. Some people get knocked out in the first quarter and they don't play the rest of the game. Some get knocked out in the second, third, or fourth quarter. Anyway, I like my analogy because I like football and I see the comparisons between life and a football game. We either win it or lose it, right?

**Blessing #14**

> *In a football game you win or lose based on points. Winning in life doesn't have to mean a financial reward; it has to do with having had a life that you feel counted for something, versus having a life that you feel really didn't count for much of anything. It has to do with peace of mind. You can get knocked out early: if I only make it to 76, that would mean I was knocked out of the game just a little bit before the end. But even when someone's knocked out early and they're on the sidelines – maybe with crutches – they can still feel like they contributed. It looks like I'm not gonna finish the game, but I contributed and played the game as well as I could. I think if you're able to look in the mirror and say, "I did the best I could," that's a great reward.*

---

## A LAST TIME FOR EVERYTHING

*The only other thing today was that I needed to buy a couple of articles of clothing. I've given just about everything I own away because it doesn't fit, so*

*I needed a couple of articles of clothing for the trip to Atlanta. So I went shopping. I bought a new casual jacket and a casual pair of pants, trousers. In both cases, I thought:* How many casual jackets have I bought in my lifetime? Maybe 50? And how many pairs of pants? *I've bought hundreds of pairs of pants. When I made those two purchases, I just couldn't help but think* This is the last jacket and the last pair of pants I'm ever gonna buy. *It was just a strange feeling.*

---

It felt extravagant to buy new clothing, like I was doing something that I didn't *have* to do. I felt guilty, like, *Do I really need to spend this money on these things?* But the other jackets I have look like tents when I put 'em on. Made by Omar the tent-maker. I just needed a nice, trim jacket that I could wear and feel good in it.

So that was my day. Thinking about my life in terms of the quarters of a football game, and how I'm not gonna make it to the end of the game, and that's OK because I feel good about the way I played the game. I haven't always felt that way, but I do now, and that's probably the most important thing.

**DAY 17 – SUNDAY, APRIL 7, 2013**

This has been an incredibly emotional day. It was a beautiful day, but very emotional.

When I woke up this morning, my primary mission was to get to church. I wanna try to do that for as many of the Sundays that I have left on this earth as I can. I haven't told a lot of people in church about my illness and the time I have left, other than the pastor. When I arrived this morning, he asked if I would stay at the end of the service because he wanted to gather some of the elders to pray for me. I said, "Sure, I'll be happy to. I would love to have the prayer." Then I sat down and I enjoyed the service.

After the service I saw a woman whom I've known for maybe six or seven years. She was someone with whom I've really bonded over the years. So far I hadn't mustered up the courage to tell her about my illness. Sometimes I don't like to tell people because I don't want to upset them. But today had to be the day.

Her name is Jane. She always comes by saying, "How ya doing? How are ya?", that sort of thing. I said, "Jane, I have to give you some bad news. My cancer is terminal."

I was entirely unprepared for her reaction. She really broke down and cried. She hugged me tight and wouldn't let go. It was by far and away the most passionate response that I've had, and I wasn't expecting it. She was truly hurting. We hugged each other for about five minutes while she cried. I was incredibly moved by the whole thing. I told her, "It's OK. I'm at peace with this; I'm going home." We talked a little bit more about our individual faith and we finally parted company, but it was an amazingly emotional experience and it was something I hadn't expected. Nobody else has reacted quite like that.

Then the pastor gathered five elders of the church together, to gather around me and pray for me. They put their hands on my shoulders, and then each of them prayed aloud. It was an incredibly powerful experience to feel that prayer and to feel surrounded by the concern they had for my circumstances. I was incredibly moved.

I asked them to pray for my friends and family, because I know that some of those people are struggling and having a hard time with what's happening to me. They prayed that I wouldn't have to endure a lot of suffering in all of this, that I could go home peacefully rather than going through a lot of suffering and anguish. I felt as though the Spirit was in that room. It was incredibly uplifting.

---

### A LAST TIME FOR EVERYTHING

*After church, I met up with Karen. We had plans to have lunch with a young couple from church, Aaron and Christina Lee. They have a 17-month-old son, their first child. Aaron is a medical student at OHSU, and he helped me find my current primary care physician.* It was a beautiful meal and I thought we had a really straightforward and interesting conversation throughout. Right now in my life there are a lot of "lasts": the last time I'm gonna do this, the last time I'm gonna do that. *I thought:* This could be my last lunch with Aaron and Christina.

---

Anyway, that's all I wanna talk about today. There were three very emotional events – Jane, the prayer, and the lunch. Each was incredibly uplifting but at the same time very tiring and draining, emotionally. I've begun to realize that some of my fatigue is not necessarily due to the illness, but from emotion. Even very uplifting experiences can cause anxiety, and that accumulates throughout the day. I couldn't have had a more beautiful day than today, but it was very tiring.

# 11
# LEAVING THE JOB

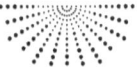

### DAY 18 – MONDAY, APRIL 8, 2013

---

#### A LAST TIME FOR EVERYTHING

*Today was interesting because this is my last week at work. Every day of work this week is the last one of that day. In other words, I worked today so now I don't have any more Mondays, which was always the hardest day of the week. Now that I've finished, that's the last Monday work day that I'll ever have! So that felt good.*

---

When I got to work this morning, I wandered around and got to thinking about my liver, and how the cancer is progressing there. There's no way to really know what's happening. There won't be any more scans because right now we're basically just waiting. I have an appointment with my oncologist after the trip to Atlanta. That'll probably be my last appointment with her, to get her final word on everything. She may offer me some sort of chemo plan, but I've already decided that I don't wanna do that.

I know I've mentioned this before, but I *really* love my coffee breaks these days. I look forward to going to the donut shop. They put my coffee in a mug, and I drink it one sip at a time, savoring and enjoying it. I have my little chocolate cake donut, with beautiful icing on it, sitting on a plate. I look around the shop, watch people come and go. It has *really* become a special part of my day. And no, even though they give me a plate, I do not eat the donut with a knife and fork!

As I sat in the donut shop today, a young couple came in the door. The girl had on a nice-looking sweatshirt with a "Triumph Motorcycles" logo on the back. That logo brought back all kinds of memories. I started and ran a motorcycle newspaper for a few years in the early 1960's, and Triumph was my second-biggest advertiser. They kept me afloat for a long time.

I started thinking about motorcycles, and how much I enjoyed riding my motorcycle back then, in my early 20's. The two big English brands were Triumph and BSA. I had a BSA. I only rode it for about three years, just when I owned the motorcycle newspaper. I sat there reminiscing about cruising across the desert in southern California. I *never* actually rode it on the street. The great thing about riding in the desert was that if you got in trouble and you came off the bike, the sand was very, very forgiving. It was a pleasant landing unless you hit a rock or a fallen tree or something. You could really come off the bike hard in the desert and not get hurt. I fell off a number of times.

Then I started thinking, *Maybe I should get a motorcycle! That would be amazing!* Get a motorcycle, ride it for two months. If you go in a motorcycle shop and talk to the salespeople, you'll find out that a lot of people get to 60 and 70 years old and, all of a sudden, they wanna ride motorcycles again. It's not such a great idea, but it doesn't amaze me; it happens all the time. I started thinking about getting one and riding it in the desert – riding *fast* in the desert. But I'm not gonna do that. It felt like a good idea while I was sitting there drinking my coffee, but I'm not gonna get on a bike. I hadn't thought about motorcycles for such a long time; seeing the Triumph logo just brought that whole wave of memories into my head.

Then I went back to work. There's a guy who lives in the building; I've seen him a few times but never really spoken with him. I ran into him today. I've been trying to just say a few things to people that I haven't talked to before and see what happens. We ended up having a pretty interesting conversation about the San Juan Islands, up in Washington State. I've never been there but I've always wanted to go. He said the islands are unbelievably beautiful. Now I wanna go there! That's still totally doable; drive up to Seattle, get on a ferry, spend the night.

That was pretty much my day. My last Monday at work, reminiscing about my motorcycle, and suddenly wanting to see the San Juan Islands. I felt great today. I had a really good night's sleep last night, and I felt really blessed all day today because I felt almost normal.

## DAY 19 - TUESDAY, APRIL 9, 2013

Today was a strange day. It wasn't a work day, so I got up, had a nice breakfast, then considered what to do with the day. Again I felt a lot of anxiety about my upcoming trip to Atlanta. I haven't traveled for a year or so. I got worn down just thinking about what to pack. I began making a mental list. Writing an *actual* list would've been helpful, but I felt I had to think the whole thing through before writing it down.

Then I found a way to completely avoid trip planning: I decided to go through my apartment and clean out more things that I know I'm not going to use, and stack them up for Frank. On Saturday he'll be around to take *more* stuff to the thrift shop. It feels strange to look around my apartment and think, *Well, I'm not gonna use that in the next three or four months or a year, so it's gotta go!* A lot of these things haven't been used for a while anyway. So I just basically bumbled around the whole morning.

It was kind of bittersweet. I thought about this apartment, which was recently remodeled. It's so new and nice and clean. Everything I had to go through to get that done – moving out for a month and then moving back in – I felt kinda sad because I won't have the opportunity to take advantage of it. It was like, brand new start, brand new apartment, brand new everything – but the cancer came back. I looked at the walls and thought about all the things I had planned to do – I was gonna put up some of the old publications that I worked on; I had this decorating plan in mind. But now there's no reason to do that. It's sad.

Later I had plans to see Ellen. She came over and brought me an extra suitcase. We had a long conversation. One thing we talked about was the MacKenzie River, just outside of Eugene, Oregon. When Ellen was a little girl, she lived out on the MacKenzie River. My family did too, for a year. Ellen and I even rode the same school bus for two years, but we didn't know each other because she was a year younger, in a different class.

The MacKenzie River is beautiful. It's designated as a wild river, meaning that you can't build on it, really; what's there is there. When I was in third grade, my parents ran a grocery store right at Finn Rock, which is about halfway from Eugene to Bend. There was a community of 40 houses across the river from the store, and a swinging bridge. Now all of those houses and the bridge are gone; there isn't a trace of them left.

Besides Ellen, I didn't spend time with anybody today. I can see that when I leave my job, I'll have to make time during the day to go out and interact with people – for as long as I can. It's really helpful to get outdoors and talk to people, rather than just staying home and working on my computer or whatever. Today was the first time that I thought about this. When I leave my job, every day will be like today. I have plenty to do on my computer; I have a lot of projects. But working on a computer can be isolating. I'll have to find ways to add social activities to my day, along with my projects. That'll have to be right at the top of the list.

Going to work has also been helpful in another way. Beyond having contact with people, on a work day you have to get up, get ready, and get yourself over there, and you get a sense of accomplishment from that. I'm going to have to replace that somehow, because I want that feeling of having accomplished something.

This has been a day of transitioning, and it has felt strange. I'm actually looking forward to going to work tomorrow because I was kinda caught off guard by these thoughts. I liked it fine when my days off were between work days because that was my chance to get caught up on things. But today for the first time, I thought, *Wait a minute, next week, or the week after that, and so on, it won't be a day off; they'll all be days off!* And it'll be up to me to figure out how to fill them and not feel isolated.

I was going to make some calls today, to catch up with people whom I want to tell about my prognosis. There are maybe ten to twenty people with whom I wanna spend some time while I'm still rational and capable. They need to know that I don't have much time and we'll need to get together soon for coffee or lunch. But I wasn't able to call any of them. I kept thinking about Jane on Sunday, where she broke down and cried and it was so emotional.

Even though I've already told a few people, it gets harder instead of easier. The more people you tell, the more varied the reactions that you get; you can't anticipate how people will respond. But it has to be done. If the roles were reversed, I would certainly wanna know if a friend was in my situation so that I could spend some time with them before it's too late.

## DAY 20 - WEDNESDAY, APRIL 10, 2013

Oregon weather has a tendency to tease us every once in a while. In the late winter or spring, sometimes we'll have these brilliant sunny days, really pretty, not much wind, everything's just about perfect. You think, *Oh wow, spring is here, how wonderful!* And then the next day the weather reverts back to its gray, rainy self. I call them teaser days. One day it's great, and the next day you feel like something has been taken away from you.

That's what my day has been like today, a teaser day. All day long I felt wonderful. I felt better than I can remember throughout my whole recovery, peaceful and in control. I felt as though my body had healed and I had really good strength. I can't remember when I had a day where I felt more normal. And my food tasted good! I thought I wasn't *sick*. And then I realized: it's not true. It's like a teaser day.

It was a work day. After work, I came home and continued going through my stuff, looking for things I no longer need. There are things I wanna bring to Atlanta, to give to Allen and his daughters. I found one of my little childhood treasure boxes, full of pocket knives and little knick-knacks, things that only a child would keep. There was a pair of dice in it; apparently at some point they were very important to me. And a little piece of flint. I also found a white stick about six inches long, from a tree that I used to love. One time I just picked up the stick and decided to hang onto it forever. It's strange, what we decide to hang onto. I was less than ten years old when I decided to keep that stuff.

Then I found my old rubber cars, which were my absolute first toys when I was just a little guy, like three, four years old. They're classic rubber cars, maybe three or four inches long and a half inch wide. They're really a treasure. Of course I also thought, *There isn't anybody else on this planet that would be interested in those old rubber cars!* I'll take 'em to Atlanta to give to my granddaughters, and I'll say, "I know you have zero interest in these, but someday you may have a baby boy, and when he gets to be three or four years old, he'll love these little cars. So hang onto them for another 15 years until that time comes." There are several things I wanna give to them and tell them to just hang onto because someday they'll come to appreciate them.

I also found all my National Rifle Association badges. When my dad gave me my first .22 rifle, part of the package was to join the NRA and take all of their rifle training and safety classes, and to participate in marksmanship contests. So I was into that really heavy for three or four years and I won a lot of awards. I was a good shot, to tell you the truth, a very good shot.

The day was so strange because I didn't feel sick. But that changes very rapidly when all of a sudden you don't have enough energy to get up out of a chair. That's when you realize that it was a teaser day.

## DAY 21 – THURSDAY, APRIL 11, 2013

When I got up this morning I felt pretty overwhelmed. I have this feeling of time being short, and I need to be as productive and get as much done as I can. I have specific goals to accomplish while I'm still physically able. That's one of the main reasons that I don't want chemotherapy and everything that goes along with it – it dulls your mind. You can't string things together or write a paragraph. So it seems like right now is the time to work hard.

One thing that I've thought about doing is a series of life history recordings about my life. I had some very unusual, unique experiences as a child. I struggled with alcohol from a very young age. I was involved with a lot of pioneering technology in the publishing industry. All of those things are part of my story. Life history recordings could be rewritten into a biographical book about my life. So I spent all day organizing materials in order to begin a series of recordings: paperwork, photographs, files, documents about my family's history. I filed 'em all by decade, starting with the 1930's when I was born, through the 2010's. I think it's an excellent way to get organized.

## DAY 22 – FRIDAY, APRIL 12, 2013

Just after I woke up today, I remembered that I only have today and tomorrow left on my job. I got up, did my regular routine, had breakfast and headed for work. I went through the day pretty much like I always do. The district manager was in today. We all got together and reminisced about the past five years, which is how long I've worked there. It was kind of bittersweet, but at the same time I'm glad the job is ending. I have bigger fish to fry now.

Today I got a call from Janine Beale. It's always a great pleasure to talk with her because her husband Ronald and I were so close. Ronald died of cancer a little over a year ago. I think Janine likes to talk with me because it makes her feel closer to her husband. At the same time, she has a strong faith so I find it very comforting to talk with her.

We were having a great conversation until she told me that her mother died of liver cancer, which I hadn't heard before. Then she proceeded to tell me what happens to somebody as they're dying of liver cancer. I said, "Hold on right there. I don't wanna know; don't give me those details." I have purposely not researched that. So we had a little bit of a conflict there.

It's not that I'm afraid of what's going to happen to me. My motivation is that I don't want to think about it every day that I have left on this earth. I want to focus on the things that *I choose* to focus on, not what's gonna happen to me down the road.

We also had a long conversation about cancer in general, for instance how long people have it before it's diagnosed. Why hasn't more progress been made in detecting cancer through blood tests? I would think there must be *some* blood test that would indicate that you have cancer growing in your body, much earlier on. Ronald went to orthopedists because he had joint pain, but that pain was from the cancer spreading all around his body. So they didn't detect it until it was too late to treat.

So much money is poured into cancer *treatment* – poured down the drain! – but it doesn't help everybody. A lot more should be poured into research on how to find it in the first place. Finding it sooner is the key, not all this chemotherapy and radiation and everything. Treatment is just after-the-fact. Much like alcohol and drugs, you've got to get to the root cause before it becomes a disease, before it eats you up. When a kid *starts* drinking a little bit, you have to do something about it. Same with cancer. It all comes down to finding it earlier, so that people don't have to go through radiation and chemo and so on. The treatment can be worse than the disease! The conversation with Janine, and all those thoughts, kinda consumed the latter part of my day.

I still have a lot of people whom I have to talk to, but every time I start to call somebody, I think of Ronald's email where, all of a sudden, he said he was gonna die in a few months. I'll never forget how I felt at that time. Tears came to my eyes and it was two or three days before I could call him back, before I could even talk to him. I was shocked. When you know how it can affect someone, it's not easy to call people up and tell them you're gonna die.

Anyway I think that was pretty much my day. I'm learning that you can be cruising along pretty well, feeling good, and then a thought-provoking conversation with a friend can turn it around really fast.

**DAY 23, SATURDAY APRIL 13, 2013**

Today is actually only about one thing. It was my last day on the job. When I first took the job, I thought it would be a very short-term thing, but it turned into five years. Previously I'd had a different job which I really liked, where I did a lot of driving. But I suffered a detached retina and couldn't drive as much anymore, so I left that job. I wanted to do something else but I didn't know what. Then I saw a notice, in the apartment building where I used to live, saying that they needed a custodian. The job paid a whopping eleven dollars an hour. I thought it would be great as a short-term, interim situation. I knew the manager because I lived there, so I applied. She said, "Yeah, I think you could do that job," and I said, "I *know* I can do it. I clean my own apartment regularly, so I'm sure I can take care of this building." So she hired me.

When I started, I had about a four-and-a-half-minute commute to work. It was the kind of job where you don't have to think much. At the same time it was good physical exercise. I was also going to the gym and doing a lot of hiking, so it was an opportunity to add to the physical stuff that I did, and listen to things on my mp3-player while working. It enabled me to do other enjoyable volunteer projects and not have to worry about additional income. At that time I had a number of entrepreneurial ideas that I wanted to get going. But my eye, the one with the detached retina, didn't respond to treatment as well as it should've. Over time I just stayed on the job; I settled into it.

## INSIGHTS ABOUT WORK AND INTEGRITY

Today I thought about what I've learned from that job. My boss used to say, "You are so unbelievably over-qualified for this job, that I can't even imagine why you're doing it." But I learned a lot in three different areas. The first was a little bit about humility. In my career in the publishing business, I was a very egotistical, competitive person. I didn't have a lot of humility. I was very aggressive and competitive in everything I did. So I found out that cleaning a toilet is a humbling experience. Cleaning up after residents of an apartment building puts you at pretty much the low end of the totem pole. Some people look at you and I'm sure they think, *I would sure hate to have that job!*

But I grew to like it. Every day I felt like I had really accomplished something. The building looked great. I knew it wouldn't last for very long, maybe only a few hours. But for a certain period of time, it looked great, and I felt really good about that.

Here's the second thing I learned from the job. I had always felt that there were two groups of people in the world: those whom I would call considerate of others, and people whom I would call inconsiderate. The inconsiderate ones don't care what they do, they just do it. It doesn't matter to them if it causes other people problems. Well, it doesn't take very long in a janitorial job to find out that there are a lot of quote-unquote inconsiderate people, who seemingly do things just to make your life miserable. For the first two or three years on this job, I had everybody in the building divided into these two categories – considerate of others in the building, or inconsiderate.

It took me a long time to learn a really important lesson and look at it a different way. There's a third category of people! The third category of people are those who are *clueless*. Nobody has ever taught them what to do or not do, with simple things like recycling, washing clothes, and dealing with other people in tight surroundings. They just don't know; nobody ever told them. There certainly are people who really *are* inconsiderate, but the vast majority are just *uninformed*. They just don't know. That gives you a softer feeling about them; you don't get as upset with them. Actually, you just feel sorry for them, for instance that they don't know how to pour detergent into the 18-inch-diameter opening in the wash machine without getting it all over the floor and the machine itself. They didn't mean to do it; it's just that nobody's ever shown them how to do it properly. That perspective really makes you feel better.

The third thing that I learned on this job was about integrity. People either have it or they don't. Fortunately I learned about myself that I do have a fair amount of integrity. On this job I could've easily sloughed off all the time, taking shortcuts and literally sweeping the dirt under the rug. It would've been easy to do. You know, as long as you spray a lot of air freshener around and people think it smells clean, you can take a lot of shortcuts. But I found that even though I had the opportunity on a daily basis to avoid doing my job, because nobody was really looking over my shoulder, I still did my very best to do the job properly.

The longer I worked there, the more I thought about integrity in the workplace. In my career I saw that many people have no integrity whatsoever in the workplace. They'll play video poker on the computer all day long, or these days they're on Facebook. We're all familiar with it: personal emails, personal telephone calls, that type of thing. Yet I found myself on this nondescript, bottom-rung-of-the-ladder job, doing the very best I could. I mean, does it really matter, whether or not you wipe all the wash machines down today? You're coming back tomorrow or the next day so you could easily skip a couple, and no one would notice. But I found myself wiping all the machines down every day, mopping the floor, doing all the things that I knew I was supposed to do, even if nobody knew the difference, even if no one was there to say, "Hey, I saw you cleaning up in there, that was great." I was the only person who knew.

It's a lot like giving a donation or a gift. There are people who don't wanna be known; they just wanna give the gift and not have anybody pay any attention. Then there are others who want you to know. One time the newspaper where I worked had a page with a list of people who had donated to some cause. It was a big daily paper in Los Angeles, and your name would be listed as a donor if you donated at least five dollars. I remember them putting the page together and printing it. The next day, I answered a telephone that I wasn't actually responsible for but I happened to be in the area. The person on the other end of the phone screamed at me. I asked, "What is the problem?", and this person said they had given five dollars to that cause, and their name was not in the newspaper! The conversation went on and on and on. So that's what I'm talking about. Some people do really good work behind the scenes and nobody knows about it except them, while others donate five bucks and get extremely upset if it doesn't appear in the newspaper.

So those are the three things that I contended with almost on a daily basis: humility, integrity, and how people are considerate or not – or clueless. Today was my last day, and after I finished cleaning on every floor of the building, I said, "Goodbye floor!" and that was that. I worked harder today, to leave the building in great shape.

# SECTION 3: RECONNECTING PAST, PRESENT, AND FUTURE

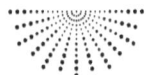

A person may hear that they only have so much time left, then live much longer than predicted. Although I don't think that'll happen with me, it *could* happen; there *is* that possibility. So I don't know that this is the last time I'll ever see my grandchildren. Why be sad when I don't actually know? I mean, if I knew that I was going to face a firing squad on Monday, then I would know, right? But I'm not! That changed my perspective, and I wasn't sad about it. I just was there to enjoy their company as much as I could.

## 12
# SEEING MY SON'S FAMILY

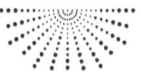

**DAY 24, SUNDAY APRIL 14, 2013**

I got up this morning and had to finish packing so that Karen could take me to the airport. Allen had booked a direct flight to Atlanta for me. I was kinda struggling and felt disoriented. I've built up a little safety nest in my apartment, and I definitely felt like I was leaving my comfort zone, taking an adventure that I wasn't absolutely sure I wanted to take. I thought, *Wow, I'm flying 3000 miles away from my doctors, my support system, everything that I have going for me right now at a very precarious time in my life.* It didn't feel like any trip I'd ever taken before: normally by the time I got on the airplane I would've been really excited about the trip, but right from the start, this trip was a mental struggle.

My son and his daughters met me at the airport in Atlanta. It was really nice to see them; my granddaughters have grown quite a bit since the last time I saw them a few months ago. I have a comfortable room at my son's house, with a private bath. It's a very, very nice place. I unpacked most of my things and I even set up my little blender in the kitchen. I brought my protein powder and everything so that I can make my morning smoothies. I lined all that up on the kitchen counter so that it feels like home to me. I'm sure it's going to be alright in a day or so but right now I feel like I'd rather be at home, in my own bed. Tomorrow will be a whole different experience, but right now, I feel anxious about the whole thing. It didn't help that my son and I had a preliminary talk about how I'm doing; that wasn't fun either.

I think once I get back to Portland, it's gonna be really hard for me to get outta town, except for a drive through the Columbia Gorge or going over to the coast. Having cancer can make you feel unsure of yourself in certain circumstances, such as travel. But I'm here now, and I'll make the best of it, have the best time I can.

## DAY 25, MONDAY APRIL 15, 2013

I woke up this morning in Atlanta, Georgia. I decided to leave my watch on Portland, Oregon time because I struggle with the timing of my meals. I decided that for my first day here, I'd operate on Portland time. So I got up at ten o'clock in the morning, local time, which was seven o'clock on my watch. I had my breakfast and nobody was around. The kids were off at school. My son's wife, Trish, wasn't home, and Allen was in his office. He usually works from an office in Tennessee during the week, but this week he's working from home.

After I got up and had breakfast, I just crashed. I was absolutely, totally exhausted! I took a nap for two hours. The trip yesterday really, really wiped me out. I think it was all the tension and anxiety about going so far away from home. Later my son took a break from work at some point, and we went outside and weeded the whole front yard. We built up a pretty good size pile of weeds. It was fun; I hadn't done something like that with him for a long, long, long time.

My youngest granddaughter came home at three in the afternoon. She's eleven years old. We had a great chance to talk and have fun. She's making videos on her iPhone, so I suggested we collaborate on a video. She showed me some of the videos that she's made so far. She selects a song and then builds the video around the song using a little program on her phone. I suggested making a video of their dog

Ginger, running around and doing all the crazy stuff she does. She liked that idea. I suggested using the song *Who Let the Dogs Out*, and she quickly found it in the iTunes library. Within two minutes, she had the background music all set up and ready to go. The opening scene is Ginger charging pell mell toward the camera. We'll have a number of scenes where she's running, and some close-ups of her little antics. We'll work on it some more tomorrow.

Both granddaughters have swim practice nearly every day for an hour and a half, a very rugged regime at an Olympic-sized pool with like a hundred other kids. Atlanta is basically the swimming capitol of America, with about twenty-five thousand kids in the city's swim program. A lot of Olympic swimmers have come out of this program. The girls are both very accomplished swimmers, in the top of their age division. They've actually gone to the state finals, things like that. Today was my first opportunity to actually see them swim so that was a lot of fun. After that, we had dinner.

I'm starting to feel that I'm *not* going to fall apart; I'm a little more relaxed. It was a beautiful sunny day. I can't begin to explain how nice that was, the first day in about a year that I've actually felt warm. Because of all the weight I've lost, I usually just can't get warm. I soaked up that warmth.

## DAY 26, TUESDAY APRIL 16, 2013

Yesterday I was really tired all day, but today I'm feeling quite a bit better. I'm trying to conserve my energy because it's gonna be a long day.

Before the trip, I was afraid that when I got here, my granddaughters and I would be sitting around staring at each other with nothing to talk about since we've had so little contact in the past few years. The older granddaughter is very busy. She's a teenager, 13 years old, with a cell phone loaded with contacts, so she has a lot going on. My other granddaughter who's two years younger isn't quite as busy, so she has a little more time. That's giving me an opportunity to get better acquainted with her.

## Blessing #15

*This evening, my son had tickets to an Atlanta Braves game at Ted Turner field. Baseball is my favorite sport, but I haven't been to a big-league baseball game in about three years. So the whole idea of going to a major league game with my son was really exciting. When we arrived, we were trying to find our seats and an usher came up and said, "Come with me, I'll get you some better seats." She took us down to a lower level to a pair of field-level seats and said, "There won't be anybody down here tonight; sit here and enjoy the game." It was tiring but we had a great time. The final score was six to three, Atlanta.*

By the time I got home, I was basically exhausted. I hadn't given cancer any thought all day. I just got up in the morning and proceeded along like a normal person on a normal vacation. At the end of the day I thought that it's kinda strange how you can completely forget about something like that for a whole day. But I did, and it was a memorable day and I thoroughly enjoyed it.

## DAY 27 – WEDNESDAY APRIL 17, 2013

I'm still in Atlanta. My youngest granddaughter and I worked on a couple video projects this afternoon: we finished the video of Ginger the dog, and started working on one about a day in my granddaughter's life.

Everybody here is on a very busy schedule. My daughter-in-law has a lot going on and she drives the kids everywhere. It's a little chaotic, just like any family with a lot of activities. We went out for dinner tonight since the girls had a break from swimming today. We went to a restaurant called California Dream, a really nice place. It was huge, with high ceilings; you think you're going into a stadium or something! I had a cheeseburger with fries and salad – a bad choice but it was delicious! But I think that pretty well wraps up the day.

## DAY 28 – THURSDAY APRIL 18, 2013

This morning after breakfast, I talked with my son for a while. He's working in his home office. He can't just drop everything to spend time with me, but he pops out on occasion to say hi and talk for a while. That's really nice. His wife has an incredibly busy schedule with the girls, but we've also had time to sit down a couple, three times a day for a little conversation.

My son's family lives at a country club. It's got a huge 18-hole golf course, tennis courts, swimming pools, and about 300 houses all the way around the complex. It's a huge gated community. They used to host a regular PGA golf tournament for the younger players, but now they host a PGA senior tournament. These players are over the age of 50 and they're still great; so it's exciting to watch. Today they had a Pro-Am round, where each of the pros plays with three amateurs. The amateurs are all ages, men and women in their 20's, 30's, 40's and so on. It's a big thrill for the amateurs but it's also a costly thrill because they have to pay a few thousand dollars to participate.

Anybody who lives in this community can attend the tournament for free. Find a hole, grab a seat, and watch the golfers. I had the opportunity to watch the Pro-Am tournament for a few hours and I got to see a couple of really famous old-timers: Tom Watson, Ben Crenshaw. It was very exciting to see them come through. I was only 50 yards off the green, sitting on a hill. My son supplied me with a nice folding chair and a backpack with a big University of Oregon "O" on it. I filled it up with water bottles and sandwiches and snacks. I sat near another guy who was there on his own, and we ended up chatting for a couple hours, off and on; he was an avid golf fan who wanted to get autographs from all these guys.

Later I got back to the house a little bit before my youngest granddaughter. She did her homework, and then we finished working on the video about her life. We got it done and everybody loved it; that was really fun. The great thing about this little video project was that it brought us all together. I don't see my son's family very often so I feel like I don't know them that well. This project was a perfect vehicle to bring us all together.

Overall it was a good day. With the golf tournament, shooting a video with my granddaughter, and then having a really nice dinner together, again I didn't think about cancer even once today. That was thrilling!

## DAY 29 – FRIDAY APRIL 19, 2013

Today I had the opportunity to see the Atlanta Aquarium. Allen and Trish picked the girls up early from school so that they could go too. I was totally amazed; the aquarium is a monstrous structure, like the size of a football stadium. The first thing after you get in the door is a "Petting Tank". I thought: *What on earth is this?* In the tank, they have very small manta rays, about 18 inches across, and they look soft. They swim around in a circle, and the kids can walk over to the rail and reach down and pet them.

The spectacular thing there is the main tank. I couldn't believe it. It holds 800,000 gallons of water, and tons of fish. They also have a whale, and little porpoises that swim up under his tummy like a little flotilla. It was really stunning.

We saw the dolphin show, in a big auditorium. They have a special tank for the dolphins, six highly-trained dolphins. They dive clear to the bottom of the tank and then come shooting out of there and they go 15, 20 feet in the air and do somersaults and everything else. It's unbelievable to watch.

I could go on and on and on about the aquarium and going for dinner and everything, but the main thing I really wanna say is that I didn't think about cancer once all day long. It just didn't cross my mind. It was an absolutely wonderful, stunning day, and cancer didn't take away one iota of the day's enjoyment. It was a fantastic experience, a tremendous slice of life.

## DAY 30 – SATURDAY APRIL 20, 2013

The girls were home today since it was Saturday. This morning I had quite a bit of time with them, two or three hours to hang out and talk until they both had to leave. One was going to a birthday party and sleepover, and the other was going to another event with a friend. Neither of them would be back until Sunday.

My son and his wife had a special event that had been planned for quite a long time, so that left me with a free afternoon. I decided to go watch more of the golf tournament. Allen loaned me a chair and a backpack and an L.A. baseball cap to wear – *his* L.A. baseball cap, which, of course, I immediately started to covet because I don't have one. I thought, *Well, is there some way I can just slip this baby into my suitcase when I go home?* He'd never know the difference because he has a lot of baseball caps! I figured, no, that wouldn't work, but I really enjoyed wearing it.

## A LAST TIME FOR EVERYTHING

*I headed over to the golf tournament, got my little chair set up, had my water, sandwiches, apples, and all kinds of snacks. It was easy to find people to have a conversation with. I talked to the steward of the hole, a television guy, and some of the spectators. I was really enjoying it... then I started thinking about cancer again, and the short time that I have left to live. This probably is the last golf tournament that I'll ever watch, because there are no golf tournaments of any size in Portland. I started feeling a little melancholy. I hadn't thought much about golf for a long time and it felt like I sort of re-discovered it this week. It was like finding a new toy and then having somebody take it away. Well, all in all I had a great time there, except for when that dark cloud of thought came across the sky and for a little while it felt as though it might as well be raining.*

Late in the afternoon I walked the three blocks back to the house, and by that time Allen and Trish had returned as well. We went to a really nice Italian restaurant for dinner. The restaurant was loaded with prom kids in tuxedos and gowns, from a senior and junior prom at a nearby high school. I was flooded with high school memories. Young people just starting out in life. The cancer thing, the little cloud, kinda drifted in again for a moment, but it didn't last very long.

The three of us had a great discussion. They asked questions like, "What are you gonna do when you get home?" The subject of cancer hadn't really come up all week. I had decided ahead of time that I would respond to any direct questions but I wouldn't bring it up myself. My basic feeling was that they really didn't wanna talk about it – they just wanted me to have a good week so they avoided the subject. But this evening they asked me some questions that were a little more probing, like whether I knew how much time I had left, whether the doctors had said I'd suffer a lot of pain, and so on. I didn't mind talking about it, but of course no one *really* knows all the answers to those questions.

In the evening I watched a movie about President Lincoln. I'm a great fan; I think he was our greatest president, and I love what he did for this country. I've read books about him. But this was a little different. I thought about how his life was taken from him, at a time when there were still a lot of things he could've done to help with the restoration of the country after the Civil War. I thought of myself, dying at a point where I still think I have a lot to contribute.

All in all it was a terrific day, even with the little cancer "clouds" that came over me a few times.

## DAY 31 – SUNDAY APRIL 21, 2013

When I woke up this morning, I was amazed that I didn't feel sad. It was my last day with my son's family. I was seeing my granddaughters and their mother for most likely the last time in my life. I'm sure I'll see my son again before this is all over but I don't think I'll see the rest of the family because it's a long haul across the country.

The reason that I wasn't sad – the reason I hadn't really been sad all week – was due to something that Karen had said before I headed out here. And I'm really thankful that she said it, because it changed my perspective enormously.

Karen had told me a story about a woman who was told she had six months to live, yet she lived another two and a half years. So a person may have a terminal illness and hear that they only have so much time left, then they live much longer than predicted by the medical prognosis. Although I don't think that'll happen with me, it was easy to think, *Well, it <u>could</u> happen; there <u>is</u> that possibility*. So I don't *know* that this is the last time I'll ever see them. It has nothing to do with hope, or false hope. It's just a case of, "I don't know."

Why be sad when I don't actually know? I mean, if I knew that I was going to face a firing squad on Monday, then I would know, right? But I'm not! That changed my perspective, and I wasn't sad about it during this trip. I didn't shed any tears. I just was there to enjoy their company as much as I could and get the most out of the trip, which I did.

I spent Sunday morning talking with them and getting ready to fly home. There was no sadness, no tears, nothing. When it was time to head to the airport, I hugged my daughter-in-law and thanked her for the hospitality. I hugged my granddaughters and told both of them that they were beautiful, talented girls and I was extremely proud of them. I just told them how I felt! And although I have no idea whether I'll ever see them again, that didn't bother me. So I appreciate what Karen said to me before the trip, and how it helped me to stay cheerful.

That's an important point – for anybody! Say something encouraging to another person when you have the opportunity, even if it's just a sentence. Those things can have a huge impact on people. We need to take time to reach out a little bit, say what we think and encourage people. Tell 'em they've done a good job, or there's still reason for hope, that sort of thing. It's critical to say those positive things to people.

I was amazed that I felt so relaxed when I left their house. It took close to an hour to get to the airport and I was glad to have that time alone with Allen. There were serious things that I wanted to talk about with him. I laid out my plan for my last few months and explained who the players are. I talked about how I think things will go and how I want my personal possessions handled. There were details that he had never heard, so I wanted to make it very clear to him. We had a fabulous exchange.

When we got to the airport departures area, we hugged each other and we both said "I love you." He and I understand each other and that's really important. Then I got on the plane and headed back to Portland.

# 13
# FINDING PEACE IN THE INEVITABLE

**DAY 32 – MONDAY APRIL 22, 2013**

*I* woke up at seven o'clock Portland time, the same time that I woke up throughout my week in Atlanta, and I felt absolutely normal. So my little plan of staying on Portland time while in Atlanta worked to perfection. No jet lag – I just felt really good.

This morning I had a lot of stuff to do, and I just blew right through it all. I made a bunch of telephone calls, and I had to get a set of keys from Josh, my former coworker. By mid-afternoon I had also caught up on all my mail, all the stuff that piled up last week while I was gone. Things went extremely well on my first day back, and I felt great. It was a beautiful, sunny day and I didn't think about cancer; I just felt like I was accomplishing a lot. I was astounded that I felt so well after the trip, so I was bound and determined not to let cancer take anything away from me today.

Today I thought about this image of a lemon. You slice a lemon and you squeeze it to get juice out of it. You wanna get as much juice out of it as you can, right? Normally, you know, if you squeeze all the juice out of a lemon but you need more, you go to the store and buy more lemons, right? That's pretty much what you do. Suddenly today

I started thinking about how I've only got one lemon left, and I can't buy any *more*; they're not going to be available to me. The lemon is similar to the time that I have left in life – I want to squeeze that lemon as hard as I can, and get every last drop of juice out of it. Today I biked down to Pioneer Courthouse Square and sat in the sunshine with a big cup of coffee, and I thought: *With everything I got done, I really squeezed a lot of juice out of that lemon today.*

## DAY 33 – TUESDAY APRIL 23, 2013

### Blessing #16

*I woke up this morning feeling pretty good. Today I needed to work on financial planning for the next few months. I have spreadsheets concerning my finances and bills. I just left my job of five years, so I have to figure out how much money I'm gonna need. My budget has tightened up considerably. I worked on that, and called my son to discuss it all, especially what's going to happen at the end of my life. Being told you have a limited amount of time left changes everything. How will the final bills get paid? How much will it cost to take care of funeral arrangements? Will anything be left over, and who will get that? That sort of thing. A lot of people can't do that because they get hit by a truck or something; they die suddenly and don't have any time to plan. So I feel tremendously blessed because I have the time to think this through.*

This afternoon I had to make a big decision regarding my next cell phone. I've been using an older-model "dumb" phone for the past two years. You can take pictures with it, but the screen is so small you can't see 'em. I didn't use it for texting, I didn't take pictures or videos, I just called people on the telephone. Ha! There's a unique idea, if you think about it, just using a telephone for making telephone calls. So I wanted a new smart phone for my last few months, so I can do some texting, and take photographs and videos.

I decided to get a phone and a plan at Walmart, and made arrangements to meet with a friend for dinner. However, to make that happen, I had to actually get to Walmart, which is several miles away. I don't have a car, and I probably won't have another one at this point. Taking public transportation would involve a bus line that I absolutely hate because the buses are always full of pushy people who are just out-of-sorts. Taking the light rail train would involve a lot more walking. So I sat and pondered that for a while before finally deciding to take the bus.

The bus was the nightmare I expected it would be. It was about three o'clock in the afternoon, so we hit a couple of high schools that had just gotten out. The bus filled up with what seemed like two hundred high school students, with skateboards and hockey sticks and all kinds of things. The driver kept screaming, "Move to the back of the bus! Move to the back of the bus!" and they answered, "We don't have any more room!" It went on and on and on. But I managed to get to Walmart and buy a new phone.

My friend Emma picked me up at the store and then we had a really nice dinner. We had a long conversation about taking or avoiding chemo. She of course understands my circumstances more than anybody that I might talk to, having been through this twice.

We've been friends for about five years; she's a cancer survivor. When we first met, she had just been diagnosed; it was terrible. She was married, with three young children, two daughters and a son. After an operation and chemo, she seemed fine, but about a year later, she went in for a scan and found out that the cancer had reoccurred. Her medical plan dictated that all she could do at that point was chemo; her doctor under that plan said that surgery wouldn't be possible so it wouldn't be covered. Fortunately, at that time she had the option to switch to another health plan; and once she switched, she found a surgeon who was able to operate and remove the tumor.

At the time, she said to me, "I wanna raise my children, so I'm willing to do anything that I can, to make that possible." After her second surgery, she went through another round of chemo. Throughout that time I encouraged her and did whatever I could to help, and we became very close friends as a result. She is a courageous person, someone I look up to for her courage.

I've wondered whether the fact that I'm *not* willing to do another round of chemo means I don't have any courage. But I'm nearly 76 years old. I don't have any children to raise and I've had a long life. My situation is very different from Emma's.

She agrees with my choice 100%. *Her* main reason for doing chemo her second time was her commitment to her children; she was only in her 40's. Under the same circumstances, I would probably have done what she did. So it was a good conversation – that kind of support and understanding are really important to me, coming from her.

## DAY 34 – WEDNESDAY APRIL 24, 2013

I woke up feeling anxious this morning. My new phone wasn't working, and I had an appointment at nine a.m. with my oncologist. Those two things weighed heavily on my mind. I had missed two or three hours of sleep, so the morning was very stressful.

The appointment was important because the oncologist was gonna review my scan from a month ago, which had shown the cancer spreading in my liver. I had seen her at least a dozen times during my three months of chemo last year. At our last appointment after chemo ended, a scan was done and it looked clear, so she had felt very good about my condition. I remember asking her, "Do you think we're doing well?" She had said, "I think we're doing terrific."

My next scan had been a few months later, after radiation, for my radiologist to see whether the radiation had done any damage. That scan showed the two spots on my liver. My final scan, a month ago, was also ordered by the radiologist to follow up on the two spots. So far I hadn't discussed that final scan with my oncologist. The last time I saw her, I'd had high hopes. Today was our first appointment since that time. Although I believed my primary care doctor was right about the cancer growing rapidly in my liver, it hadn't been confirmed yet by any other medical professionals.

So I went to OHSU pretty upset because this would be, in a sense, the final word on the subject. Also if any other treatment were possible, I would've found out today. I've already made up my mind about declining further treatment, but I certainly wanna hear what people have to say. Between that and my phone not working, my blood pressure was up to 161 over 78 – the highest blood pressure I've ever had!

I waited patiently when I got to the oncologist's office. A few minutes went by, then fifteen minutes, and I got more and more nervous. When she finally came in, I was very happy to see her. I really, really trust her, and I really wanted to talk with her about my condition. She sat down on her little stool and rolled over close to me. She had her computer screen there, and she said, "The final scan, the last one you had, absolutely confirms that you have cancer growing in your liver."

I could tell she was upset. The look on her face showed that she was sad about it. I asked, "Well, what options do we have?" She replied, "The only thing we can do now is give you more Gemzar, which you had before, intravenously." A Gemzar infusion takes about an hour to administer, and it'd be once every two weeks for the rest of my life, or until I got to the point of being in a hospice situation.

I asked, "OK, what's the bottom line? What would that do for me? It's not gonna cure the cancer, right?"

She said, "No, that's not possible. It *could* add six months to your life if you're lucky."

In other words, it might extend the diagnosis of six-to-twelve months out to twelve-to-eighteen months. But she wasn't guaranteeing it, and even if I picked up an additional six months, I'd be sick all the time as a side effect of the chemo.

I said, "It doesn't make sense to me, choosing to be sick for twelve months and not have any quality of life." Chemo drugs kill blood cells, and you have no energy, you can't think, you can't take walks. It just wipes you out. My oncologist suggested trying it for a couple of weeks to see whether it would really be that bad. I thought, *Yeah, but I don't even wanna be sick for the next two weeks because I don't know how long I have left, and there are things I wanna do right now.* I asked, "What's the point of no return for making this decision?"

She replied, "You'll have to decide within a few weeks. Let me know by May 15th."

I told her I would think about it.

That confirmed the diagnosis I had received from my primary care doctor. It was a second opinion: now there's no turning back from the fact that cancer will take my life within six to twelve months, maybe a little longer if I start treatment soon. I felt relieved because now I knew for sure. Having chemo at this point would not be a cure, it'd just be prolonging a sick person's life.

Dr. Benito also confirmed something else. I didn't wanna do radiation after my chemo last year. I had thought that if the cancer was going to spread, it would spread into my liver, which they can't radiate. They radiate the organs *around* the liver, to prevent cancer from starting in the pancreas, intestines or stomach. So I asked whether it might've been a good decision if I'd chosen to forego radiation at that time. She said, "In retrospect, absolutely." Without radiation, I'd still have ended up where I am now; the same thing would've happened. It felt good to hear that because it turns out that I was right to be skeptical.

We had a good discussion, and I really appreciated it. I could tell from her face that she considered this to be a major defeat. She thought we had won this battle but we didn't. She looked very disappointed. As I started to get up to leave, I noticed that she had positioned herself between me and the door, facing me. I sensed that she wanted to give me a hug. I didn't think it'd be appropriate for me to initiate it, but then she put her arms out and hugged *me*. It was a nice hug, a very reassuring kind of thing. It was really special to me. She's a medical provider, an oncologist, whom I didn't know prior to a year ago, but we had bonded in a very special way through this cancer. And I could sense that she was sad.

After my appointment, it was only ten o'clock in the morning. I walked out of the office with a feeling of peace. Now I truly have to accept the fact that my life will just be a matter of months; it's been confirmed.

I still had a good day ahead. Josh, my former coworker, had offered me the use of a house on the Oregon coast for five days, and Karen was planning to join me. It was time to go home and make plans and meet up with her for the trip. But I still had the phone situation going on, which was absolutely driving me crazy. The phone still wasn't connecting to a network and I had no idea what to do about it. I was having a meltdown because of that phone! Once Karen arrived, we were able to resolve the problem. We figured out that the salesperson in the cell phone department had installed the sim card backwards. Once we installed it properly, it worked just fine.

Overall my day was pretty darn good. I received confirmation on my cancer situation – sad news but now I felt at peace about it. We managed to get my new – extravagant! – telephone working. And when we got to the coast, the sun was shining and it was warm. The Oregon coast on a sun-shiny, warm day is one of the most beautiful places in the whole United States. So it's a thrill to be here. My day ended beautifully, with time at the beach, and I feel eager to get up tomorrow morning, and to see what my remaining months have to offer.

## DAY 35 – THURSDAY APRIL 25, 2013

This was a transition day for me. I had a couple hectic days in Portland and then Karen and I drove out to the coast yesterday. Today I was getting used to the new surroundings, this house in the city of Gearhart. OK, Gearhart feels more like a village than a city. I've been here before, but never for an overnight trip.

My thoughts have been similar to what I thought when I used to go hiking. I used to do a lot of day hikes; I just loved it. I often experienced this: I'd drive out from the city, my head filled with junk and clutter and thoughts about work. It would take a while to get used to the idea of being in the wilderness. After like two or three hours of hiking, I'd finally get the feeling that I wasn't in the city, and the problems that I brought along with me started to melt away a little bit. That's what it was like today in Gearhart – it took time to get used to the idea that I wasn't in Portland; I was at the beach. Kind of a transitional feeling. This morning we went for coffee at a little bakery in downtown Gearhart, and I say "downtown" loosely because there's really not much of a town here; it's just a few buildings.

## A LAST TIME FOR EVERYTHING

*All day my thoughts kinda bounced all over the place. It's another day of "lasts", meaning the last time I'm gonna do this, the last time I'm gonna do that. We took a walk on the beach today, and found a bench up in the grass, looking out over the ocean. At one point we saw three ants in the sand, all trying to pull the same piece of debris in three different directions, just going in circles. Ha! I don't know if they ever got to wherever they were going. But I had the feeling as we sat there, that this was the last time that I'll ever see the Oregon coast. Those feelings don't necessarily make me feel sad. I just wonder, is this really the last time? It's just a question that enters my mind when I'm doing something really pleasant. Will this be the last time I'm gonna do this?*

It was a bittersweet day in a lot of ways. The house where we're staying is a real blessing because it's very comfortable. It's extremely special to be spending time with Karen at the beach. At the same time I still have carry-over from my conversation with Dr. Benito, the final pronouncement by a second physician that my situation is real. So it's been a mixed-bag day: beauty, sunshine, comfort, food, friendship, companionship – and the realization that this is short-lived.

# 14
# VISITING THE OREGON COAST

**DAY 36 – FRIDAY APRIL 26, 2013**

Today was a wonderful day. I got over the sense of transition that I mentioned yesterday, where I was mentally split between the city, my problems, the cancer diagnosis – and just being here. Today I felt more like I was experiencing the environment, experiencing *this* place, and enjoying it. After breakfast this morning, I suggested going to my favorite beach in Oregon, a very small beach called Indian Beach. It's near the city of Cannon Beach, and once again the sun came out, for the third day in a row – at the Oregon coast!

It was overcast this morning, and I was skeptical when I first looked outside. Then Karen said, "There's a little ray of sunshine coming through the clouds there." Soon after that, the sun broke out. It was very beautiful; the temperatures were even better today than yesterday.

After breakfast we headed for the city of Cannon Beach. Ecola State Park has a panoramic view of the ocean, including the famous rock near the shore in Cannon Beach, which is called Haystack Rock. It's an Oregon icon. Everybody knows Haystack Rock. You see that, and all the other rocks just off the coast, and you can see a lighthouse offshore, which was built like a hundred years ago. It was used as a lighthouse for 76 years, and now it houses people's ashes. It's a columbarium. You can pay to have your loved one's ashes stored in this lighthouse a few miles off the Oregon coast.

When I read the sign about storing a person's ashes off the Oregon coast, I got to thinking about whether I'd want to do that. I thought about it for a while, but no, I'm not interested in that. I don't get it, really. Ha! I mean, putting your ashes in a container in some *place* doesn't make any sense to me. Pouring out the ashes over a piece of ground that you love, or into the ocean or a river – *that* makes sense to me – but just storing them somewhere doesn't make sense. I had always felt that I wanted to be buried. But I changed my mind on that over the last couple years; cremation is the way I want to go now.

I was overcome by the beauty of the place, the coast and the rocks, so I decided to shoot some videos of the trip using my new phone. Next we drove over to Indian Beach. It has high rocks around it, and it's loaded with driftwood and debris. It's really pretty. It has two or three streams that run into the ocean and they're always interesting.

We got down to the beach and found a nice place to sit. I had very little energy. I can go for a while but then I gotta sit down and rest. The cancer is really starting to rob me of my endurance. I used to hike ten to twelve miles, out in the Columbia River Gorge, up mountains, down mountains. The idea of a ten-mile hike today is out of the question, it's ridiculous. One or two miles would be the absolute max now. I run out of energy without warning. I'll be walking along and all of a sudden I just get wobbly. My body says, "Wait a minute, you're doing too much, you have to stop!" It's been kinda shocking to me but I've had to get used to it.

---

### A LAST TIME FOR EVERYTHING

*Indian Beach was every bit as beautiful as I remembered it, sitting in the sun watching the water and the little streams running into the ocean, and the rocks. I pulled out my phone and shot more videos. I didn't wanna leave! I could've sat there all day long. But eventually we had to go get lunch; we ran out of snacks. And once again, just that little twinge of thinking,* Am I ever gonna see Indian Beach again? *Every time that I'm really enjoying something: am I ever gonna see this again? I felt that as long as I could stay there, I could see it and enjoy it, my favorite beach in Oregon.*

---

Next we went to have lunch and look around downtown Cannon Beach. It's a commercial city with all kinds of stores and antique shops. I've always been puzzled by how people drive to the Oregon coast to see the scenic beauty of the magnificent ocean and coastline, yet then they spend the day *shopping*! That's just not my thing, so I wanted to get out of town as soon as possible. We headed back to the house, and I worked on figuring out my new phone and the video camera and how to edit my photos.

### Blessing #17

*In the evening Karen and I drove to the center of Gearhart, parked the car and walked through the dunes and the tall grass out onto the beach. We took a really nice long walk. On the way back, it started to get chilly as the wind kicked up. We were getting uncomfortable but then we spotted a driftwood fire that somebody had left to burn out. I said, "No one's over there; let's go sit next to that fire." We didn't have any marshmallows or hotdogs; we could've had a nice little feast. But sitting there in the warmth of the fire and watching the sun set – that was really special. In all it was a really, really special day, and I'd like to end the day on that scene: two people who really care about each other sitting on a log in front of a driftwood fire watching the sun drop into the Pacific. I don't think there's anything more beautiful than that.*

## DAY 37 – SATURDAY APRIL 27, 2013

All I can say to summarize this day is that I'm sure that if you're dying of cancer, there are certain things you can do that will probably shorten your life. For example if your liver is infected with cancer and you're drinking a lot of alcohol, that would undoubtedly shorten your life, beyond what the doctors have told you. But I *also* think there are things that can *lengthen* your life. A day like *today* is one of those things.

Even though I'm really tired, it was truly a terrific day in every sense of the word. After breakfast, Karen and I decided to explore more of the Oregon coast. One thing that I had never seen was the northwest corner of the state of Oregon. I've been to the northeast corner, the southeast corner and the southwest corner. I'm talking about the actual corners, where border meets border. At the northwest corner, there's the Columbia River, which flows into the Pacific Ocean. Today we decided to go find that corner if we could, explore it and see what it looks like. It's in Fort Stevens State Park but we weren't exactly sure where.

We set out on our exploration around 10 o'clock in the morning. First we headed to Fort Stevens and drove out onto the beach. We discovered the wreck of the Peter Iredale, which ran aground at this spot in 1906. It was a four-masted barque. I'm looking at a photo of the ship, taken shortly after it ran aground, while it was still intact. Now all that's left of it on the beach is the bow, and some of the masts sticking out of the sand. A lot of it has just been covered by sand, but it was still interesting.

Then we decided to drive as far as we could along the beach, and ended up at a jetty that cuts across the beach and heads out to sea. We weren't sure whether that was actually the northwest corner of Oregon. We drove back and got off the beach, found a road heading farther north, and saw road signs indicating the Columbia River up ahead. We continued 'til we reached the river. Now it looked like we'd have to walk westward two or three miles along the beach to get to the point where the river meets the ocean. I yearned to take that walk, all the way to the ocean. I'm always fascinated to see where a giant river enters the ocean; it's fun to see where they come together. But I knew that I would never make it in my present condition. So I didn't get to the exact northwest corner of Oregon, but I got within a mile or two. It was a goal that I'd had for a long time, so that was very exciting.

After that we roamed around the state park and made more of our ridiculous little videos, using our phones. We visited a wildlife viewing bunker, where we didn't even see *one* bird. Ha! There were pictures of birds on the wall but no *real* birds. I guess all our talking and laughing scared them away. Later we went to Fort Clatsop, where they have a replica of the buildings where Lewis and Clark spent the winter of 1805 to 1806. We imagined what it might've been like for 34 people to spend the winter in close quarters like that. I don't think I've laughed as much, in one day, in I-don't-know-how-long. We laughed and laughed and laughed and laughed. It was a thrilling day for me.

There was only time that the thought of cancer crept back into my life today. It's very difficult to get through an entire day without cancer invading my thoughts, even if I'm having the best day I could possibly have. It just sneaks its ugly head in and turns things down for a while. We stopped at a coffee shop and sat in some really nice chairs. As I've said before, my little daily coffee breaks are really special moments for me. This afternoon was especially great because we had seen so much and enjoyed the day so much.

But as we sat there, I noticed an older couple close to my age in the shop, wearing spandex bicycle riding gear and jackets, first-class stuff. I would guess that with the gear they had on, they were probably taking a really long bike ride. There were some great trails out there in Fort Stevens and people could have a marvelous time on a bike. That's when the cancer thing came up again. I had the body for long bike rides: I had the heart and the energy and the healthy blood pressure and everything else to go along with it. And just a year and a half ago I could've jumped on my bike for 10, 15, or 20 miles and it would've felt great. I would've been tired, but I could've done it. I just watched this couple for a little while as I drank my coffee, and I got a little envious. They're able to do all these things that I can no longer do. That was the only time today that the cancer managed to get involved, where it kinda came back.

### Blessing #18

*Today was a marvelous day. If I were on chemo right now, this day wouldn't have been possible. I would've been able to drive out there, but I wouldn't have felt like doing anything, especially making little videos and things like that. That reinforces what I've said a number of times, that I just want a few good days like that, rather than an extra three to six months of feeling sick. Combine that feeling of validation with a marvelous day like today, and I just feel so blessed.*

### DAY 38 – SUNDAY APRIL 28, 2013

Today was the dreaded transition day after a really nice vacation. Karen and I had the opportunity to go to the coast, and we spent time looking at the ocean, taking walks, and being in the fresh air. Even my allergies were getting better! And the sunshine. Sunshine at the Oregon coast is such an incredible thing. It's like a myth, you know? "When was the last time we saw any sun here?" We stayed in a really nice house that someone let us use and we were very happy and thankful for that.

Vacations always progress a certain way. There's the anticipation of going, and then the transition day where you get ready and travel – you're on *vacation* but you're traveling so it's not really a vacation day yet. Then you've arrived and you have the actual vacation. At the end there's another transition day or two, depending on how far away from home you are, where you're not really on vacation, you're just heading back home. Today was a transition day. We cooked a really fun breakfast in the morning and then we went out on the beach for a little while. It wasn't as sunny but it was still pleasant. Then, unfortunately, we had to put the bags in the car and head back to Portland.

As I started loading up the car and we began our trip back, I started feeling anxious. I think it was because tomorrow I have to see a doctor that I've been dreading talking to. I started projecting into the next day and having to face the reality of the cancer all over again. Out at the coast, it had just been there in the background. At the end of a vacation, you wanna go home, right? You wanna get back to where you're really comfortable. But by the same token, in my situation, home is where I have to face reality again. That makes it difficult.

On the drive home, I started feeling out-of-sorts, and that resulted in an unpleasant incident between Karen and me. *She* likes to start a long drive with a full tank of gas. *I* looked at the gas gage and said, "We have way more than enough gas for this trip; let's just go and not worry about it." She was upset by that and wanted to stop at the next gas station. It set up a bit of conflict between us, which really disturbed me. During the drive, she asked me a couple times what I was thinking about, but I didn't answer.

Without getting into a lot of psychological mumbo-jumbo, I really think I was just dreading my appointment tomorrow. This doctor and I are going to discuss the point in my life where I no longer have any control – where I'm still alive but unable to function on my own anymore and I can't even get out of bed. That's the part of this whole experience that's the most frightening, the idea of not having any control during the last weeks, or maybe months, of my life.

What brought that to the forefront of my mind today is the fact that I don't have my own car anymore. I've driven at least a million miles in my lifetime; I calculated it once. Not everybody can say that! It's based on how many years I've driven, and my average annual mileage. Working in sales, there were many years where I drove thirty to forty thousand miles a year. So here I am, riding in Karen's car, and I know there's enough gas but we're arguing about stopping for gas, and what it came down to was that *I had no control*. It wasn't my car and it wasn't my decision. And with tomorrow's appointment in the back of my mind, the gas situation magnified itself. I wasn't in control in the car, and further down the line, I'll have even less control. I like knowing *what's* going to happen and *how*, and *who's* going to be involved. So those thoughts resulted in a bad couple of hours for Karen and me, a dark cloud on what had been a few beautiful days.

The whole experience of having cancer happens in stages. Here I'm talking about the stages of what happens in your life, not the stages they use to describe how far the cancer has progressed. The first stage is when you hear you *have* cancer. There's the initial shock, and telling the people you're closest to. The second stage is about what the doctors plan to do to fight it. In my case it was surgery and chemo and radiation. In the third stage you're wondering whether they managed to get it into remission. At this stage, you don't know whether you'll have years of peace or whether it's gonna come back. The fourth stage happens if it comes back. Each stage has its own set of problems.

I'm at that last stage. My faith helps me tremendously in dealing with the reality that I'm going to die in a short period of time. It's very comforting and helpful to me. But the one thing that's out there that still scares me is the question of how much time I'm going to be incapacitated by this illness. Who's going to help me with *that* problem? Tomorrow I'll find out a lot more about that. I'm not looking forward to tomorrow, but I'm certainly thankful for the past few days.

15

INTRODUCTION TO HOSPICE

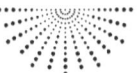

DAY 39 – MONDAY APRIL 29, 2013

*I* woke up this morning feeling very stressed. I was thinking about today's medical appointment. Dr. Gould is an oncologist but his specialty is, basically, helping people to end their lives. Palliative care. He'll be preparing me for hospice. He'll be the one prescribing pain medication and working with my primary care doctor to keep me going as long as possible. I got there about a quarter to twelve and went through the entire procedure, checking blood pressure, temperature and all that while I was waiting.

Finally he came in and introduced himself. His first question was, "How did you end up here?" I explained that after months of cancer treatment, scans indicated that I have cancer in my liver and it's terminal. Nothing can be done about it except prolonged chemotherapy, which I've decided not to do. It took a few minutes to explain the whole thing. Then he looked at me and said, "That's the most clear-eyed and peaceful explanation of someone's diagnosis that I've ever heard from a patient."

I was shocked and amazed to hear that! But I think I remain peaceful – even though I'm dying – because of my faith. It also helps a lot to talk about my experiences on a daily basis. Every evening I think through the events of the day, and Karen records me retelling it all. That keeps me very focused on what has happened, day by day by day. I think that's what led up to the focused presentation that I gave when he asked me that question. But I was still shocked by his response.

Next we got into the nitty-gritty of what this doctor is going to do for me. It was difficult news because, basically, he said, "I'm going to help you die. My job is to help you stay physically fit as long as you can, to provide pain medications as needed, to set up nursing care in your home, and to make a determination as to when you should go to hospice to end your life." It was like no other medical appointment I've ever had! All my life, doctors have been about getting you back to good health. Not this one; it's too late for good health.

Dr. Gould explained what he thinks might happen. I had figured the cancer would continue to grow in my liver until the liver shut down. But *he* said that the liver is an amazing organ which can actually continue to function even when 90% of it has been destroyed! I was astounded. He said that people's lives typically end due to other complications, meaning situations that arise because the liver isn't functioning at 100%. Heart failure, an infection, pneumonia. He also encouraged me to continue exercising.

To my surprise, I came away from the appointment with a lot of positive feelings. The thing that I worry about more than anything else, even pain, is how long I'll live after I'm incapacitated. When I can no longer take care of myself, how long will it be before I die? No one wants to be in bed for two or three months, unable to care for themselves, while cancer finishes its job. But the encouraging thing was that my body is physically in very good shape, apart from cancer. My heart, my lungs, my kidneys, my cholesterol levels, all of those kinds of things are very healthy. I can still exercise. The doctor talked about giving me steroids and other drugs to help me have more energy. All of those things can help me stay out of bed and remain mobile for a longer period of time. I have more hope now, knowing that I may be able to shorten the time that I'm incapacitated, with exercise, good nutrition, anti-oxidants, that sort of thing. Those are some things that I *can* have some control over! I felt very good about all of that. But it was a very difficult appointment and I'm glad that it's over.

## DAY 40 – TUESDAY APRIL 30, 2013

When I woke up this morning, I was still reeling from my appointment with Dr. Gould on Monday. I was thinking about everything we discussed, and the things I will have to do. At some point in this process, I'm faced with the possibility of being incapacitated and unable to do anything for myself. That's the scariest thing because I don't wanna leave my apartment, my home. I don't like the idea of being someplace else, in someone else's house, and having them take over my care. I'd prefer to have people come to my apartment and help me here.

The other thing about yesterday's appointment is that this doctor is very different from the other doctors I've seen. There was the surgeon, the oncologist, the radiologist, the primary care doctor and others who helped me with my initial diagnosis and treatment. Each one did their thing and sent me off to the next one. I keep thinking about how Dr. Gould doesn't have any more doctors to refer me to – he's the end of the line, the one who's going to help me until the end of my life.

Because of the finality of that appointment, I see that I have three or four days' work ahead of me that I hadn't planned to tackle right now, to really nail down some final preparations. I already have an Advance Directive filled out from when I had surgery, along with a list of people to be contacted when I die. Karen and I had loosely planned a memorial service and talked about cremation, and what to do with the ashes. When I went for surgery, the chances of dying on the operating table were about ten percent, according to my surgeon. But now the chances of my dying are 100 percent! So I re-read my Advance Directive, and got copies made for my doctor. I'm also going to have to review that contact list and revisit my plans for a memorial service.

I've always had an emergency packet just inside my front door, in case paramedics have to come and they need to know know what medications I'm taking and who to contact. Dr. Gould had me update that by filling out a POLST form – a paramedic can look at that form and know immediately if there are things that I don't want done to prolong my life, in case I'm not capable of telling them. It's a legal document; Dr. Gould went over all of it and we both signed and dated it so it's official. So that's hanging on my wall now.

Today I finally told my next-door neighbor, Faye, that my cancer is terminal. I had told a couple of people in the building but I hadn't talked to her yet. People start asking me about the future, with questions like, "What do you think about this or that, down the road?" And I think, *Wait a minute, I can't discuss that now.* If I don't tell them right then, when's the right time to bring it up? It'll just go on and on. But I don't like to tell people and upset their day.

So I told Faye, "I haven't told you this before because I hate to upset anyone. My cancer is terminal and there's no treatment for it. I've been given just a short time to live, like six to twelve months." She got very emotional about it. We've been neighbors and good friends for like three years. She often brings me little things like custard pudding. She took the tack that a lot of people take, that it's just not fair. I said, "It's not a question of being fair. And it's OK; I'm at peace with it."

When I tell somebody, I say, "Look – I don't want to upset you, but I think that it's important for you to know, and if I *don't* tell you, I feel like I'm deceiving you." She said, "Oh no, I definitely wanna know." Everybody says that! "Oh no, I'm so glad you told me, I *do* wanna know that." It's validation that it wasn't a mistake to tell them. They do, in fact, want the information, even if I feel like it's something that no one would want to hear.

I think that will make it easier for me to tell more people, that and the fact that I'm at peace with it. If I wasn't, I'd probably get all anxious and teary-eyed about it, and that wouldn't be good. But I've been able to reassure people – we all face death, and mine is going to happen soon. But I was glad to get that conversation with Faye out of the way.

## DAY 41 – WEDNESDAY MAY 1, 2013

I woke up this morning looking forward to breakfast: a milkshake and a bowl of hot oatmeal. As I ate, I thought more about this concept of having to plan for a period of time when I can't take care of myself. I was encouraged because Dr. Gould said that I can probably cut that time down by continuing to exercise and keep mobile, and by eating well and taking vitamins. I don't know if it'll work but that's the concept I'm gonna go with. I'll push myself as hard as I can every day – and take my vitamins.

Another thing that has given me a lot of encouragement is the fact that my friend Ronald, who died of cancer just a little over a year ago, was only in a hospice situation – where he couldn't take care of himself – for about two weeks. I visited him on his last coherent day, the day before he died. What gives me hope is that he was very active – very busy, always going places. He always walked really fast. I think the cancer was killing him but he didn't know it, and he just kept going, and going and going. He's kind of a role model for me! If you just keep going and going, while the cancer does what it has to do, maybe you can shorten the period of time where you're incapacitated.

Today I also thought about what happened at the end of my adopted mother's life. I actually have an incredible amount of experience with this sort of thing! My mother had a stroke, and I managed her in-home health care for eleven years. I coordinated everything: the people who came to take care of her, the medical appointments. I wasn't her caregiver myself, but she was always cared for at home. In the end she died – peaceably – at home. When she had her first major stroke, she spent a month in a nursing facility. Her doctor told me that she would never walk or speak again. I was told, "You will not succeed. She's a heavy-care patient and it won't work out to have her at home." My reply was, "Well, we're gonna try."

I didn't know what it was gonna be like, but she came to my home, and I worked with her on physical therapy, like a gym teacher. I really like working with people when they're trying to help themselves. Within three to four months, she was able to walk *and* talk. So I know that people *can* be managed at home if they can put the right resources together. I'll just have to draw on that experience and have faith that it can work.

As I've said before, I want to stay in this apartment for as long as possible. There's a remote possibility of maybe moving to the second floor where the residents are totally disabled and they have 24/7 medical and personal care, but I am adamant about staying in this building – they'll have to *drag* me out. That's all there is to it! I started the ball rolling myself by making some calls today, to my health insurance provider, to find out what's available to me for home health care. I'm gonna contact Medicare as well; I'll just go through the list and find out what resources I can put together on my own, to stay in my own apartment. Within the hospice program, there's also a social worker involved. That's one of the calls I'll have to make.

After thinking through all of that, and figuring out what steps I'll have to take, the situation was no longer terrorizing me. I moved on and did a lot of work on my finances, paid all my monthly bills. Since I left my job, all I have left is my social security and a small pension, so I experienced some sticker shock there. But I'll be OK for this month, and we'll see what happens after that.

Then I decided, *you know what? It's a beautiful day and I'm gonna take a really long bike ride.* I wanted to see how far I could ride, how strong I am. I rode down to the waterfront. Portland has a beautiful waterfront along the Willamette River. I rode up the west side, crossed the Steel Bridge, came back on the east side and crossed the Hawthorne Bridge; it was several miles. It was my first time making this big loop in over a year. I was tired but I felt great. I decided that now that the weather is warmer, I'm gonna try to do a longer bike ride every other day.

On the way back from my ride, I met another person whom I know fairly well, Lionel, whom I hadn't told about my cancer. We became friends as a result of my taking a portrait photo of him awhile back. I told him about my situation. He had prostate cancer but he's been cancer-free for four or five years now, after going through radiation. He's a cancer survivor. But he would understand my situation; anyone who's had cancer knows the feelings that are involved. So I told him, and I really liked his reaction; it was the best I've experienced so far, just really peaceful.

Lionel is a very quiet, peaceful person. He looked at me, and reached over and touched my arm, and said, "Oh Don, we all face death; it's inevitable. We just don't know when or how. But I'm really sorry to hear that." It was comforting, very comforting. I replied, "You know, Lionel, I'm a person of faith, and I'm really at peace with this." He said, "I understand; that's wonderful." It was a great conversation and I wish every conversation I have with people about this could be like that. It was heartfelt and honest but not overly emotional.

When I got back to the apartment, I saw that the manager was in the front office. I marched right in and sat down and said, "You know, I have terminal cancer, and I have a diagnosis of from six months to a year. I want you to know that I have every intention of staying in my apartment until the very last possible moment. It's my home and I wanna stay there, and I'll need whatever help I can get to make that happen." She replied, "We'll do whatever we can." We talked about getting extra keys made so that it's easier for certain people to get in and see me. I asked if it would be a problem if I end up having a live-in helper for a month or so, and she said that that would be fine; I'd just need a doctor to sign off on it. The building manager will do everything she can to accommodate me so I can stay here. It was extremely reassuring to have taken that first step in getting this whole thing mobilized.

I would say it's been a great day. I faced the tiger, you know? This morning, fear was chasing me around. But I thought, *Wait a minute, I've had tons of experience with this type of thing; I just have put it to use!* So I set out to start that process, and I feel a lot better tonight than I did this morning. Plus I took a huge bike ride! And I took my vitamins and drank my protein shakes. I'm doing whatever I can to make my liver feel good. So I feel like I made a lot of progress today.

## DAY 42 – THURSDAY MAY 2, 2013

My usual schedule is to have breakfast and then sit at my computer and figure out what I'm doing for the day. I have a calendar on Google which I've been using for a while. Today I concluded that I have to finish all the top priority stuff in my life right now before moving on to more fun projects, including some where I might be able to earn some money. So I decided to work on my priorities.

First I tackled my contact list, making sure it included everybody whom I want contacted after I die. When my mother passed away, she didn't have this kind of list and a big group of people who knew her got left out. After the funeral they were very upset because they hadn't been notified. I learned a lesson there!

Next, I investigated the Medicare system to find out what they do for people in the hospice program. Hospice is a whole-nother program in Medicare. I looked at the website and made a couple of telephone calls. Now I have a complete list of services that Medicare provides under hospice. One thing that I found interesting was that once you're in hospice, Medicare doesn't cover any kind of care that's designed to cure your terminal illness. They won't cover chemo or radiation or prescription drugs to cure you. In other words, once you're in hospice, all they're interested in is helping you to finish things up, you know? Medicare says, "OK, you made a choice and you're gonna have to live with it!" Or die with it. Ha! They pay for you to die. It just struck me as humorous. You sign that paper, get set up with hospice, and now you're supposed to die.

You're eligible for hospice if your doctor certifies that you're terminally ill and you're expected to live six more months or less. Instead of seeking care for your illness, you accept comfort care only. You have to sign a statement saying that that's your choice. I haven't signed that thing yet, since my prognosis isn't down to six months or less yet. I'm gonna see Dr. Gould again in a month to review it. It's interesting – the Medicare website says that if the doctor initially states that a patient has six months to live, and then he or she lives longer than that, the doctor can renew it. My doctor could say, "Oh, we guessed wrong," and we sign up again. "He's eating right and exercising but we don't think he can make it *another* six months."

I was glad to find all this information online. It sounds like I'll get whatever I need, including if I need people to help with cleaning, meals, that sort of thing. The only thing hospice doesn't cover is a 24-hour caregiver. So I'll have to work that out another way, but I have a lot of ideas. I don't think I'll be in that situation for a long period of time anyway, where I need 24-hour care. I know a couple-a three people who are totally disabled and they have a lot of care at home, so I'm gonna talk to them.

In the afternoon I decided to take advantage of the beautiful weather. I took another long bike ride, starting with the same route, over the bridges. Then I rode farther on the east side, past OMSI and out toward Sellwood, before coming back. I tacked on another mile to what I did yesterday. I decided that I'm gonna ride my bike *every* day until I can't ride it anymore, not just every *other* day. I feel free as a bird when I'm on my bike! It doesn't matter what the weather is like because I have rain gear. Well maybe I'll take a break on Sundays, but the other six days of the week, I'll take a bike ride.

My whole body felt so relaxed today after my ride, so I think biking will help me a lot with my anxiety. I feel *normal* when I'm on my bike; I feel like everybody else. I'm riding along and keeping up with other people. If I fall off my bike and land in the river, so be it!

# 16
# HOW PEOPLE RESPOND TO SAD NEWS

**DAY 43 – FRIDAY MAY 3, 2013**

*Blessing #19*

> *When I woke up this morning, I felt well rested and invigorated, and I think that's totally because of the bike rides that I've done the last couple of days. I felt great! My body felt great, as though I wasn't sick at all. That's a huge blessing, having that kind of a feeling at this particular time, it's really a major thing.*

This morning I looked outside and it was another beautiful sun-shiny day. Having several sun-shiny days in a row in the late springtime is kind of a miracle in Portland. It's usually a very wet, soppy time of year. Nicer weather improves everybody's spirits, no matter what kinda shape you're in.

After breakfast, I was committed to finishing preparations for the end of my life here, so I got back on my computer. I'm not really gonna be able to concentrate on anything else 'til I feel that plans for my final days are in place, my memorial service is planned, and the cremation thing is taken care of. And my contact list – I don't wanna neglect anyone that I might wanna talk to before I die. There may be things to resolve with some people, and I just won't feel comfortable until I get everyone onto one list.

Working on my contact list reminded me of a joke. If a woman says she'll call you, she means she'll call you today. If a man says, "I'll call you," he means he'll call you before the end of his life. I really like that joke because it's kinda true, at least for me right now!

Around mid-morning I took a little break and went down to the ground floor lobby. There are these two guys who have scooters, who park at the front window of the building every morning. They look out the window and talk about people. People going by, people who live in the building, whoever. They say stuff like, "Well whattaya think of *that* guy?" and "Look at that lady coming down the street." Today some lady walked by and they said, "Uh-oh! That's the lady who killed her husband," or something like that. *What?* They sit there and talk about people, every day. I stop and talk with them once in a while.

One of these guys is Ike. He's 94 years old. He's a marine hero, all the way from World War Two. I really like him; I think he's tremendous. The other guy is Fred. He has lived in this building since the day it was built, 28 years ago; he was one of the first people to move in. Today there was also a lady sitting nearby, whom I don't really know. She wasn't really talking to them but she was sitting in close proximity.

I walked in and started talking to Ike and Fred, and they asked, "So why aren't you at work?"

I replied, "I don't work anymore."

They asked, "Why don't you work? What happened to your job?"

I said, "I had to leave the job. I didn't feel like doing it anymore."

They kept pressing me about it! I finally said, "I can't do the job. It's too physical for me now, and I only have a few months to live. I have terminal cancer."

They both knew that I'd had cancer treatment, but this was the first they'd heard about it being terminal. They both looked at me for a minute, and then Fred said something like, "Well, it's really a beautiful day outside today, isn't it?"

Then Ike said something totally off the subject also, and they started a whole different conversation. I thought, *Well, this is one approach I haven't seen before!* It's the ostrich approach. You tell somebody something like that, and they immediately stick their head in the sand and say, "I don't know anything about any of this; what *else* is going on?"

Then all of a sudden the lady who had just been sitting there said, "Oh, that's awful, I am so sorry to hear that. I'm so sorry." I thought, *Well, at least somebody here heard me and understood what I was saying!* She didn't say any more, but she gave me a really compassionate look, which was very sweet. I thanked her. Then I looked back at the other two, and they were back to looking out the window and talking about something going on outside. I thought, *Well, that was an interesting conversation!*

It was really strange. There was absolutely no compassion from either of those guys. But I understand it. They don't wanna hear about it. They're both fragile too, in their own circumstances. They just don't wanna talk about it. If they had, they would've said something, right? But neither of them said anything. They may have felt compassion but they didn't know how to express it or what to say. They both probably thought about it as the day went on, but at that moment they didn't have an answer. That's the first time something like that has happened to me. Surprisingly, it didn't bother me at all, but it sure was interesting.

After that I thought, *It's time to do something fun.* I decided to do a post on Square People, my Pioneer Courthouse Square blog. I haven't posted much over the past year because of my illness; prior to that I was doing over 70 posts a year.

Recently, a local hotel set up a sample of one of their newly renovated rooms in a yurt on the Square. I took pictures of it from two or three different angles, and then I wrote what I thought about it. It was the first time I've ever put up a negative post. In the past, if I didn't like what I saw on the Square, I just didn't report on it. Anything I *did* report, I was enthusiastic about. But in *this* case... People who put up stupid displays in Pioneer Courthouse Square usually give you something: a lollipop or a cheap plastic trinket of some kind, so you feel like it was worth your time to listen to them. These people could've at least given away water bottles with the name of the hotel on them, or maybe some cheap pens, you know? Or at least hand out ice cream or cookies. You can't just go down there and not give anything away!

It was also stupid because 99% of the people strolling across the Square will *never* stay in that hotel for $200 a night; they already live here! So no one had any interest whatsoever. There were some hotel representatives off to the side, but they were just sitting around instead of mingling with people. One thing they *did* do was to set up a webcam in the yurt, and let someone spend the night in there. So you could get up in the middle of the night and watch this person sleeping if you wanted to. How lame is that? I mean, yeah, I've always wanted to get up at three o'clock in the morning and turn on my computer to see a webcam picture of a guy sleeping in a hotel room on Pioneer Courthouse Square. That's great stuff, huh?

After I finished my blog post, my ex-wife Ellen came by to pick me up to go for coffee at Starbucks. We had a really fun conversation. We've had kind of a resurgence of our friendship as a result of everything that's happened. We had been friends for years anyway, but we'd only talk on the phone maybe once every two or three months. Now we talk pretty much every week. It's really nice!

After she dropped me off back at my apartment, I decided to go for my bike ride, for the 3rd day in a row. I took a similar route down to the waterfront, across the Steel Bridge, and all the way down to OMSI. Today, instead of coming back across the Hawthorne Bridge, I backtracked so I basically did the whole route twice. I was actually shocked at how much my endurance has picked up in just three days: I was out on my bike for two and a half hours. I stopped every once in a while to watch people go by. In Portland, when this kind of weather comes along, people just come out of the woodwork. They're everywhere! Where have they been? Downtown and the waterfront were deserted just a week ago.

***Blessing #20***

*There's just nothing like sunshine to warm your body. There's no better source of warmth known to man. Fire will keep one side of your body warm, the side facing the fire. That feels good, but your other side stays cold. On the other hand, sunshine wraps around you. It provides warmth all the way around your body; it's phenomenal. I've been cold for so long because I've lost so much weight. So these warm sunny days are such a blessing.*

## DAY 44 – SATURDAY MAY 4, 2013

When I woke up this morning, I looked out my window and saw sunshine again, beautiful sunshine in a clear sky. For Oregon in early May, that is really amazing.

I felt good. I'd had a very good night's rest. I don't have any particular symptoms right now except for fatigue. I get tired early at night, but I feel good in the morning after a good night's rest. I start off feeling almost normal, which is kind of exciting because – for the first couple of hours of the day – I don't feel any different than I did two or three years ago.

The other thing that hit me today was that it's Saturday. I always enjoy Saturday. It's sort of a leisurely kick-back kinda day. You usually have errands and things to do, but it's very leisurely and you don't have that feeling of pressure. I love Saturdays. After breakfast I decided to take an early morning bike ride. I thought I'd make a short loop, maybe three to four miles, and end up at the Fred Meyer grocery store to do some shopping.

As I wandered around Fred Meyer, I thought I saw a couple people looking at me a little strange. I realized that with my trip to Atlanta, the trip to the coast last week, and all the sunshine we've had this week, I've been getting a lot of sun and I look like it. I've noticed that kind of thing for years – if I get a sunburn, people give me strange looks. Like, "Doesn't he know the sun is dangerous, and he shouldn't let himself get sun-burned?" Portland is the only place I've ever lived where people wear safari helmets and things like that in the summer. They look like they're ready for a hike in the Serengeti plains, with these big hats that have canvas that hangs down their backs so they don't get any sun on their head or neck or face. There's an awful lot of people here who are terrified of the sun!

I've always loved the sun. I lived in Los Angeles for 25 years and I was out in the sun a lot. And I hate using sunscreen because it irritates my skin. It's a Catch-22: sunscreen makes me miserable, but without it I get sun-burned. But now? I'm not worried about skin cancer! It's not an issue for me anymore. I get that sun exposure can be very dangerous. But at this point, for myself, I really don't care; I enjoy the sun on my skin. I have had several little skin cancers removed over the years, so I do think everybody *else* should use sunscreen. But I don't know about those safari hats.

---

## A LAST TIME FOR EVERYTHING

*The Kentucky Derby was today, which I was very excited about. It's another thing that I've really enjoyed for years and years and years. I realized that this is probably my last Kentucky Derby – I won't know who wins it next year. I watched it in the community room where we have a really nice 50-inch HD television. I got there early to get the TV turned on and set to the right channel, since our community room TV is on a first-come-first-served basis. I was afraid I'd get there and find someone watching Gunsmoke reruns, but there was nobody there so I tuned in to the Derby way ahead of time.*

---

A lady walked in, whom I've spoken with a few times, and sat down on the couch nearby. She said, "I've been meaning to tell you, you really look great since you had your surgery."

"Well thank you very much."

"You were very fortunate that the cancer was caught in time, and that you've recovered so well from it."

At that point I was sort of dumbfounded. I said, "Well, actually, the cancer is not under control. It's in my liver and it's spreading. It's terminal."

"Oh, I will pray for you."

I thanked her and she immediately launched into *her* cancer tale, about how she'd been diagnosed and had gone through chemo and radiation. It all happened ten years ago so now she's a cancer survivor.

I started feeling jealous! I thought: *Why are you telling me this story?* I was happy for her, but I was kinda jealous. I wanted that too – to be a cancer survivor. So the whole conversation just went south for me. I lost interest.

She went on and on and on about how fortunate she was that they caught it when they did. I just didn't wanna hear it. Besides that, I was waiting for the Kentucky Derby to start.

That kind of thing has happened to me a couple of times. When somebody says "I'll pray for you" and then launches into their own story, it's just confusing and it doesn't make me feel good. It's nice of people to say they'll pray for me, assuming they really will do that. But when they go on and on about how they beat the cancer, the whole conversation turns out badly and I feel resentful.

After watching the Kentucky Derby, I returned to my apartment and got a phone call from my friend Larry, a guy whom I see about once or twice a year. I enjoy talking with this guy. We're not all that close as friends, but we are faithful about talking on the telephone and it's usually about sports. He went to Washington State University, and I briefly attended the University of Oregon, as well as growing up in Eugene near the U of O. I love the Oregon Ducks and he loves the Washington State Cougars, who are rivals. We always have a really fun conversation; I like his sense of humor. He was really upbeat today. He plays trombone and he wanted to tell me about some upcoming gigs, and he had plans to go on a date tonight with a new lady he had met online.

I thought, *I really need to tell Larry about my situation because he's someone I'd like to sit down and talk with one more time. I'd like to meet for lunch or a coffee.* But I couldn't do it today. I just couldn't! Finally I said, "I gotta go; but email me about your next music gig and I'll try to come out and see it." So we hung up. It was a great conversation, and this just wasn't the time to talk to him about my circumstances.

There's never a good time to bring up my circumstances. If people really care about you, that kind of news spoils their day. I know that that kind of news would spoil *my* day. It was just too nice a day, and he had high expectations about a lotta things and I didn't wanna ruin it for him. I'll have to call Larry back on a rainy day in the next couple weeks, but it's not gonna be easy.

Next I rode down to Pioneer Courthouse Square to see what there was to photograph. They were setting up for an event tomorrow, the Cinco de Mayo 5K, which starts and finishes at the Square. There were all these trucks, and people running around unloading stuff, a frenzy of activity. Initially I felt like I didn't have the energy to take any pictures, and my trip over there would have been for nothing. In the past, I've photographed actual events; none of my blog posts covered a situation where people are setting things up *before* the event. Then I thought, *Why not?* I started feeling energized about getting a different type of story, and I ran around the Square taking pictures. I think I got some nice photos and I'll put that post together in a couple days. It seems that having energy can sometimes be a psychological thing instead of physical.

**DAY 45 – SUNDAY MAY 5, 2013**

It was a beautiful day again today, and I can't remember experiencing a stretch of weather like this in May in the time I've lived in Oregon, twenty-something years now. This morning I was also looking forward to going to church, since I hadn't gone for three weeks. I enjoy going, to hear about Jesus, and to see friends. Everyone whom I know and consider a friend at this church now knows about my situation, so I'm comfortable there. I also really like the music. Most of all, I enjoy Communion, the way it's done at this church.

I enjoyed the sermon. Lately I've noticed something about sermons, though, given the short time I have left to live. Some sermons are more timely than others: some things really resonate, while other things make me think: *Well, that's not gonna affect me much longer.* When the pastor talks about the Book of John, where Jesus speaks specifically about heaven, and about how he's preparing a place for us in heaven, those things really resonate with me. On the other hand, when the sermon is about how to live as a Christian, and what we can do for other people, it's hard to envision those things as long-term goals. For me, that's not as relevant.

On my way home from church, I stopped in the Safeway store to pick up some items. There's a Starbucks in the store, with a group of tables where you can sit and drink your coffee. As I walked by that area, I noticed someone I knew. I couldn't remember his name but I've talked to him a number of times. I like him because he's a fellow Christian and he has what I consider to be a bona-fide street ministry. He befriends people in the community and helps them in various ways. He was sitting with a guy who was severely disabled. He had taken this guy to church and was now spending some time with him having coffee. That's the kind of ministry he does; helping people and getting them to church and things like that.

I was really happy to see him. He asked, "How ya doin'?" and I told him, "You know, I've been battling cancer."

He said, "Yeah, I remember you telling me about that. How's it going?"

I said, "It's not going well. I only have a few months to live."

He said, "I'm really sorry to hear that! But you are a Christian and you know what the outcome of all this will be."

I said, "Yes, I do."

I spent the rest of the day with my friend Karen.

## 17

## RUNNING OUT OF MARBLES

**DAY 46 – MONDAY MAY 6, 2013**

*I* woke up this morning, looked out the window, and guess what – another beautiful sun-shiny day. I was dumbfounded yesterday and I was dumbfounded again today. I checked online and it looks like it'll be five more days of this; zero percent chance of rain 'til Friday. It just doesn't seem possible to have so much nice weather at this time, but there it is.

After breakfast I had to get back to the drudgery at hand: working on my list of contacts. I pulled out a notebook from when I lived in Los Angeles. It had a whole group of contacts, although there's nobody in there that I actually wanna talk to now. But I got all caught up in it because it brought back so many memories of all the people I dealt with in that city. I ended up looking through it for about an hour and a half. I started googling people to see if I could find anything out about 'em online; people whom I hadn't thought about for over 20 years. I got kind of distracted for a while there.

After lunch today I went over to Safeway. I pretty much go there daily; it's as much a ritual as it is about actually going shopping. I like to go over and see what's going on, and it's full of interesting people.

Walking in, I bumped into a woman I know, but I don't remember her name. I've shot portrait photos of a lot of people in this neighborhood; once you've done that, you don't forget their faces. They remember me too, so we have an immediate bond when we see each other – but I don't remember all of their names.

So this lady came up to me and said, "Oh, you look wonderful!" That's a very disturbing comment to me right now! She had no idea that I was battling cancer last year. I was wearing my mirror sunglasses, and she asked me where I got them. They're actually safety glasses from my former job, but they're really cool so I still wear 'em anyway. So she was just going on about how I looked, with my sunglasses and my suntan and all that. I guess normally I would've said, "Well thank you, I appreciate that." I kind of felt like saying, "Well, you don't know the truth, you don't really know what's going on." But, naturally I couldn't say that.

It upsets me when people tell me that I look good right now; they don't know what's happening inside my body. Appearances don't mean anything. I see this all the time when I look at people now. They look great, but a moment later I'm wondering if they have anything going on in their life that's similar to what I'm going through. And it's disturbing! People think you look good but you're not well at all. But with people who are just casual acquaintances, I don't want to go into what's really going on.

Later on I decided it was time for another bike ride in this magnificent weather. I rode the same loop that I've been riding lately. It's one of the most beautiful bicycle loops that anybody could ride, on both sides of the Willamette River and across the Steel Bridge and the Hawthorne Bridge. It was a great ride and I felt good.

## DAY 47 – TUESDAY MAY 7, 2013

Today I remembered a strange idea from somebody that I used to be friends with. This guy wanted to track the remaining years of his life using a jar of marbles. He decided that he had X number of years left, maybe 35 or 40. He filled a jar with that many marbles, and every year, to commemorate where he was at, he would take one marble out. It was his way of keeping on track. Each year when he took out another marble, he'd think back on the past year: *What did I accomplish last year? Do I need to make any adjustments or course corrections?* It was an interesting idea, tracking life with marbles, and focusing on having a time frame to get specific things done.

It was another gorgeous day today so I went on a bike ride again. Then I ended up at Pioneer Courthouse Square, where I had a cup of coffee and met a couple, three interesting people and got some photographs for a future blog post. I really felt well today; it was amazing.

## DAY 48 – WEDNESDAY MAY 8, 2013

This turned out to be a very confusing day, as well as a milestone in my journey. Late Tuesday night, I started feeling really disoriented. Basically I was unable to concentrate on anything. I felt unable to focus on what I was doing. At first I figured it would pass, because I've had little neurological problems over the past year or so. I thought it was just another one of those little neurological blips on the radar. But it turned out to be far more serious than that

Around 10 or 10:15 pm, I was going to brush my teeth and get ready for bed. But I couldn't figure out how to work the Waterpik. I couldn't even figure out how to brush my teeth. My right hand felt totally detached from my body! I sat down on the bed and became really, really frustrated and disoriented. I didn't know what was going on. My first thought was that I'd had a stroke. But my mother had strokes, and I know all the drills that my mother had to go through – I did those drills with her if I thought she was having an event. You raise your hands over your head, and smile, and check all your facial expressions. I wasn't having trouble with any of those things, so it didn't seem like I was having a stroke. I began to feel extremely anxious.

I called Karen and said, "I can't figure things out." I even had trouble figuring out how my phone worked; I just couldn't put the pieces together. Initially I thought I would just ride it out and see if things would clear up. But it got worse and worse and finally I called 911. I was very upset, and I got in a little tangle with the paramedics when they arrived, because I didn't know *what* I wanted. Should I go to the hospital or just have them check my blood pressure? The paramedic got upset and asked, "What did you call *me* for?" We got into it pretty heavy but then we both calmed down because I realized that we weren't getting anywhere, and I didn't really know what to do; I was so confused. I finally said I just wanted to go to the hospital, to get some help to find out what was going on and why I was so disoriented. It was scary because I didn't know what to do! I just didn't know what my next move was.

They transported me to the hospital. The doctors started the process of figuring out what was going on, and they did a pretty thorough exam. I explained my cancer situation and said that I didn't want any heroic efforts to be made; I just wanted to feel oriented and know what was going on.

One of the doctors wanted me to have a CAT scan. The other doctor wasn't adamant about it; she seemed a bit skeptical about the whole thing. I certainly didn't feel that a CAT scan would do me any good. One doctor said it could be that the cancer had metastasized to my brain. It didn't make much sense to me; I thought it was a neurological event, not necessarily related to cancer. I've had some neurological problems that have gotten worse over the years because of my detached retina, my inability to see well in one eye, and the confusion that comes as a result of that. A neurologist confirmed a while ago that I have vision and hearing problems that will probably get worse over time, and as far as I knew, that had nothing to do with cancer.

But we weren't getting anywhere. The blood test showed decent liver function, and they pretty much ruled out a stroke because I didn't have any of those types of symptoms. My electrolytes looked fine, so it wasn't dehydration. My white and red blood cells were OK. Somehow, other than some neurological problems – and cancer – my health is actually quite good right now. I'd even been on a bike ride yesterday for a couple hours and felt wonderful. So this just came on out of nowhere and really threw me into a tailspin.

If I were a healthy individual, without a prognosis of just a few months to live, I would've had that CAT scan and seen another neurologist, to try to figure out what's wrong with my brain. I mean, if everything else is OK, you wanna try to figure out what's going on and save your life! But it doesn't make sense to start a whole series of neurological testing *now*. I've got an appointment with Dr. Pine tomorrow, my primary care doctor, and we're gonna discuss whether it's time to enter hospice care now. If I'm entering hospice care, this is all just a moot point because we won't treat any of that neurological stuff. If it's not time yet, then maybe this *is* a neurological problem, and we'll investigate it a bit. It'll be up to the doctor tomorrow to figure that out, and there's not much else to say until I have that appointment. This has all been very confusing, to say the least.

## DAY 49 – THURSDAY MAY 9, 2013

Today was more-or-less a blur because of what took place toward the end of the day.

I had a doctor's appointment at four o'clock, and I was waiting for that all day, so I don't really remember much of what I did earlier in the day. I was scheduled to see Dr. Pine, to evaluate what had happened in the emergency room Tuesday night. The E.R. doctors thought perhaps I'd had some sort of brain episode, but they weren't sure what it was. They suspected the cancer had spread from my liver to my brain, but they were more-or-less guessing. So I was waiting to get to my doctor and find out what his take on it was.

When the doctor arrived, he said he had looked over the test results from the emergency room, and he concluded that the cancer has indeed metastasized to my brain. He was just guessing because we haven't done any scans, but he was fairly sure. He didn't think it was a stroke, and he said that because I'd had a variety of different symptoms, it was likely there's more than one tumor in my brain. I could have a scan, but he didn't insist on it.

I've had a couple other symptoms now too. There was blood in my urine today for the first time; I don't think I've ever had that. I've also noticed some pain in the area of my liver, kind of a throbbing pain. It's nothing severe, but it has just kinda felt the same every day and it's not getting better. If you combine those symptoms – blood in the urine, the slight pain, and the big episode the other night which clearly indicated that something went haywire in my brain – it all points to one thing, that the cancer has probably metastasized to other parts of my body. When I started this journey 49 days ago, we had just found out that the cancer had spread to my liver. Now it's in several areas; it has spread quickly during that period of time, and the amount of time that I have left has been diminished considerably.

The big thing today is that I'm now officially enrolled in the federal government's hospice program. Now any medical care that I need will be provided through hospice, covered by Medicare. It wasn't going to be official until my next appointment with Dr. Gould in June, but things have accelerated. So what that means is – well, I don't know. Nobody knows what it means. I thought I was doing incredibly well physically, with a tremendous feeling of wellbeing. So this was a huge shock! I'm changing my thinking rather drastically regarding what I have time to do while I'm still here on this earth, and what I won't have time for. The way things are going, it could be only two weeks! Nobody knows. Or it could be months. It's a huge shock, now that it's all official. I haven't really grasped it yet, but we all know this is not gonna take very long.

I'm relieved to be in the hospice program. That's because I have somebody I can call if I need any help immediately. Before I was in a sort of no-man's land, as far as what to do if I had a major medical event. I wasn't in hospice yet, but there was no imperative to save my life at all costs either. I'm relieved that there will be a nurse showing up at my door tomorrow to get a plan going, whereas before, there really wasn't any plan in place concerning home care.

I took a walk to Pioneer Square late this afternoon after my appointment. I thought about the finality of what happened today: *I'm officially dying, and my time is short*. The only thing I feel bad about is projects I might not have time to finish. I'm thinking a lot about my faith, and about the people I care about. I need to talk to some people very soon. I've been putting it off for several weeks: I need to tell them how I feel about them. I'd like to be able to speak to more people who share my faith.

I don't feel scared, because of what I believe in. I believe in God, I believe in Jesus, I believe in the resurrection and I believe I'm going home. I'm going *home* – so I don't fear death. My fear – I think everybody's fear – is the possibility of suffering a great deal of pain, and not wanting to be alone in a time of need. Fear comes from not knowing what's gonna happen, with something like this hanging over your head. You don't know how many days you have left. You don't *know* anything. You just do the best you can, every day.

# SECTION 4: HOSPICE CARE BEGINS

It's an overwhelming turn of events to have people show up at my doorstep and tell me, "Yes, in fact, you are going to die, sooner rather than later." I *knew* this was coming, but people keep reinforcing it, talking about hospice care and pain medication and all those things. It's not, "At some time we'll evaluate and get you into the program." It's, "You *have* been evaluated and you are *in* the program." This kind of thing just comes at you all of a sudden in a rush.

# 18
# MOTHER TERESA, BILLY JOEL, AND FAITH IN ACTION

**DAY 50 – FRIDAY MAY 10, 2013**

What an unbelievable day! I got up this morning and right away I started worrying about my meeting scheduled for one o'clock this afternoon. I tried to do some work but I kept getting all discombuberated thinking about that meeting. It was going to be about hospice care, which my doctor initiated yesterday. A hospice nurse was coming over to do a medical intake. She arrived with a hospice social worker. Also a friend of mine stopped by to help sort it all out, so there were four of us in the apartment, all trying to get acquainted and figure out what was going on. I didn't have enough chairs, but the nurse said she was comfortable sitting on the floor.

These two ladies – the nurse and the social worker – do what they call "hospice intake". They don't work on the actual case long-term; they specialize in collecting the intake information. They both have powerful notebook computers and they're flying from the minute they get in the door, asking questions and recording stuff on their computers.

I learned that once you turn your life over to hospice, the hospice doctors make the decisions on what kind of care you're gonna get, as well as what kinda care you're *not* gonna get. You can quit at any time; you're not obligated to stay in hospice. For example if I got a kidney infection and wanted to see my regular doctor about clearing that up, I would have to get out of the hospice program first. I could die from a serious infection; if I stayed in hospice in that situation, I'd basically have to ride it out. So hospice is actually a huge decision. But of course I wouldn't be faced with that decision if I wasn't dying of cancer.

The nurse said that she has had a lot of experience with hospice, including brain and bile duct cancers. She said that bile duct cancer, for some reason, really likes to metastasize to the liver and the brain; those are some of its favorite places. It tends to bypass all these other organs. That was pretty interesting! She said that that can have an upside and a downside. It can be fairly painless – it will kill you, but probably won't cause agonizing pain. She has had people die of brain cancer, who didn't have any pain at all. In a way, that was encouraging.

The nurse and social worker asked me everything they could possibly ask. Where do you live? Who's your next of kin? It just went on and on and on for almost four hours. Non-stop questions. It was absolutely totally overwhelming and I can't even begin to cover it all right now; I'll have to revisit this whole thing tomorrow.

But I do want to mention one key point: I'll never have to call 911 again. To me, that is really exciting. If I have a crisis in the middle of the night – if I have extensive pain, or another bout of disorientation – I pick up the telephone and call a special nurse, and they dispatch someone to my home. It might take them a while to get here, of course, because they're not an ambulance and they have to stop for traffic lights. But they will show up.

They will give me a home kit for pain, and train me on how to use it. A morphine kit and some other pain killers. If I experience severe pain, they can instruct me over the telephone on how to administer the pain medication for myself, while they're on their way over. They don't have anything to do with emergency rooms; they're not into that. They try to resolve the issue at home. To me, that's all really comforting. If I call, somebody's gonna come over and guide me through the crisis. I'm gonna remain in my home and not be taken away somewhere. That gives me a sort of in-the-middle-of-the-night feeling of security, which is a big bonus in all of this right now.

Anyway, I'm overloaded. It was a brain-numbing four hours. One question after another. Four hours! All I was able to do today was answer their questions and just try to absorb all the information they gave me.

## DAY 51 – SATURDAY MAY 11, 2013

It's another day and I would *like* to say that I feel all warm and fuzzy, but I really don't because I still have a lot of unanswered questions about hospice and how it works. Also – I didn't notice this until today – my doctor's notes regarding my appointment on Thursday said that he anticipated this process could take as little as two months. I had assumed that the amount of time I have left would be shorter now, but when your doctor writes something like that down on paper, it adds a lot of power to the statement.

I feel like I've deteriorated quite a bit in just the past few days. I don't have anywhere near the energy I had before. I'm not enduring any pain, but my quality of life has dropped off considerably in just three or four days, from the standpoint of how much energy I have, what I can and can't do. I have to reconcile what's going on with my feelings about the finality of it. All along I was thinking, *It's gonna be a nice summer and I'll have the opportunity to visit the Columbia Gorge a few times; a friend wants to take weekly hikes; other friends want to get together.* Suddenly I'm realizing that none of that is gonna happen, at least not to the extent that those kinds of things *used to* happen.

So I'm looking at this huge folder on my desk, labeled *Providence Hospice and Palliative Care*. I've looked through some of the pamphlets and letters in here: *Dear Patient and Family, Helping You Live Independently at Home*, flyers about Hospice Aides, Certified Nursing Assistants, bathing, skin care, changing the bed, toiletry needs. They also have volunteer services, where volunteers will come to your home once a week for a couple of hours. Here's another flyer: "Help us help you. Ask if you have any questions or concerns. Do not be embarrassed about asking questions; we want to help you understand your care." A couple more pamphlets: *Know your Risks*, *Disaster Preparedness*, *Emergency Information*. All of these are enclosed in this giant folder. There's a comfort care journal, with diagrams on pain and how to report pain. I think they want you to keep journal entries in here, which may or may not happen.

Here's one for family members, called *Anticipatory Grief*. "How can I address my grief yet be a comfort and support for my loved one?" Here's a booklet that discusses what may or may not happen at the end of your life, and here's a quote from Mother Teresa: "In this life, we cannot do great things. We can only do small things with great love." I once had the incredible privilege of meeting Mother Teresa when I worked at Twin Circle Publishing. She made a trip to the United States. At that time I was general manager of the National Catholic Register, so she was invited to our offices. That was a great honor.

I'll always remember another thing that Mother Teresa said, that really touched me. She was in Calcutta, and she had a home to care for people. She didn't have a lot of money, so her mission was a bare-bones operation. During an interview, she was asked, "Don't you feel completely overwhelmed by everything that you *can't* do because you don't have the resources?" She replied, "Not at all. God didn't put me on earth specifically to help people; God put me here to be faithful." That always struck me as a beautiful thing to say. I'm here to be faithful, and do my work, and show up every day, do everything that I can, and not cry and moan and groan about what I don't have.

So yesterday – at the same time that the social worker was going through the pamphlets and explaining things to me, the nurse was constantly firing questions at me about my medical history. It was a double-barrel shotgun approach, nonstop, bam-bam-bam-bam-bam, one thing after another. My friend who was here sat over in a corner with his head tilted back, totally overwhelmed by the whole thing.

They covered all the medical problems that I have ever had or *could* still have.

They both complimented me too, similar to something that Dr. Gould had said. They said they had never really heard anybody explain their situation better and or more concisely than I did. Once again, I think I can do that because Karen and I talk about this information and record it, and that gives me an opportunity to digest it. So then when I have to tell somebody what's going on, I have a very concise approach and I say what I mean to say. Even the doctor in the E.R. on Tuesday night said something similar! So this was the third time that someone has said that to me, about being clear and concise and at peace about my situation.

It's an overwhelming turn of events to have people show up at my doorstep and tell me, "Yes, in fact, you are going to die, sooner rather than later." And I *knew* this was coming, but people keep coming along and reinforcing it, talking about hospice care and pain medication and all those things. It's not like, "Well, at some time we'll need to evaluate this and get you into the program." It's, "You have been evaluated and you are *in* the program." I don't care who you are, this kind of thing just comes at you all of a sudden in a rush.

And I'm disappointed – not because this is the end of my life, but because I thought I'd have a little more time, especially during the summer months, to just go out and enjoy the scenery. In Oregon we wait a long, long time for nice weather, and I really don't wanna die in the summer time. It was a huge blessing to be able to get out and ride my bike on all those days recently, really feeling like I used to feel before my operation.

Another thing about the discussion yesterday. An awful lot of medical knowledge was thrown around, including a lot of medical terms, a lot about the business of dying. But there was also a lot of personal stuff. In between firing questions at me about all the medical things, they were also trying to find out who I am and what I'm doing here, what kind of a person I am.

For example, on my wall, I've got a little set of antlers, from the first deer that I ever shot. That's mounted with a cap pistol from when

I was a little boy, along with an old hunting knife. I used to track down all sorts of bad guys with those weapons. Ha! There's also a BB gun on the wall.

The nurse and social worker looked at my wall, and the social worker asked, "Is that gun loaded?"

"No, that's a cap gun. It can't possibly hurt anyone."

She pointed to another gun, "What kind of rifle is that?"

"It's a BB gun," I said.

"Is that one loaded?"

"No, I only use BBs in it, but it's not loaded now; it's just hanging on my wall."

She seemed apprehensive, like, *Wait a minute now, we can't have anybody armed around here, we're gonna have nurses coming in and everything.* Maybe she was afraid I'm gonna shoot *myself* to avoid all the aggravation of dying! It was just funny, but I could certainly understand it. You don't want weapons and guns lying around when people are coming to help, in a hospice situation.

Then my friend who was sitting there said, "Don, you should tell them some of your stories! Tell them about Billy Joel!"

"What about Billy Joel?" the nurse asked.

I asked, "First of all, do you like Billy Joel?"

She goes, "Oh we love Billy Joel!"

So I told the story. When I lived in Los Angeles, I used to go to a bar called The Executive Room, on Wilshire Boulevard. There was a guy who was a phenomenal piano player, just absolutely unbelievable. Far better than any piano player I'd ever heard in a piano bar. And he sang, too. I saw him there, maybe a couple times a week, for like six months, and just loved his music. But I didn't really think anything of it.

A few years later, I think I was watching *60 Minutes*, and they were interviewing Billy Joel. Maybe it was more like 20 years later. The subject came up that he had had a big contract dispute with his first two records. He didn't make any money; actually he lost money because everybody was trying to cheat him. So he hired a lawyer, and the lawyer said, "You have to hide out until we get your contract straightened out." He'd already had two big hits but the lawyer advised him to disappear. So he decided to disappear in Los Angeles, at the bar that I used to go to. So I found out from watching this *60 Minutes* interview that it was Billy Joel that I had been watching 20 years earlier, at a time when he went by the name of Bill Martin. It was unbelievable! Billy Joel's signature song, *Piano Man*, was about that bar that I used to go to. I knew everybody in that song; they all hung out there. I *always* used to ask him, "What are you doing here?" I would hear him play and I'd go, "I don't get it!" I had a lot of conversations with him; I told him about a couple of country and western stars that I liked to listen to, like Marty Robbins.

At the time, I didn't know who he was. I did *not* know. After he became famous a few years later, I still didn't pay any attention, and didn't realize that he was Billy Joel. He looked different, and besides, I thought the guy I had seen was Bill Martin, not Billy Joel.

The nurse and social worker loved that story and had a lot of fun with it. Then the social worker asked me, "Does your faith help sustain you through all of this?"

I said, "Absolutely, my faith is the most important thing that I have, through everything that's happened to me over the last year and a half. Every day that goes by, I'm sustained by my faith."

My faith stems from personal experiences. Not just once or twice, but hundreds of times. Throughout life, I have struggled in many different ways, and I feel as though I've been given a generous portion of grace. For instance, when I heard that my long-time friend Ronald was ill with terminal cancer, his wife Janine told me, "You have two, three months to get up here and visit him." She knew it would be a struggle for me to get there quickly, since they lived just outside Seattle. At that time I had already started feeling the effects of cancer in my own body, although I didn't know yet that that's what it was. I figured it was anxiety, or something like that, and it'd go away.

But I suddenly had this overwhelming desire to visit Ronald. Absolutely overwhelming. I called Janine and said, "I want to come and see him *now*."

She said, "Well, we're just bringing him home from the hospital.

He's in hospice care now, and this might not be the best weekend to visit because there's a lot going on – people coming and going, a hospital bed being delivered, that sort of thing."

But I was persistent. I said, "I need to come up and visit him *now*." I wanted to go on a Thursday; I only had that one day because I was still working at the time. I figured I could rent a car and make it to Seattle and back in a day if I left early in the morning.

Janine reiterated, "Maybe this isn't the best time," but then she talked with her daughter and finally she said, "OK, it might work out."

So I rented a car and got there just before lunch. Ronald was phasing in and out. Sometimes he was very alert and able to talk, and other times he seemed to be dozing. We'd known each other for 50 years, starting down in Los Angeles, so we reminisced. We had both been in the publishing business, so we had all sorts of wild and wacky publishing stories. We *always* enjoyed each other's company, even on that day. At that time, I still figured that I'd be able to make another trip up and see him again.

Around four or five o'clock, I could see that Ronald was getting really tired so I decided it was time to make the long trip home. Before I left, his daughter said, "I'm amazed by the conversation you had with my dad. He's a really private person, and I'd never heard a lot of those stories before. It was extremely interesting!" Then I went over to Ronald and I hugged him, and he hugged me back. I believe we'd never hugged before. He said, "Don, it's a beautiful place we're going to." We were both crying. I said, "I'll see you. I love you." And he said, "I love you." Then I said goodbye to Janine and their daughter, and I started driving home.

It seemed like it should all have been incredibly sad, but it wasn't. I had a feeling of elation, that Ronald was going to be in a better place, maybe in a month or two. At that moment he was in a terrible place. I had a great feeling of thankfulness, all the way home, knowing that he wouldn't have to suffer too much longer.

That was on a Thursday. The next day I didn't hear from anyone so I assumed Ronald was settling into his hospice situation. Later I found out that on Saturday his pain got very bad, and he was taken to the hospital for better pain control. He passed away sometime Saturday afternoon. Janine told me later on that as far as she could tell, I was the last person on this earth that he'd had a coherent conversation with. I was just overwhelmed by that! Before going to see him, I just knew that I had to make that trip, *on that day.*

That has been one of the most powerful experiences in my life. It goes back to my faith. This type of thing has happened many times throughout my lifetime, where coincidence just doesn't enter into the picture. It wasn't pure coincidence; something inside of me *told* me that I had to be somewhere at a certain time. I often think about Ronald, especially since my own cancer diagnosis and treatment and the whole process started. His face is right there in front of me; it's amazing.

The hospice nurse and social worker were also interested in the fact that I want to keep riding my bicycle and going outdoors, and that I want to spend as much time as possible walking around, even when it gets difficult. I told them I want to continue living my life as best I can.

Today has been a setback. I've had trouble with my speech a few times. I've had a little difficulty trying to pronounce words and string thoughts and sentences together. I'm definitely slipping. I took a small bike ride today, and I was extremely cautious. I only rode through streets that were really clear, and I walked my bike across all the intersections. I spent an hour and a half on what would normally take me 20 or 30 minutes to ride. I'm not capable of doing what I was doing just a week ago. But I was very happy about that deep conversation with the nurse and social worker, sharing my personal philosophy about taking care of myself and getting outdoors.

19

# STARTING TO LOSE GROUND

**DAY 52 – SUNDAY MAY 12, 2013**

The last 24 hours have been pretty difficult. Between last night and this evening, I feel as though I've slipped quite a bit. Hopefully it's just a temporary setback, from feeling a lot of stress and anxiety as a result of the day's events. In the past, I've had a couple bad days followed by some good days, so maybe tomorrow will be different. But today I really feel that I've sustained a major setback in how I feel.

Last night when I went to bed, almost immediately I started feeling hot and feverish. But I didn't even check my temperature because I felt like it really didn't matter. I felt surprisingly content. In the past I've always been alarmed by a fever. I would think, *What is it? What's gonna happen? Do I have an infection?* I had a lot of terrifying nights during chemo because above a certain temperature, I was supposed to go to the emergency room and I hated that idea. Some nights I would check my thermometer every ten minutes! But last night I had an incredible feeling of peace and I just dropped off to sleep. Maybe it was because I knew that if it got really bad, I could just call the hospice phone number for help.

Last night I also thought, *What would happen if I just passed away in my sleep?* That would be a wonderful blessing. I'd be on my way home, and I wouldn't have to worry about drugs or chemo or any of those things ever again. I almost felt like saying, "Bring it on! If this is a fever and it's gonna be fatal, so be it!" I was astounded that I felt that way.

This morning I wanted to go to church. Without that to look forward to, I would have stayed in bed for a couple more hours. But I felt a tremendous need to go to church, mostly so I could take Communion with my fellow believers and experience the sensation of being in Communion with the Lord. I struggled to get out of bed because my body told me that I needed more rest. I also struggled with having breakfast because my hands were a little dysfunctional; they didn't operate as well as the day before. I felt like I was kind of reeling around. I didn't fall down but it was all very discomforting. Tonight I'm having a little more difficulty with speech too. I'm losing ground to this disease.

Anyway I did manage to make it to church, although I was very wobbly. I wasn't able to stand up when the congregation sang hymns; I just sat there. I didn't feel like I could join in. So my church experience today was marked by thoughts like, *I've slipped; I've fallen behind here.* I did get up for Communion, and after the service I got up to talk to the people there that I care about. Seeing my friends was very helpful. When I was ready to leave, I sort of wobbled out the door. I didn't feel like I was gonna fall down, but I felt very wobbly.

After that, I made it over to my favorite place: Safeway. Ha! I wanted to see what was going on there, and whether I needed any groceries. I also stopped to check my blood pressure with the machine that they have in the store. I know those machines aren't *terribly* reliable, but they can be an indicator if something's *really* gone haywire. Another fascinating thing that's happened to me since being in hospice is that my blood pressure has really dropped. I'm no longer concerned with emergency rooms and this and that, and there's something about it that's really peaceful and relaxing.

I was very concerned about getting my hair cut today. It's not a vanity thing; I just like my hair cropped fairly short. I've always ridden my bike over to my favorite haircut shop, about a mile away. But today I just knew I wouldn't be able to do that ride. Unless I experience a turn-around tomorrow, it seems like I'm going to have less mobility than before. I don't know if I'll have enough energy for long walks, like going down to Pioneer Square or downtown for some shopping. I can walk around two or three blocks without a problem, but the idea of just going out into the street all alone suddenly seems scary. If I lose my ability to walk to Pioneer Square and take one- to two-mile walks, that's going to be difficult. It seems like my life is starting to become compressed a little bit by what's happening.

## DAY 53 – MONDAY MAY 13, 2013

This was a confusing day. I'm still having trouble putting it all together. Time seems to drag when I try to figure out how to do various things. Also I got up pretty late today after sleeping really well, so my day got off to a slower start than usual. I felt like I really needed more rest because I was stressed out from everything that happened last week.

After breakfast, I started getting telephone calls from people on my hospice team. It's time to start meeting and talking to everybody and I'll probably be doing that for most of this week. The hospice situation has developed a life of its own!

The first person to call this morning was the hospice social worker. He wanted to come by around 10:30 or 11:00. His name is Rome, R-O-M-E; a shortened version of Jerome. He's an interesting guy; he was a social worker in Washington, D.C. for many, many years. He told me that he loved D.C. but he couldn't live there anymore; it was just too much, with crime rates and traffic and everything. He's fairly new to Portland so he doesn't know the city really well, but he has friends here.

Overall we had a really nice conversation. He explained that he'd be helping to coordinate various aspects of the hospice team and he'd help me resolve any problems. He'll come to see me every two weeks. I said, "One thing that you could help me with right now is that I can't get enough hot water in my bathtub in this newly-renovated apartment. The new water heater isn't big enough. How do *you* feel about that?"

He replied, "I feel that that's very wrong. For someone in your situation, a really nice hot bath can be very, very soothing and comforting, and I definitely feel that something should be done to fix that. I'll talk to my colleagues and see what we might be able to do. That's really not fair in your situation."

It's true: there's enough hot water to take a hot shower, but when our apartment building was remodeled, they put in new water heaters and they simply don't produce enough hot water to fill the bathtub. That's been very difficult for me. I wouldn't normally take a bath every day, but a couple times a week would be nice, to just relax and soak it up. But I haven't been able to for several months now. The building manager keeps saying, "Well, we're working on the problem and doing this and doing that." It's the same old run-around that you get when people don't wanna fix a mistake. I don't know whether Rome will be able to help me with this, but I felt comforted that he was concerned.

Rome and I went over a few other basic things, including contact info for the people in my life. He wanted to know everybody's names – who all the players are in this situation and what their roles are, that sort of thing. He kept calling me "sir" and "mister" and I said, "Please, don't call me 'sir' and 'mister'; 'Don' is fine." So we got that straightened out. Anyway I think he's gonna be fine and I'll enjoy working with him.

About 45 minutes after Rome left, my new hospice nurse, Susan, called. She sounded like a very nice lady; I really liked her. We talked about my medical treatment, including the emergency pain kit that recently came in the mail. It's a sealed package with boxes of morphine and various other things, and she will come by soon to review it and show me how to use it in an emergency situation.

We also talked about the steroid pills that were delivered to me last week. I'll test them out to see if they help relieve pressure that I've been feeling in my brain, which might help me to speak more clearly and move around with less dysfunction. She said to start taking those pills tomorrow morning, and that you can usually see an immediate effect if they're working. You take steroids in the morning, as soon as you get up, with food. They get you jacked up and hyped up, and increase your appetite, and then you have a lot of energy in the morning. By the time the afternoon rolls around, the effects kinda wear off and you go on with your day. I will try it and see how that goes.

The nurse also said that she would like to order a four-wheel walker for me. That's for taking longer trips, if I wanna be more mobile but I'm feeling a little insecure. The walker will have a seat on it, so if I get tired, I can just sit down on my own chair. I hate to have medical equipment in my house. I know I'm going to need a walker at some point but I just don't want it now. The only reason I *would* go for something like that is because I would like to take longer walks. Having a place to sit and rest would give me a feeling of security. Maybe I can disguise the walker somehow so it doesn't look like a piece of medical equipment; make it look like a skateboard or put a bicycle wheel on the front of it. Instead of a walker, it'll just be something that I cruise around on.

The third phone call I got today was from a pastor. He wants to come by to chat and see what's going on. I explained that I have a pastor and a church that I go to. He said, "That's OK; I'm part of the team, so I'll come by to see you." I think the hospice people try to prevent social isolation; they check in often. That seems to be part of their strategy.

Later I went to the grocery store. I think I really will be more secure going to the store with a walker. I could put my shopping bags on the walker, and pretend it's a shopping cart. I'll cruise right by, and people will just think I've got a little shopping cart. The bags will camouflage everything nicely!

While I was at the store, I had kind of a strange incident. I knocked a couple things off the shelf. One was a jar of peanut butter. Fortunately it didn't break, and I picked it up. But then later I just ran into a wall and knocked something down. Obviously my field of vision isn't right and I'm not as coordinated as I used to be.

Another thing that I noticed today was that time has been running very slowly. I thought I was doing a lot of stuff but now the day is almost gone and I haven't done much of anything besides answering telephone calls and trying to come to grips with my new situation. I'm dealing with a whole new scene and a whole new group of people, and I don't know how to react to it all.

## DAY 54 – TUESDAY MAY 14, 2013

This was a strange day. I woke up this morning thinking about the possibility of taking a new medication, which might help my head feel better by relieving pressure due to tumors. If it's gonna help, it'll kick in about the 2nd or 3rd day. If it's not gonna help, we'll know by the 4th or 5th day. I don't like taking medications; I am *very* anti-medication. I looked at the bottle for about 10 minutes this morning, trying to decide whether to go ahead with it or not. I opened it up and looked inside. I poured one out and then I paced around, trying to reconcile how I felt about it. But I finally decided to try it, so I popped one pill.

After that, I wasn't able to focus on much of anything. I kept looking at things I wanted to do and thinking, "Nah, that's too much – I can't do it, I can't figure it out." I ended up just doing odds and ends, bits and pieces. I suddenly feel overwhelmed, and anything I consider doing seems like it'll take way more effort than I'm capable of. For a couple hours, I got hung up on my old telephone directory again – my giant notebook full of business cards from people I knew in Los Angeles, from the early 1960's through the 80's. It reminded me of places I've been, and people I knew and have long since lost contact with. I finally thought about throwing the whole binder in the trash because I don't need it, but then I thought, *Well, just because I don't need it doesn't mean that I have to throw it away right now.* I ended up putting it on my bookcase. Ha! I may never look at it again, but it's there on the shelf.

At one point I decided to take a little stroll around the block, to help me figure out what to do next. Down in the lobby, I ran into an acquaintance whom I call Scruffy Joe, and I had a funny encounter with him. He's about, I'd say 67 years old. He fondly remembers playing baseball as a child. About six or eight months ago, he started asking me if I would play catch with him. He loves to play catch. I do too, so the idea actually appealed to me. I thought we could go out in a little park somewhere and play catch. So what if it looked really strange, two old dudes throwing a ball around! We talked about it several times.

Scruffy Joe knows that I have terminal cancer. He has actually handled it really nicely; he's kind about it without going overboard. That's how I like people to deal with it: they know you have a terminal disease but they don't belabor it, they carry on as usual.

So today he said, "Well, I guess we're not gonna be able to play catch."

"Yeah, I don't think I'm really up to it anymore. It would require some good mobile dexterity."

"Well that's too bad. I was really looking forward to playing catch with you. But I'm never gonna ask anybody to play catch again."

I asked, "Why not?"

"A few years ago, there was another guy that I really liked, and we were gonna play catch. We talked about it a few times, and then he got cancer and died! So I'm never gonna ask anybody else to play catch."

Ha! Well, I still think he should go out and find somebody to play catch, but we'll see how that all works out.

I ended up doing one errand today. I wanted to go to Staples for a box of clear plastic pushpins. I figured Staples would certainly have them. I got to the store and looked around where one employee told me the pushpins would be, and they didn't have any clear ones. The bin was completely empty so I looked around for a suitable alternative. The manager came by and said, "I thought we had 28 packages. The computer says they're in stock, so we shouldn't be out. If you can wait, I'll go look for them."

I said, "That's fine, I'll wait. I don't have a big agenda, just need some pushpins. If you can accommodate me, I'll stay here as long as it takes." Ha! So I sat down in a chair, and he was gone for about ten minutes.

When he came back, he said, "I'm so sorry. I'm having trouble finding them, but I'm sure they're here somewhere. You still wanna wait?"

"I'll wait. I really wanna wait. I want these pushpins."

"OK, if you can wait, I'll keep looking."

So another ten minutes went by. This was so contrary to my nature, sitting in a retail store waiting for pushpins. A year ago, I would've been out of there in under a minute, to go look someplace else. But today I had no intention of leaving. I probably would've stayed there 'til six o'clock if this guy hadn't come back with pushpins!

After about 20 minutes, he came back and said, "This is really perplexing! We shouldn't be out of those pushpins but I can't find them. I'll tell you what, I have a special offer for you. I happen to have a 200-count box of pushpins that has been opened. It doesn't have exactly 200 because I've used a few. But they're clear plastic, just like you want. Here's what I'm gonna do. I'll sell you this box for a dollar."

I said, "Wow, that's a great deal!" A 60-count box sells for $3.99, so was like seven or eight bucks' worth of pushpins for a dollar.

"You've been so patient and accommodating," he said. "I just wanna help you out here." Then he shook my hand and said, "We're really big on customer satisfaction. Would you mind going online and giving us a good rating?"

Ha! I said, "No problem, everybody's good here, and I've had a wonderful time sitting in this chair." So now I have all the pushpins I need for my project, exactly the kind I want. You know, if you're patient and willing to wait, good things do happen!

After Staples, I wandered down to the waterfront for close to two hours. The weather was incredible today so I just didn't wanna go back inside. Tonight I'm gonna haul out some of my 8 x 10 photographs to pin to the wall; that's why I needed the pushpins. I'm not gonna bother with buying frames.

Anyway I had some good laughs today; I enjoyed that. And I'll know in another couple days how this new steroid drug will make me feel.

20

# JOHN AND JOHNNIE

**DAY 55 – WEDNESDAY MAY 15, 2013**

For several years I've had a website called The Book of John, which has all 21 chapters of the book of John from the Bible, accompanied by space photos. I really like it but I haven't really had any particular purpose for it. It's out there and I feel good about it, but so far I haven't had any place to go with it. Recently I've been thinking about turning that concept into a blog. That's a project that I could work on daily, from right now until the end of my life. But so far I haven't had an angle for it; I couldn't figure out how to turn it into a blog.

Meanwhile, this morning I decided to get up early and go to a church group that meets in downtown Portland. I'd heard that for a long time they've had a Wednesday morning Bible study, only two blocks from where I live, and I'd been wanting to go to that. I just never had the energy to get over there at 6:30 in the morning. But today I woke up around four o'clock, wrestling with the concept of the blog. I got all churned up about it. When I finally got up and went to the Bible study, I still hadn't solved the book of John problem. I didn't know what to do.

I showed up at the church and there were about ten or twelve people there. The leader of the group started out, "This morning, we're going to be studying chapter 16 of the book of John. Let's start with verses 25 through 28." I thought, *Wow, that's amazing!* I mean, I finally got up early enough to get to this Bible study, after being awake much of the night thinking about how to start my blog, and the subject was a specific chapter of the book of John. As I listened, I thought, *Those are the perfect verses to start off my blog!* In those four verses, Jesus explains that he's leaving the world and going back to his father. He lays out where he's going and why. Well, that's where *I'm* going – my journey, going home to the Lord. That's all I needed, to start my blog. That was it!

So I launched the blog today. It's brand-new, it's on the internet today for the first time. It's called John in Cyberspace. Why "John in Cyberspace"? Because it's all about the internet. And cell phones. And tablets. And all of the other electronic devices that people now have, to study the Bible and find out about Jesus. Each day's post will have verses from the book of John, whichever ones I'm focused on each day, with a beautiful photograph from outer space. I love the concept of combining space and time and God and Jesus. The photos are from the Hubble scope, put out by NASA, and you can use them if they're not copyrighted, as long as you give NASA credit.

I got home from the Bible study around 7:30 am, and completed my first blog post around 9:30. I think that's pretty amazing, considering I didn't even know what I was gonna do with it before I headed to church this morning.

It really turned my day completely upside down because it was essentially the launch of a whole new publication. Throughout my career in publishing, it was always a thrill to see the launch of a new publication, and it was really exciting this time to see it happen on the internet. Fifty years ago when I was starting out, that would've been impossible. And now a person can publish something like this on a cell phone, and it will travel all across the globe. To me, that's stunning! You can compose beautiful pieces of literature on a *cell phone* and send it to anybody in the world. Most people have no idea, no clue how it used to happen in publishing. In the 60's it cost millions of dollars a year to run a printing plant. Millions! We take it for granted now.

Centuries ago there were scribes. They were responsible for the printed word. In junior high school, as part of a special arts project, I hand-lettered the names on all the junior high school students' diplomas in old English script. It took hours and hours and I almost went crazy by the time I got them all finished. As a scribe, that would be your job, day in and day out! You couldn't make a mistake. You had to know the language, how to read it and write it. Not everybody learned how to read and write. And you had to be meticulous with your work; you couldn't spill ink all over everything. It required an incredible amount of discipline. And where would we have been without the scribes? Think of the Dead Sea scrolls, from like 3000 BC. They included parts of the Bible and the Koran and a lot of ancient literature also. Those were all put together by scribes. And now a child can put together a blog, with just a little bit of creativity, and have it seen by a billion people all over the world. That is pretty amazing.

I spent much of the rest of the day scrambling to catch up on sleep after getting up so early.

## DAY 56 – THURSDAY MAY 16, 2013

Today was a difficult day. Yesterday I completely wore myself out, so I woke up this morning feeling really tired. I stayed in bed until almost 10 o'clock, which is very different for me, but I felt like I needed the rest.

Since entering hospice, there's all this social activity. People call me all the time for all sorts of different reasons. A lot of people are paying attention to my situation – I love that and I've met some wonderful people – but I'm really dealing with a lot of telephone calls, and many of 'em are confusing. Truth be told, I don't really wanna deal with all of them. People ask for information, like: did you get the medication that we sent you? *Yes I did*. Well, do you have any questions about it? *No, because I talked to the nurse about it.* People are just trying to be helpful, but I don't think they realize how many different people are in contact with me all of a sudden.

I felt really dizzy all day, dizzier than I've ever been. I've had a lot of dizzy spells since this started. They usually only last for a minute or two. I think the dizziness comes from anxiety, because I have so many things going on and I don't know what to do about all of it. Today I got another call from the hospice pastor. I like him; he's a nice guy. But he wanted to know when we could get together – this afternoon? The next day? Back and forth. I don't know when to have him come and visit. So many decisions!

I went to the store around noon, after answering all the phone calls and dealing with all these people. On the way back, I was about to cross one street when all of a sudden everything just started reeling. I grabbed ahold of a telephone pole to kinda steady myself. I didn't know what to do! I was standing there, traffic was going by, and I had this hopeless feeling, like *How am I gonna get myself out of this and get home?* Eventually I calmed down a bit, and I kinda got my bearings. I thought, *All I have to do is make my shot across the street here.* The last thing you wanna do is just give up and say, "Well, I can't do this."

Finally there was a big, long break in traffic. I felt *really* wobbly, but I went across the street. I didn't run but I went pretty fast, because I was afraid that I might fall down in the middle of the street. I got to the other side and I got ahold of the nearest building; I put my arm up against it. That way I was able to navigate OK. I worked my way along the building for a block without leaving the wall, then turned the corner and walked the next block down to my apartment building.

Once I was back in my apartment, I sat down and had a little bit of a panic attack. *What if I can't walk anymore? What am I gonna do?* I looked at my walker, which was delivered a couple days ago. I thought, *Well... I guess I can try walking with this thing; it is a beautifully designed piece of equipment.* I decided to just go out in the hall and walk around with it and check it out. I walked up and down the hall a couple of times, and realized that this walker could get me just about anywhere I need to go. There's no reason to be all panicky; this'll be great!

**Blessing #21**

> *All of a sudden I felt a lot more peaceful. Now I knew I could get to the laundry room, I could get to the store, I could get around the block a few times. No question – the walker is sturdy and handy and convenient. I had this enormous feeling of being blessed to have it because, going forward, I don't know how I'll get anywhere without it.*

I stayed home for a while 'cause I felt pretty overwhelmed. This is the first time in my entire journey where I've had to face the fact that I can no longer just head outside and take off down the street. Obviously the cancer is progressing, and it's gonna be more and more difficult. But I'm really glad to have this walker. I decided to name it Johnnie Walker.

Later I thought, *It's time to take Johnnie Walker out for a trial run, to see just how well it performs under fire. This is it, I gotta do it.* I got my grocery bags together for another walk to the store, and I ventured out. First time using it outside. First time anybody's seen me with a walker, and a lot of people know me around here. I started walking and it was *really* comfortable. It's three blocks from my door to Safeway – I walked all the way over and it was great; I was totally at ease. I would not have been able to walk back to the store without Johnnie.

I walked into the Safeway store and suddenly I realized that when you have a walker, you get involved in a whole big congestion situation. There are so many walkers around, and scooters and carts and other things vying for space. If you're not involved in it, you don't pay any attention to it. But if you *are* involved in it, you're constantly looking at everybody. I must've encountered a dozen people with walkers and scooters, and we were all looking at each other trying to figure out which way to go! This is something I'd never noticed before; it's like a whole new world. Before, I would just walk around them; I wouldn't pay any attention. I'd just sidestep them or whatever. But all of a sudden, I'm part of it! Now I *have* to pay attention.

It was all too confusing so I went to get a cup of coffee instead. I pushed my walker up to the counter, ordered my coffee, and then realized I had to deal with the two handles on the walker *and* hold onto my coffee cup. I'm gonna need a cup-holder for Johnnie Walker. I managed to get to a table, and I sat down with my coffee and realized how happy I was to have that walker. I would've been *done* without it; I wouldn't have even made it to the store. And I thought about how, when I head home, I'll just sit down in my seat and rest if I have to. That gave me a feeling of peace and contentment.

Late in the afternoon, I sat out on the deck for a while. I've taken a big step backwards in the last couple of days. That doesn't mean I won't be feeling good – or maybe even feeling better – tomorrow, but I almost had tears in my eyes. My bike was sitting out there on the deck, and I thought, *I'm probably not gonna be able to ride that bike ever again.* It was really sad. Forty-three years of riding my bike. Now I don't ever see myself being able to ride around downtown Portland ever again.

One thing amazed me about today. I used to think that when it came time to give everything up, I would feel a lot of anxiety. Yet, even though I feel some sadness, I feel surprisingly comfortable. That walker is the next-to-the-last step here, you know? But it's wonderful to have it. It's all about reconciling yourself to the fact that things are gonna change.

One last thing about today; I got a second blog post done on my new website, John in Cyberspace. It's an extremely difficult chore; it takes me so long to do anything. I have trouble figuring out the words in sequence; it takes me a while to put them in the right order. But I found the verses from the book of John that I wanted to use today, a few verses from chapter 14. I feel really, really good about it. Jesus tells his disciples not to worry because he's going to prepare a place for us in his father's house. It's incredibly comforting to me. I believe what Jesus said, that he's gone to prepare a place for me.

## DAY 57 – FRIDAY MAY 17, 2013

Today was difficult. I'm taking a new medication, which I mentioned a few days ago: steroids. They're designed to help decrease swelling in my brain. If the swelling gets out of control, that can cause pain. The problem is that the steroids make me anxious. They hype me up and make me think, *Oh wow, I gotta do this and I gotta do that*, but I really *don't* know what I wanna do! I feel like there are all kinds of chores piling up, but they're nothing that I really *have* to do. The steroids do give me energy and increase my appetite and make me talk really fast. But they don't help me focus. I haven't actually had any pain related to my brain, so taking steroids is just precautionary at this point.

I have never liked taking medication. If a doctor sends me home with a prescription, I usually cut the pills in half or smaller. The steroids are probably worth the effort to make me feel more comfortable, but the problem is that I'll have to add another pill on top of that to help with the anxiety. They prescribed Phenobarbital, which is really, really old-school. I think it goes back to the 1940's because I used to hear about it in movies way back then. Apparently it's a good anti-anxiety medication, designed to work well with steroids. Perhaps I'll start taking that tomorrow.

Today I'm having a lot of difficulty reconciling the fact that I've lost a tremendous amount of mobility. I knew this day was coming, but I didn't want it to come quite this soon. I still envisioned myself taking bike rides, being out in the sunshine, walking down to the waterfront, and having complete mobility. I thought I'd still be able to walk around and enjoy everything. Now, suddenly, a walker is part of my life, and I'm struggling with that. Nobody wants a walker to become part of their life! On the other hand, I feel blessed to have it. Without Johnnie Walker, I'd be confined to this building, unable to go anywhere. This gives me the chance to remain as mobile as possible for a while longer.

I did a little graphic design project today. I realized that I could get into a situation with my walker where I'm unable to talk or express myself clearly. I made a tag for the walker, which lays out who I am and whom to call in case of an emergency. So if I'm just sitting there in my walker, unable to speak, I can just show someone the tag. Anybody can see it. I designed it using PageMaker, my favorite program. I printed it and trimmed it and made it look really good, then took it to a copy place to get it laminated. They helped me attach it to my walker. It looks pretty good!

The whole idea is that I don't want anyone to call 911 if there's an emergency involving me; I want them to call hospice. Someone from hospice will figure out a way to get me home, get me the medication I need, and go from there. I'm doing everything in my power to avoid the 911 syndrome.

I went to the store today. With the walker, again I really noticed all the other people with walkers. We were all kinda glommed up and running into each other and trying to get out of each other's way. I look around, thinking *Uh-oh! How am I gonna get by this guy? Or avoid colliding with this lady?* We were all juggling for position. Then there are all the people with big shopping carts. They're not disabled but they take up a lot of space. With a walker, you're constantly figuring out how to get to where you're going; it's a traffic jam. I was amazed. But I managed to navigate my way through the store, putting my items on the seat of the walker. Basically I've got this nice little personal shopping cart so I don't have to carry everything.

### Blessing #22

*The hospice volunteer coordinator called me today. She told me that they found someone to work with me one day a week for two hours. We're gonna try for a morning next week. The volunteer will help me with light chores. This is another comforting aspect of hospice. It's another set of eyes and ears, and they come in and help out for a couple of hours. I would imagine that to be a difficult job – spending two hours a week in someone's home and trying to comfort them when they're in the process of dying. People like that are heroes. I just can't imagine; I think it would be very, very hard to do. So I'm very grateful for my new volunteer.*

This has been the first week of hospice. There's been a lot of figuring out who everybody is, who all the players are, how we're gonna work together, what's gonna happen, and all of that. But I feel blessed! I feel incredibly blessed that all these people wanna help me. It truly is a wonderful, wonderful thing. But I can see that it's also gonna be kinda tiring, with all the phone calls and coordination.

21

# CONFUSION AND COMPASSION

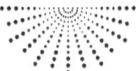

**DAY 58 – SATURDAY MAY 18, 2013**

Today was a day of confusion, from the standpoint of taking new pills and getting used to the idea of needing a walker. I'm having a problem with the steroid pills. I can feel that I'm all hyped up and anxious. I have a really good understanding of my body and how it's functioning. For instance I can tell when my blood pressure goes up; I can actually feel it. It has been going up every day with these pills. So I'm trying to figure out how to stay a little calmer and relaxed, and avoid stressful situations and people.

I went to the grocery store again today. I got really confused about my groceries, like how to put 'em in the bag and get everything organized. I became very anxious. The whole process of running into people with my walker added to my state of confusion. On top of that, the store itself was in total chaos because the refrigerator and freezer cases weren't working. Employees were packing ice bags on everything, trying to protect the perishables. That took much of the staff away from the check stands, so when I went to check out, with Johnnie Walker and my groceries, there were about 15 people lined up at each check stand. The lines were all moving incredibly slowly, and I got more and more anxious. I just wanted to get outta there! It took at least 45 minutes to get through the line. But I finally got outside and made it back to my apartment. I don't need that kind of chaos right now; I need peace and relaxation.

The second leg of the Triple Crown, the Preakness Stakes, happened today. Every year I look forward to it. I usually watch it with Scruffy Joe; we have a lot of fun with it. We always have a big bet on each race: going into today's race, I owed him two dollars. We had a lotta fun talking about the race and arguing over the money. The Triple Crown is three races, so we're not paying off until the last one, which is when we find out who's the overall winner in our gigantic jackpot. Today, *his* horse won, so now I owe him *four* dollars.

My plan for the evening was to go and see a big band show. I wanted to see my friend who plays in the band but it was a struggle to get going. I felt so disoriented from the pills I'm taking. I thought it might be too much for me, a situation with bands and noise and a crowd of people and all that. This is all new for me; I've never felt this way before. But I had the opportunity to go, because Ellen's daughter Renee had volunteered to drive me and her father, Jeffrey, to the performance.

The concert was in a bizarre location, in an industrial area in North Portland. We walked into this warehouse, a manufacturing plant, and found out that the event was a fundraiser for a local elementary school. There were tables and chairs and food and the band and all these people. It was a super-confusing environment but I chose to embrace it; it looked like fun. We found a table and got situated. Renee had brought her four-year-old son. He was wearing a Spiderman suit and seemed to fit right in. We must've been a little bit early. They were serving food but it was the worst food presentation I've ever seen in my entire life; nothing but chips and guacamole, which my stomach can't handle anymore. All of a sudden Renee told us that she had to leave because her four-year-old wasn't allowed to be there since the venue was serving alcohol. She said to stay and enjoy the band and she'd come back later.

So there I was, with Renee's father, Jeffrey. With everything going on, I felt totally confused. Jeffrey is somewhat older than me, and he has memory issues. So now we're sitting at this table all by ourselves, trying to figure out what's going on. The band hadn't started yet. There was nothing I could eat, so all I had was a glass of water. Jeffrey had a drink. A guy came over and I asked him, "Excuse me, could you tell me basically what's going on here this evening? I'm a little confused about it." He explained that it was a charity auction for a school, plus a concert. That made sense to me.

Then he asked, "What are *you* guys doing here?"

I said, "I'm here to listen to one of the bands, because my friend is playing in it. Why are *you* here?" He explained something about teaching an aviation class at Portland Community College. I said, "Aviation? My friend Jeffrey here was an aerial photographer back in the day, taking pictures of construction sites and stuff."

So he started talking with Jeffrey. As I said, Jeffrey has some memory issues. He proceeded to tell the guy that over the course of his career in aerial photography, he had owned seven airplanes. He had really only owned *one*. Ha! But the guy was totally enthralled by this story, so he asked Jeffrey if he'd come and talk to the students at his junior college about aviation. Jeffrey said that he'd be happy to, so they exchanged email addresses and telephone numbers.

Then I said, "Do you know what else Jeffrey has? A radio-controlled helicopter with a webcam on it. He's going to take aerial pictures with that." And of course the guy was like, "Oh! I wanna hear more about *that!*" It turned out to be one of the funniest conversations I've ever overheard, because I was the only one who knew where Jeffrey was stretching the truth.

Eventually I got kinda bent out of shape because nobody was paying any attention to me, so I asked, "What else do your students wanna hear about?" I thought maybe they'd be interested in hearing about my publishing career. But he said, "No, we don't talk about anything except aviation." He kinda cut me off! That upset me a little bit, but the guy finally just went away, absolutely delighted that he had found this new friend to address his students about aerial photography.

After that, we just hung out listening to the band and keeping an eye on each other. Jeffrey would wander off to take some pictures and I'd say, "I'll wait here 'til you get back." And I'd watch him the whole time. Then I'd wander off and go to the restroom or whatever and I'd say to him, "You stay here 'til I get back." It was like the blind leading the blind. Just about the time the band was finishing up, Renee came back to rescue us.

Jeffrey and I go back many, many years. We met in 1954 or '55. I was still in high school. I was dating Ellen, who became my first wife, but there were a couple of times when we split up. One of those times, I heard that she was seeing someone else, a trumpet player named Jeffrey Barron. I had been totally shocked, and I was very upset. I also heard that the guy was like six years older and had his own apartment. It just didn't seem right to me; that was unfair competition! So I decided to drive over and have a little talk with him about the situation.

More than a talk, actually. I was prepared to have a confrontation over it. I brought a friend, for backup, since I didn't know if this guy had roommates. I knocked on the door. He opened the door and I confronted him. "My name is Don McCall and I heard through the grapevine that you were seeing my girlfriend." He asked me who I was talking about. I said, "Her name is Ellen, and I wanna know what's going on."

He said, "Well, look... I'm sure there's just been a misunderstanding here. You guys look like you could use a beer. Why don't you come in so we can sit down and talk about this?"

My friend and I thought, *Yeah, we could use a beer.* We were underage, but a beer sounded good. Actually we had already had a few beers, or else I wouldn't have been there in the first place! We sat down at his kitchen table. Jeffrey attempted to explain the situation, and it all seemed to be very logical. He said, "I have been seeing her, and she's a really nice girl, but I don't know what's gonna happen. I don't think there's anything for you to be upset about. Why don't you have another beer?" So we had another one, and before long we seemed to have it all worked out, miraculously. I found out that he was a very charming guy. After a while my friend and I got up and thanked him for the beer, and we got back in my car and drove the 40 miles back home.

Ellen and I eventually got married, but we divorced after 12 years. Then she ended up marrying Jeffrey, with whom she had two daughters, Renee and Lillian. Ellen and Jeffrey eventually split up, but that's how we all ended up together at a concert in North Portland on a Saturday night. It was a wild and strange evening; I would say it was almost psychedelic. I'm not a drug person, so when I use the word "psychedelic", I don't really know what I'm talking about. But it was almost psychedelic, for me. Lights and music and people, not understanding where my own head was and what I was doing there. On the way home we talked about taking that radio-controlled helicopter out to a big field and flying it. We'll see how that works out! By the time I got home, around nine o'clock, I was exhausted.

## DAY 59 – SUNDAY MAY 19, 2013

Waking up this morning, I felt good. I usually feel pretty good for the first hour, hour-and-a-half that I'm awake. The anxiety doesn't start to build until a little bit later in the morning. It comes from the medication, which I take with my breakfast. Within about half an hour after taking it, I begin feeling anxious, and everything seems out-of-whack.

I was excited today. I've been working on my John in Cyberspace blog. It gives me something to focus on every day, where I have to use my brain and work on the computer and organize some photographs. I really enjoy working on it. It takes me about an hour, hour-and-a-half to put together a post, which would've taken me 15 or 20 minutes in the past. That's because of the dysfunction in my brain. It's hard to distinguish the letters on the screen, so I make spelling errors. For example I can't figure out whether it says "l-o-o" or "l-e-o". It doesn't happen *all* of the time, but enough that it takes me a long time to get it done. If I didn't have spell-checker, I wouldn't be able to do it. But I've already found that doing the blog adds a lot to my day.

This morning I wanted to go to church. Emma was gonna drive me over to a church she sometimes goes to. She and I first met at that church about five years ago: just before Easter that year, I received a postcard in the mail from a new church that was starting to meet at a school near my apartment. This new church was renting space in the school cafeteria, starting on Easter Sunday. I thought *that* was really interesting, so I wanted to go and lend my support.

Two of the first people I met there were a couple, Emma and Phil Larken. I really liked them; they were very friendly. They had two daughters and a son. We hit it off and our friendship grew pretty quickly. They hosted a Bible study at their house, and I became involved in that. Not long after we met, I had a detached retina and I was in pretty bad shape. My vision was almost shot; I thought I was gonna lose sight in both eyes. It was a hectic time. Emma and Phil were very supportive and helpful; it felt great to have them in my life. Sadly their marriage eventually ended, but Emma has made the effort to maintain our friendship. So I was anxious to see her today and have the opportunity to go to church with her. I was also looking forward to seeing a few other people at that church.

We arrived, found seats, and the service started. I noticed a guy, Arthur, who I knew had just gone through a personal tragedy. At one point I stepped out of the service, and Arthur came out and we started a conversation. I hugged him. He lost his wife Janet about four or five months ago. They hadn't been married all that long. She had been a remarkable woman, a very free spirit, into biking and hiking and outdoor things like that. She had been in the process of starting a new bike shop. She had a whole new concept on how to sell bikes, and was really starting to get a wonderful business going. Arthur is a Lifeline helicopter pilot, someone who goes out to pick up people involved in crashes on back country roads and all over the place.

Janet died of cancer. Almost a year ago she developed a brain tumor, outta nowhere. She was 50 years old. Arthur was devastated. Of course you don't expect something like that to happen; he thought he would be spending the rest of his life with her, and all of a sudden, it was all cut short.

Arthur and I talked about her, about how her life ended, and her spirit, and how she had demonstrated great courage at the end of her life. We talked about the grief that Arthur was still suffering as a result of that loss. I also told him about my situation. An amazing bond developed between us fairly quickly. I recognized that his grief was substantial. He's selling his house and he quit his job at Lifeline. Suddenly I was no longer focused on *my* situation, facing death; I was seeing it from *his* perspective. When someone dies, that's the end of their suffering. But the living have to continue and go forward after that.

*Blessing #23*

*After the service, Emma came out and I explained that Arthur and I had been talking for quite a while, going back and forth on the tragedy in his life, and what's ahead for me. It had been a wonderful, enriching conversation. We got in the car to leave, and Emma looked at me and said, "You know why you came here today, don't you? You and Arthur were meant to meet today and have that conversation." I agreed on that. I'm really thankful because there are several other churches I coulda visited today, or I could even have just stayed home, resting in bed. But seeing Arthur and spending that time with him was a tremendous blessing. I felt a close bond with him, stopped thinking about my own problems for a while, and gained some perspective on what it could be like for people who love me, when I'm gone.*

## DAY 60 – MONDAY MAY 20, 2013

Today was another Battle of the Steroids. When I woke up today, I'd had a wonderful night's rest; I felt great and I was very thankful for that. After breakfast, I took my steroid pill. I usually start the day feeling calm and relaxed, feeling like I'm going to have a pretty good day and be able to function pretty well. But within about an hour-

and-a-half after taking the steroid pill, I become very anxious. Anything that goes wrong creates a real anxiety situation.

This morning the shower curtain rod broke while I was taking a shower. It looked like it was gonna fall down, and that was very upsetting. I need my daily shower! The curtain rod is brand new; it was just installed when the apartment was renovated. I went to find the maintenance person and got it fixed, but that took an hour or so. By that time my anxiety was starting to build up.

Today I had the dreaded task of paying a few bills. I felt really concerned and my stress level was starting to build because I don't see numbers all that well now. I had to write out several checks, and get stamps, and put everything in the right envelopes, and my brain was not functioning very well on all that. Everything is different. I have to figure it all out, use the calculator, double-check all my numbers. I persevered, but it took me a *long* time. What should've been a half-hour job now takes three times as long.

One thing has gotten easier though! Normally I've always kept all my receipts from the store. I'd reconcile my checkbook by looking at my account online, comparing the store receipt with the online posting. I don't do that anymore; I just throw the receipt away. I don't care about it! I eliminated that step; it's another piece of paperwork that I don't need right now. I look at the number online and just assume it's correct. Frankly, I don't believe it's ever been *in*correct! That gives me a certain sense of freedom, just throwing those receipts away.

I had another errand to take care of today, which had a lot of disappointment connected with it. I'd had a business bank account for a while that I was going to use for various projects. For instance, the recycling-related ideas that I've had – projects which I thought would provide enough income to carry me through a decent retirement. It's been sad to admit that that's never gonna happen. The bank account had just dwindled down to ten dollars and some-odd cents. Ha! But I had to close the account, and it was the sad ending of a dream.

The bank teller told me, "You have to meet with a personal banker to close a business account." I replied, "No, just gimme the ten dollars and fifty cents and close the account; I don't need to meet with a banker." We got into it over the personal banker until I felt like giving *them* the ten dollars and getting out of there! But the monthly fee would've continued to add up, so I figured, *Well, I'll just have to sit it out to get this thing closed.*

The personal banker came over and I explained my situation. I started to get frustrated discussing the numbers, so I told him, "Look, I wanna apologize, but my brain is not functioning at 100%. I've had health problems and I've had to take steroids, and I just haven't been able to make sense of everything." He replied with understanding, "In junior high school, I had an emergency appendectomy and everything went wrong. My heart was punctured, and then I was in a coma for a while. When I came out of the coma, I had to take steroids. I went to school, but I didn't know who my teachers were or which classes I was taking, and I didn't understand anything. It went on for two months, struggling through my classes and trying to figure out what I was doing there."

I thought, *That was just what I needed to hear right now!* The banker was very compassionate about my situation, especially by sharing his own personal story. He looked like he was only around 25 years old. And then he even helped me to get my walker out through the door. I walked out of the bank feeling a lot better; I really needed that wonderful personal touch.

All in all it was just a steroid struggle kind of a day; that's the best way to put it. I was confused by dealing with numbers and math, and that made me anxious. The highlight of the day was that young man taking time out to explain all of the trials and tribulations he experienced with taking steroids. It made me feel normal! It was so much better than hearing it from a doctor or from somebody who's never experienced anything like that.

## 22
# MEETING THE HOSPICE TEAM

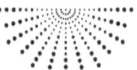

**DAY 61 – TUESDAY MAY 21, 2013**

This morning started out in a very chaotic way. The last part of remodeling my apartment was putting up new blinds. A couple weeks ago I received a notice and I thought it said that somebody would be here at nine o'clock this morning to do it, so I set my alarm for eight. I was sleeping really well and I didn't feel like getting up when they actually showed up right at eight. I just jumped up and grabbed my breakfast. They had to move furniture around to install the blinds, which took about an hour. My day got off to a really raggy start because I couldn't figure out why they showed up an hour early.

After they left, I sat down and finished a post on my John in Cyberspace blog. I struggled with it this morning because I was very foggy and out-of-sorts. It seems like with the steroids and treatment and medication and everything, I really need to have a little routine going. I get upset when my routine gets knocked out of kilter, even just a little bit. I did manage to pull it together, and then I decided to continue with the process of cleaning out my apartment. I worked on organizing things and pulling stuff out and throwing things away.

I cleaned out photographs from the past. They were scenic shots of the Pacific Crest Trail and Mexico and various places I've hiked. I'm the only one who could make any sense out of them; no one else would have any idea where these pictures were taken. I had put them into photo albums but never labeled them. They were beautiful, but basically worthless when you really think about it! So I made this huge pile of photographs on the floor, to get rid of. The only ones I decided to keep were photographs of people, and I started putting those up on my wall. They won't mean anything to anybody *else*, but right now I want to remember these people. About three quarters of them have already died. Stuart's no longer here, Charlie's gone, David Shaw has died – I've outlived all of them.

Eventually I picked up my giant pile of color photographs and walked down the hall to the trash room. On the way, I saw Scruffy Joe. He asked, "What are you gonna do with those?" I walked on past him into the trash room and tossed 'em in the dumpster. When I came out, he was standing there with a disappointed look on his face, like, *Did you just throw all of those away?* I told him that I got rid of them because nobody would know what they were anyway. He said he would've liked to look at them. So I went back in the trash room. The photos were just lying on top, not buried in garbage yet, so I grabbed them. And Joe really wanted them! He took most of 'em back to his place. I really didn't expect that.

Going through my stuff today reminded me of how I felt years ago when I worked at a self-storage place and I had to throw someone's stuff in a dumpster. This guy's storage unit had been filled with all of his personal stuff for like 12 years, but we couldn't locate him or anyone associated with him, so it had to be emptied out. I've never forgotten that. I felt like I was violating his life! It was chilling to think of a total stranger just taking another person's stuff and throwing it in a dumpster. It's harsh, and I feel that if somebody's gonna throw my stuff in the dumpster, it should be *me*.

## DAY 62 – WEDNESDAY MAY 22, 2013

Today was an interesting day. Before I went to bed last night, I realized I couldn't find my reading glasses. I looked everywhere for over an hour. Everybody knows that feeling; you misplace things and you think you've looked everywhere. It's especially bad for me because, with the steroids I'm taking, everything gets confusing really fast. So I thought, *I gotta find these reading glasses quickly.* I looked around until I remembered that my new hospice volunteer was coming to meet me at ten o'clock this morning. So I figured that would be our project, finding the reading glasses.

When the volunteer arrived this morning, I asked her to come on in and sit down and talk for a while, since I've never had a hospice volunteer person before and didn't know what to expect. She explained that she would come once a week for a couple hours, to help me with whatever little tasks I might have. She told me that she had lived on the east coast for most of her life. She lost her husband about 17 years ago, and has been volunteering with hospice since then. She moved to Portland about three years ago. She's a cheerful person with a very bright spirit.

Then I said, "The first thing we need to do today is just find my reading glasses. I've looked everywhere, and it's going to take a fresh set of eyes to make this happen. I *know* they're in this apartment!" We checked the recycling bin and the garbage can. We checked all the drawers and plastic bins and cupboards in the kitchen. We got a flashlight and checked the little slot between the refrigerator and the cabinet. We finally gave the kitchen a clean bill of health.

We checked the hall closet; I looked at the top shelves, and she checked inside all the shoes. She found the sunglasses that I was missing last week, but no reading glasses. We gave the closet a clean bill of health as well. We moved on to the living room. I have a large leather recliner, and I thought the glasses might've fallen behind or under it. So I pulled the recliner out from the wall, and then I found the reading glasses stuck down inside the cushion of the chair. So our first mission was a success! We found the reading glasses, *and* we found a bonus pair of sunglasses.

That's pretty much all I want to talk about today. The visit from the volunteer was a really wonderful, uplifting and helpful experience.

## DAY 63 – THURSDAY MAY 23, 2013

My day started out with the usual thing of looking at my calendar and finding out who, if anybody, I had to talk to today. Today my social worker was on the agenda for 11 o'clock. In the morning I get going and have breakfast and work on my computer for a while, and then I start to get a little anxious when it's time to expect people to show up at the door. I don't know why I get anxious; I actually love having people come over. Maybe it's because I'm not sure how they're gonna get in. I can buzz them in with my phone, but it doesn't always work. Sometimes they sneak through the front door behind somebody else although you're not supposed to do that. So I never know if they're gonna come right to my door, or call me from the front door, or call from down the street, or I might have my phone shut off and miss their call. I just wish I didn't have to keep track of all these people!

Anyway, the social worker, Rome, arrived on time. Right now he really doesn't have much to do besides stopping by; he'll be more important when I need him to arrange home health services and that type of thing for me. We talked a little more about my bath water issue, how I don't get enough hot water for a bath here. I'm pretty sure he's not gonna be able to resolve that for me; my doctor is probably the only one who can really do anything. Other than that, we talked about the hospice volunteer, and my meds and everything. One thing I see about hospice is that you may not have anything pertinent going on, but they stop by anyway to keep track of how you're doing.

Today it has been pouring rain like crazy outside. All day. I've been afraid to take my walker out; I don't want to get it soaking wet. It's brand new. Also when you walk in the rain and it's kinda cold, you stick your hands in your jacket pockets. With a walker, you have to keep your hands out on the handles, and if you don't have good waterproof gloves, your hands get wet and cold. There are some drawbacks there. So my walker is sitting here, in a beautiful dry room, and so far I'm skeptical about taking it out.

I had a big crisis this afternoon where a well-meaning friend who knows my situation decided to take it upon herself to contact another friend of mine, Gene, whom I've known since childhood. She found him on the internet, called him on the telephone, and told him about the whole situation, and he got very alarmed and upset. He lives about 150 miles away, and he didn't know what to do. He called me and sounded frantic. It was really unpleasant because I have been trying to call people in an orderly way and take care of notifying them myself. Gene has a lot of health problems, and the last thing I want is for him to think he has to jump in the car and drive 150 miles over here. So that was a mistake. I know people are really well-meaning, but they don't have to take on the job of notifying my friends for me.

The only other thing that happened today was a bit of confusion. A couple of people tried calling me but my phone ringer was off so I didn't know they were calling. So they called Karen and asked her to check on me, and of course I didn't answer her call either. Then Karen called my next-door neighbor, Faye, right around the time that I went to the store, maybe five or six o'clock. I had finally taken Johnnie Walker out for the first time today – it was only two blocks and I figured Johnnie wouldn't fall apart from getting a little bit wet. On my way back, I ran into Faye coming down the street, all upset. She had put on her rain gear and come out to track me down, and she found me about halfway between our building and the store. She asked, "Are you OK?" I said, "Faye, thank you so much, I really appreciate you coming out, but I'm totally fine." So we got that straightened out. Then I realized I had voicemails stacked up all over the place and couldn't figure them out.

So it was a chaotic day from the standpoint of communications. I'll have to figure out how to avoid having people get alarmed and confused and upset.

## DAY 64 – FRIDAY MAY 24, 2013

Today I worked on my blog, John in Cyberspace. I'm really enjoying it. The blog gives me something to focus on and it lets me pretend that I'm still in the publishing business. I don't know if it makes sense to anyone else, but it makes sense to me! Right now I think that's the most important thing, having something that I really enjoy doing. I love the book of John, and I love putting it up on the internet with these space photographs. It's absolutely fascinating to me.

Today I met another hospice team member: my nurse, Susan. I really love this woman; she's amazing. The doctor that she works with concluded that I should not continue taking steroids because they're not helping me; they're just making me anxious. Susan told me to discontinue them, and we'll see how it goes. No one really knows whether or not there's any swelling in my brain; I just know something is drastically *wrong* in my brain. The steroids just seem to keep me awake at night, and give me a little too much juice. For instance, I love baseball, and with the steroids, sometimes I feel as though I could really hit a good home run ball. I *do* seem to have a lot of strength; I feel all jacked up. So we'll see how I feel in a few days without steroids.

**Blessing #24**

*There's a lot more to my conversations with Susan and other hospice people than just medical stuff. Hospice people are a different breed. They're concerned about you in many ways; they want to help with medical stuff and also a lot more. The conversations aren't long, but they're nice and personal and you're not gonna have that kind of conversation with everyone in the medical profession. It's nice seeing Susan and Rome and the volunteer, Edith. I'm already really beginning to appreciate all of these people.*

After Susan left, I decided to go for a walk with my walker, since it was nice out. I took off and went quite a ways – *too* far, I'm afraid. On my way home, I was getting a little bit wobbly. I can see that my range has been cut down a bit.

On my way home I ran into another person whom I know from the neighborhood, through the photography that I've done. This lady was kinda shocked that I had a walker. Well, I went from a bicycle to a walker pretty quickly! So she wanted to know all about it, and I told her that I had cancer and that I needed the walker now for my balance and to be able to get around. Then she told me that *she* is a cancer patient too, but she knows a cure that will eat that cancer up. I asked, "What? Really? What's the cure?" Apparently my surgeon, my oncologist *and* my radiologist had absolutely no idea about this!

She said, "There are four main ingredients, and you have to eat these every day. You can eat whatever else you want as well, but you *have* to eat these four things, and that will eat the cancer: fresh celery, garlic, and dark grapes. And you have to drink coffee; coffee is very important." So: coffee, garlic, celery and dark grapes will get the job done. She told me she had had cancer for six years but now she's clear of it. Of course it was these four foods that took care of it, right? I'm totally delighted that she's free of cancer; it's a wonderful thing. But I'm a little skeptical about the cure! I already eat grapes and celery and I drink coffee, but I don't eat a lot of garlic; maybe that's my problem. Ha! Anyway, it was a sweet conversation. She was honestly trying to help me.

At that point I was still coming home from my walk, and I ran into another person on the street who knew me and hadn't encountered me with a walker yet. We got into a very, very disturbing conversation. This person appeared to be absolutely devastated that I was using a walker. "Why? What happened? What are you doing about it?" and so on. I tried to explain as best I could, but this person just kept going on and on about how awful it was. I started feeling totally disoriented; it was too intense to try and explain it all. I finally just had to say, "I gotta go. It's really difficult, and I tried to explain it but I can't."

I came home, and by that time I was really feeling bad. My head was spinning and I felt like, *What is going on here? Why do I have to keep trying to sort this out for other people?* It all seems pretty clear to me, but other people get really concerned and they don't know what to do. They don't understand how a person can go from riding a bicycle a week or two ago, to using a walker now. I believe they're actually concerned for their own health; they see something like this happening to *themselves*. And it's scary! It really is scary as you get up in age, and all of a sudden you think, *Whoa – this could happen to me!* They don't say it, but that's what they're thinking. And it's very disorienting for me.

When I got home after my walk and my conversations with these people, I felt like I had taken a pretty big step backwards. I felt disoriented by people's concerns and not being able to explain the situation, and from really wanting to get *out* of the conversation. So it was a difficult day. But I'm sure that tomorrow will be better.

23

INSPIRED BY NATURE

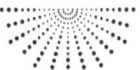

DAY 65 – SATURDAY MAY 25, 2013

*L*ast night was really, really strange. I had many odd dreams, very psychedelic and vivid. I've been told that steroids can cause difficult sleep patterns and dreams. I was on steroids for almost a week, but as of today I'm *off* of them. I'c started getting used to them – all the extra energy and talking fast and that sort of thing. Now I'm in sort of a detox situation, going in the other direction, where now I have to adjust to *not* taking the drug.

Today I had an appointment with my friends, Frank and Chuck. I've known Frank close to 20 years, here in Portland. He's been one of my very best friends. In the past we used to do a lotta hiking; the biggest connection we've had over the years has been our time outdoors. He's 20 years younger than me and sometimes he'd want to hike faster than me, but he would always take time to let me catch up if I was a little tired. He has always been there for me, and I've really enjoyed his friendship. I don't know his brother Chuck as well.

Frank and Chuck came over this morning around 10 o'clock, and we hopped in the car and went over to Fred Meyer's for a cup of coffee, and so I could pick up a few things that I needed. Then we came back to my apartment. We had a tremendous conversation, reminiscing about places we've gone hiking together. Of all the things I've seen and done, what I've enjoyed the most in life has been my time outdoors: being outside, getting away from the city and all the people, just enjoying nature as it exists. I believe that God reveals himself in nature. Going outside and observing nature is a way to experience God.

**Blessing #25**

> *I recall one time when I was hiking Mt. Shasta. I was alone, at a very high altitude, probably about eleven or twelve thousand feet. I didn't have time to go to the summit; I had to turn around and go back. But just before I turned around, I looked up at the summit. If I'd had the time, I would've had about 2000 more feet to climb. It was a beautiful, clear day, and as I stood there looking at the sky and that massive peak, I felt like I could reach out and touch the face of God. I felt like it was right there. It was an amazing feeling. That's the kind of thing that I'd experience outdoors, and it has been a great blessing.*

In the end I got really emotional, talking with Frank and Chuck. I told them that their friendship has been amazing and I sincerely appreciate it, and I love both of them. I really expressed to them how I feel about them. That's something that men don't often do, but it felt really good.

After dinner, I decided to attempt to take a bath. I realized that I had to find my own solution to the problem of not having enough hot water. Ha! I figured out how many gallons of hot water I would need in addition to what I'm getting from the hot water heater. I have some really nice new pots and pans, and I thought, *Well, why not do what they did in the Old West?* They'd just boil the water on the woodstove and pour it in the bathtub. I filled up a two-gallon saucepan and three other pots, which totaled five gallons altogether. I put them all on the stove and started boiling them. As the the pots heated up, I ran my bath so it would coincide with the rest of the water boiling. When I poured in the hot water from the stove, I had made an amazing hot bath with all the water I needed. With plenty of steam.

Sure, there's some danger involved in carrying pots of boiling water from the kitchen to the bathroom, but I was very cautious. I didn't burn myself. My pots and pans have big handles on them and they're very safe to carry. But the most important thing here is that *I won!* It took me a long time to think of that solution, but now I can have a hot bath. So I no longer care whether my social worker or the building manager ever get the water heater replaced; I'll just boil my own water.

And that's where I wanna end it today, with my good hot bath.

## DAY 66 – SUNDAY MAY 26, 2013

This morning, I felt that I had had a great night's sleep – because of my bath! The hot bath really relaxed me and I felt wonderful last night. The first hour I was up today, I felt almost normal. After that, I started to get anxious. I was planning to go to church today and bring my walker for the first time. Nobody there had ever seen me with a walker. From what I've learned from bumping into other people in the street, I think that's going to be a stressful situation, people seeing me with a walker for the first time. So I was starting to get anxious about that, but I managed to get it together.

I took off and headed to church with my walker, and it was a very nice morning; the weather was great. The church is three blocks from where I live. It was built, I don't know, a hundred years ago, a hundred twenty years ago, something like that? Trust me when I say that it would not receive ADA approval. They've only got stairs; it's really hard to get in! No ramps or anything like that. I was persistent; I dragged my walker right up the stairs. Then the front door of the church was closed; I opened the door with one hand and literally drug my walker into the church. I didn't know the two people who were handing out the order of service at the front door, but they looked pretty shocked to see me come in dragging my walker along.

I enjoyed the service immensely. Afterwards I went to the back of the church where there's another entrance with six or seven steps down to the sidewalk, as opposed to the front door where there are only four steps. I opened the back door on my own, and drug the walker out and all the way down the stairs. I went down the longer stairs intentionally, probably just to see if I could do it. I was being stubborn. And, there again, a couple people were walking by, and I'm sure it looked a little odd to them, to see some guy dragging a walker down the stairs. They probably thought I stole it. I mean, if you can get down the stairs dragging a walker, you probably don't actually need it!

On my way home from church, I decided to walk an extra two or three blocks before returning to my apartment. I was rolling along down the street, and I got to this intersection. I forgot that now I'm basically a somewhat disabled person and I can't jay-walk anymore. Jay-walking has always been my modus operandi! Everybody in Portland jay-walks; I never see anyone stop and wait for the lights to change. I checked for traffic and there weren't any cars coming, but the light had just turned red for me. I forgot about how much I've slowed down; I started out into the crosswalk against the light, and all of a sudden, two or three cars whipped around the corner about a block away.

They were speeding, and all of a sudden they were right on me. There I was like a deer in the headlights, with two cars nearly on top of me, crossing against the light. They're all looking at me like, *You idiot, why are you in the middle of the street with a walker?* So I actually smiled and said, "Hey, how's it going?" And I shot across the street – to the best of my ability. Once I reached the opposite sidewalk, I realized that jay-walking is now out of the question. Not only that – I can't even start out into the crosswalk unless the walk sign has just come on. It was scary! In the old days, I would've been able to outrun 'em, but not anymore. That was the big lesson of the day – no more jay-walking.

Later in the day, I started thinking about what's most important to me right now. The most important thing is letting the people in my life know how I feel about them, as much as possible. We all have regrets like, *Oh I wish I had told so-and-so about this, that or the other thing.* Often it's our parents, or spouses, or ex-spouses. So many things are left unsaid because people don't take the time to really express their feelings.

I also thought about wasted time. I've been a Dodgers fan since my 20's, and I've been an Oregon Ducks fan since I was eight years old. Those teams have been important to me, and I have spent many hours reading statistics and talking to people about them, going into great detail about their games. I would get up in the morning and pore through the daily scores, statistics, and standings, for all the major sports. But today? I have no interest whatsoever. I don't even know where the Dodgers are in the standings. OK, I think they're in the cellar, but I got that from something I only glanced at a couple, three days ago. The point is, *So what?* Seriously, what difference does it make? If I live another week, or a month, I really don't care who's leading the National League West in baseball. The Dodgers are on their own!

I wish people could see what life looks like from my perspective right now, and realize that the most important things while you're still on this earth are love, the other people in your life, how you feel about them and how you express that love. That's the way I see it right now. I wish that I could've seen it many, many, many times in my life before now, so I could've taken the time to express how I felt about people.

I've begun to feel more compassion for people in my apartment building who have limited mobility. What they go through has become crystal clear to me since I got my walker. At the grocery store, I see the people with walkers and chairs and scooters. I didn't notice them before; they were invisible to me. Suddenly *they're* the predominant people, not the others who are able to go wherever they want, dodging around the store. Suddenly the people who are struggling are the most important. It's not easy to get through a store with a walker or a wheelchair, and everybody else just takes their own mobility for granted and doesn't see these people.

One last thing for today is something that I've started feeling anxious about. I'm concerned about the people around me; I want to make sure everything will be alright for the people who are left behind. Things like figuring out how to get rid of my stuff, who to contact when my life is over, planning a memorial service, getting set up for cremation and what to do with the ashes, all of that. The anxiety comes from wondering how I'm gonna get that all figured out and who's gonna deal with it. Somebody advised me, "You can't do it all, you just have to let some things go." That's really, really difficult to do, letting go of trying to help to make sure everything is in order.

Anyway, that's *enough* for today!

## DAY 67 – MONDAY MAY 27, 2013

When I woke up this morning, I felt pretty good. Matter of fact, I felt *very* good. I felt like the steroids had started to dissipate from my system a little bit. I felt really relaxed when I woke up, after a great night's sleep.

After breakfast I put some coffee on and start working on the next post for my John in Cyberspace blog. That has really become an exciting part of my day; I just love working on it. I see this blog as my last publication. In my career, I worked on literally hundreds of publications, and helped maybe another hundred people *start* publications.

I think back on some of the people that I worked with for brief periods of time, to help them get their publications going. It really was a fascinating trip. I remember two young guys in their early 20's who wanted to start a bullfight magazine, covering the bullfights in Tijuana. I helped them as a consultant. It was a crazy, crazy scheme. They went down there every week, and then they'd come back up and put the publication together. They'd eat hotdogs all night long when they were working on the paper. I didn't like bullfighting: it certainly wasn't my thing, but they really wanted to do it, so I helped them. That went on for maybe three or four months. That's just an example of the types of people that I ran into.

So I'm looking at this little blog as my last publication. It's the last thing that I'm going to put out there. It's amazing to me that it's in cyberspace. Billions of people in the world have basic access to a cellphone; the whole concept of self-publishing and smartphones and all of that is just mind-boggling. It's kind of a thrill for me to be capable of attempting to stay in the game, even after all these years.

In the afternoon, Karen came over and we were considering taking a drive through the Columbia River Gorge. At first I was a little confused about it – I wondered how long it would take, when we should go, whether traffic would be a mess, and so on. To be honest, I felt like I was a little out of my comfort zone with the idea of driving clear out into the Gorge. I love it out there. But little fears cropped up. *Uh-oh, what if this or that happens? That's scary!* We managed to work our way through that, and as soon as we were headed out on the highway, I felt like it was a great idea.

I love the Columbia River Gorge more than any place on this earth because I've spent so much time hiking in the mountains out there, watching the waterfalls, and climbing over rock crevices. While we were out there today, my anxiety level went way down. I think probably 90 percent of the people on this planet never go to a place like the Gorge. They hang around in cities, travel to Rome and Paris and places like that. Most of the people that go up the Gorge drive up there, take a few quick looks around at Multnomah Falls, hop in the car and drive back home. And they say, "What a beautiful day it was."

But that's not how you experience a place like that. You have to go out there and get your boots dirty, you have to get *wet*, and climb, and exercise – then all of a sudden you start to see nature as it really exists. You can't just drive out, take a quick look and come home; it doesn't work that way. That's like merely looking at a picture postcard. You have to get your feet dirty and enjoy the incredible views.

---

### A LAST TIME FOR EVERYTHING

*It was a bittersweet day. As I sat there looking at the Columbia River, which I've done hundreds and hundreds of times before, I couldn't help but have the overwhelming feeling that this was probably the last time I'd ever see it. I may feel like going back out there again – and I hope that'll be possible – but the way my energy level is going down at this point, it's very likely that this was the last time that I'll see the Gorge. Although I know that this is what's meant to be, and I'm reconciled with the fact that my life is ending, letting go of some of the most beautiful things in my life is really, really hard.*

---

Tonight, after experiencing those incredible views and spending the time out there with Karen, I feel like maybe I'm ready to lie down and go to sleep and that'll be the end. But I doubt that'll happen; I think I still have a little bit of time left here. For one thing, I have to get up tomorrow morning and work on my blog, right? That's what I wanna do tomorrow morning when I get up.

That's really all for today. I wish everybody on this earth could find a place of their own, where they can get that kind of joy from experiencing nature.

## DAY 68 – TUESDAY MAY 28, 2013

The day started off really really well; I woke up this morning feeling excellent. I enjoyed being out in the Columbia River Gorge yesterday. I've noticed this residual effect for years, the day after spending time outdoors in a beautiful landscape. I've had a lot of Monday mornings where the carry-over from a hike the previous day is just amazing.

But even when my day starts out well, anxiety starts to build because the day is up in the air and I'm not sure what I'll be doing. I may have a plan, but I don't know how well it's going to go. What kinds of complications will I run into? There's no way to know. So I become anxious, even without steroids.

I've begun starting every morning by working on the next post for my John in Cyberspace blog. I love looking for the photographs and getting the post put together. But after I finished today's post, things started to go haywire. I needed to set up a spreadsheet to keep track of all of the posts I've done. I've already used a lot of different verses from different chapters of the book of John, and if I don't record them properly, I'll forget what I've already used. So I had to bite the bullet and create a spreadsheet to keep track. Right now I've only got 14 posts up, but in another week that could be 21, and it will get really confusing. Working on the spreadsheet turned into a nightmare.

I'm used to working with Excel, the world's leading spreadsheet program. But today it just got super confusing. I had difficulty with all kinds of things that I hadn't had any difficulty with in the past. As I got involved in the cells and trying to pull everything together, I got more and more frustrated. I thought, *Well, unfortunately this has to get done today so that I can feel some peace of mind.* I worked on it for an hour or so and then I decided that I'd had enough; I couldn't figure it out.

I decided to take a walk instead. I grabbed Johnnie Walker and headed out. I ran into some people I know and talked to them for a while, did the social thing for an hour and a half or so. Then I went back to the spreadsheet... At one point I had two or three different versions of it. Trust me, in the past this would've been a half-hour job! I had a clipboard with a printed copy, and an electronic copy on the computer, and I was going back and forth between the two. I walked out on my deck with my clipboard and stared down at the pavement below, and I felt like throwing the clipboard as far as I could throw it, clear out into the street! But I didn't; I stayed with it and finally got the thing done. It was overwhelming. I've made hundreds and hundreds of spreadsheets over the years and never had any problems like that.

This afternoon I ran into a lady who lives on my floor, who has two cats. I did a portrait photo of her with her cats a couple, three years ago. She's a very nice lady. I saw her in the lobby and she said, "You know, one of my cats was very worried about you this morning. She ran all the way down the hall and was scratching at your door. I called her and called her and she finally came back. She has been looking out the window into the hallway ever since! Would you do me a favor? When you go back upstairs, please knock on my window and let her know you're OK."

I said, "Sure, I'd be happy to do that." When I went back up, I walked down to her apartment, and the cat was right there. I tapped on the window and she looked at me, and I didn't know what to do. I said, "Hi, how ya doin'?", and I walked away! That was a strange turn of events. Who knows? It's interesting to think that an animal was looking out for me today.

## 24

# FACING REDUCED MOBILITY

**DAY 69 – WEDNESDAY MAY 29, 2013**

*E*very single morning when I wake up, the first thing I think about is, *Am I still able to walk?* I've been lying down all night, and I know my brain is doing some really strange things. So when I swing outta bed and put my feet on the floor, I wonder what will happen. Until that moment, I don't know yet.

**Blessing #27**

*I boost myself up off the bed, and it's just a great feeling when I'm able to put my feet on the floor and get up and take a few steps. I'm never sure ahead of time because my brain is really starting to react negatively to so many different things. So it's always really exciting when I can get up and walk. Every day I'm a little more wobbly than the day before, but I'm still walking, and that's a huge blessing.*

Having breakfast has gone from taking about 15 to 20 minutes to taking about two hours. It takes me longer to prepare my breakfast; then I do a little web-surfing while I'm eating. Then I wash the dishes and straighten out my bedroom. By the time I get all of that done, it's about 10:15, and I usually get up at 8! I think, *What have I done for the past two hours?* And I have no idea. I just move so much more slowly. Then I work on my blog post for the day, which is also taking longer and longer.

This morning I went out for a walk. I went down 12$^{th}$ Avenue about six blocks, then I turned and came back up on 11$^{th}$. On my way back I felt a little tired. Actually it wasn't so much feeling tired as just wanting to stop and let the day go by a little bit. So I stopped. My walker is incredible; all I gotta do is back it up against a wall, and I've got a great seat. It was a really pretty day and I just sat there enjoying the sun and the view. A guy walked up to me on the sidewalk, and said, "Hey! Don! How are you? I haven't seen you in a long time!"

I couldn't recall who he was, but I'd say he was in his late 30's. He said, "It's really good to see you; I've been having kind of a rough time." I asked what had happened, and he started telling me that he had relapsed on drugs. I still couldn't place him, but obviously we'd met before because you don't tell a complete stranger about relapsing on drugs. He said, "I've stopped using but I'm struggling right now, and it's really good to see you. You're an inspiration to me." At that point I realized that we must've talked previously about alcohol as well as drugs.

I've had problems with alcohol but I haven't had a drink in over thirty years. So he came to the right person. To anyone who's involved in recovery and struggling with addiction, anybody else with a history of recovery has tremendous validity. They know they're talking to somebody who perfectly understands what it's like. I reassured him, "Don't beat up on yourself for the fact that you relapsed." He said, "I know, I'm struggling with that too." I said, "Well *don't* do it. You're starting over; you're starting fresh. Don't take any guilt from that relapse into this new experience." He wanted me to encourage him. He didn't say so directly, but he wanted me to spend time with him and help him get through the next day of his drug recovery. In recovery, we have this saying, "One day at a time." I said, "Focus on that right now, and continue doing everything you're doing to get back on track to a healthy lifestyle."

The conversation lasted about a half hour. He finally said, "I've gotta go, but I wanna thank you. It's really amazing that you happened to be right here!" It *was* amazing that I was right there at that moment. When you've just relapsed and now you're back to walking the road to recovery again, every day is precious and you *need* people in your life who will encourage you. I couldn't have been happier about having that opportunity, sitting on a walker on a sidewalk in downtown Portland, to share that time with him and provide that encouragement, even though I still can't remember where I'd met him before!

That's where I wanna end for today, because that experience was important for me, and I hope and pray it was important for him too.

## DAY 70 – THURSDAY MAY 30, 2013

When I woke up this morning and took my first few steps, I realized that I had lost a lot since yesterday. I knew that it wasn't just a case of not getting enough rest, 'cause I'd had a good night's sleep. I was definitely feeling better a couple-a days ago, and I had an overwhelming sense that losing ground every day is now going to be the norm. In the morning my arms and my feet felt a little bit disconnected from my body. I've had that sensation before but usually not until much later in the day.

It's very disconcerting to sense my mobility becoming more and more impaired. The frightening thing about that is that eventually I won't be able to move around and go outdoors, or hang out and talk to people; at some point I'll be confined to this apartment. It's a nice place to be confined to, meaning that I really like being here, but I don't know how I'm gonna deal with it when I don't have any choice.

After breakfast I worked on my blog. I had trouble typing on the keyboard. My eyes and my fingers don't feel connected with each other. Let's say I want to type the letter *P*. I hit the *P* key, but then I look and somehow I've typed a *T* instead. It's very confusing! That confusion slows me down. But I managed to get my post together and

I felt good about it. The blog has gotten a lot of hits so far. If you're in the publishing business, or you've put something out on the internet, it's always encouraging to see that somebody's actually looking at it. If nobody's looking at it, it becomes an exercise in futility!

After that, my day started to spin completely out of control. It started with a telephone call from my hospice pastor. Every hospice patient has a pastor on their team, whether they're a believer or an atheist. The pastor and I have talked about three or four times now, and this afternoon seemed like a good day to finally meet him. He called and asked if I'd be available around 1:30, so we agreed to that and hung up.

About 15 or 20 minutes later, the phone rang again and it was my hospice nurse. She said, "It just so happens that I'm gonna be in the area; can I stop by today?" I told her that today wasn't good, and she asked me why. I explained, "I'm OK today, and I'd rather see you on another day when I'm not OK or if I need something. I appreciate it, but let's make it a different day." We went back and forth and she finally agreed to call me next Monday. I told her, "I wanna try to eliminate people just dropping in; I need time to understand who's coming and when."

Then I received a couple more telephone calls. I was getting anxious. I needed to go to the grocery store, and kept getting distracted by phone calls, which was frustrating. I felt like my head was spinning around. I thought, *I am going to get to the store today even if I have to crawl over there on my hands and knees!*

When I finally got to the store, I was walking down the aisle when the telephone rang yet again. It was the hospice pastor. He said, "I just had a chance to contact your son and we had a nice conversation and –"

I interrupted him, "Wait a minute, you and I have an appointment in an hour. Why did you contact my son?"

He replied, "I had a note here to call him."

I was so confused. I said, "My son lives in Georgia, 3000 miles away. Did you call my son in Georgia?"

He replied, "Uh, well, I don't think he's in Georgia."

I said, "Well, he *is* in Georgia. Are we talking about the same – what are we talking about?"

I was thoroughly confused. And so was *he*, obviously!

I finally said, "I'll tell ya what ... I don't know *why* you talked to my son, but now I wanna cancel our appointment this afternoon. I'm so confused right now, I don't want any visits today. I'm not upset with you, but I *am* very confused. I have all these people calling and trying to make appointments. I appreciate what you do, but for today I don't want anything. Let's talk again next week." He said he'd pray for me and I thanked him, and then we hung up.

Then a little later he called back one more time, to apologize. He said he had made a mistake; it was someone else's son that he had talked with earlier.

Today was just a day of confusion: people calling, messages on my phone that I didn't understand, people who called and *didn't* leave a message. One piece of chaos and confusion after another. I'm having a really difficult time sorting out facts and figures and things like that. At one point I just sat down and felt like saying "I'm not talking to anybody anymore." Then I realized, *That's not right, I just have to come up with a plan.*

I decided that from here on out, I won't make arrangements to see any more than one person a day. And I'll screen my telephone calls. It'll just be a different program altogether, to try to cut down on the confusion and anxiety.

## DAY 71 – FRIDAY MAY 31, 2013

Every morning I wonder if all of my body parts are gonna be working, if my arms and my legs are going to function. It's a tremendous relief when I get up, to find that they *are* functioning at least well enough for me to get around on my own. So that's a blessing every morning. I understand my illness and I know what's happening to my body. But no one wants to lose control of their bodily functions or their ability to move. That's gotta be one of the most scary things that anybody could go through.

On another note, I had a funny thought when I went to the store this morning. I was walking down the aisle to find my Gatorade, and I noticed the greeting card section, in particular the birthday cards. My birthday is tomorrow. I thought, *What kind of a birthday card do you get for someone who has a terminal illness?* They have all these categories for birthdays: grandma, grandpa, sweet 16, your boss, all of that. What about someone who's only expected to live a few more months? Maybe a "your last birthday" card? Ha! That'd be a strange category. I don't know, it just struck me as funny all day long.

The big event today was going to Pioneer Courthouse Square with Karen in the afternoon. I started my Square People blog in June, three years ago. I decided that today would be the last time I go there to take pictures for a blog post. Working on this blog is how Karen and I first met three years ago, the day that I started the blog.

On June 22$^{nd}$, 2010, Karen showed up at the Square to do a recording series called Question of the Week. I got there and thought, *This will be an interesting place for a photo blog because it's considered the city's living room.* There are hundreds of events there every year, the light-rail trains come in from everywhere, people are always crisscrossing the Square. It's a marvelous, magical place in the middle of the city. People love to go there even if they have no reason whatsoever for being there besides hanging out and watching other people. And it's not just the fun events – there have been some major protests there. People sometimes use Pioneer Courthouse Square as a place to gather and focus on their causes. That's the thing I like most about the Square, the feeling that people can go there any time and express their beliefs. That makes it exciting.

Anyway, that's where Karen and I first met. It's bittersweet for me because I don't think I can continue doing that blog. One of the annual Square events is called the festival of flowers. They pick a theme and they arrange potted plants and flowers to illustrate that theme. This year it's called "Tattoo Portland", so the plants are laid out to look like a giant heart tattoo with "Portland" in the middle of it. Around twenty thousand flowers make up the entire display. I'll use that for my last blog post. I got a really nice picture of Karen sitting within a pretty arrangement of flowers. It'll be a fun post to put together, but also sad.

It's interesting that a blog just stays on the web even after your life ends; Square People could continue to get hits from all over the world! That pretty much wraps it up for the day.

## 25
# BIRTHDAY, BILLS, BATH WATER

### DAY 72 – SATURDAY JUNE 1, 2013

It's June 1st, 2013. It's the 72nd day of my journey. And it's my *birthday!* I was born on June the 1st, 1937. Today I'm 76 years old.

This morning when I woke up, I put my feet on the floor and wondered for a minute whether my body would work when I stood up. Then I felt incredibly good and I was filled with anticipation. It's like I've made a milestone event here; I've actually made it to my 76th birthday. I'd had my doubts – I didn't know if my brain or some other vital organ would fail and I wouldn't make it to this birthday. Why did I care whether I made it to my 76th? I don't know, but I feel that it has been a huge accomplishment to get through this past year. I haven't been well, really, since before my *last* birthday: it's been a constant struggle with chemo and radiation and a lack of energy. In the entire past year, I never really reached the point where I felt like I was recovering. When I was younger, if I got hurt or got sick, at some point I'd suddenly realize that I was starting to recover. I'd realize I was going to get better and stronger, and it would continue until I was back to 100%. Over the past year, I haven't been near 100%, and at no time did

I feel like I was ever on my way to 100%. It was a hard year. So I felt great joy that I made it through the year at all.

Also I was really excited about the day – excited about having cake and ice cream, and people wishing me *Happy Birthday*. I realized that it doesn't matter if it's your *last* birthday, it's still fun and exciting to celebrate getting through another year.

When I was about ten or eleven years old, I had a friend who had a special birthday party every year. What made it so special was that his mother would invite eight or ten kids over, and instead of just baking one cake for her son, she baked one cake for every kid that came to the party. She knew ahead of time what kinda cake each kid liked. I liked angel-food cake with a hole in the middle, and it was an incredible thrill every year to go to this birthday party because not only did you get to have fun and eat cake and enjoy the party, you got to bring home your own full-size cake. I didn't know anybody else who ever did that. It was her tradition, and I was always excited about that kid's birthday because of it.

Today, my ex-wife Ellen had told me that she would bring over a birthday cake around 11:30. When she arrived, I went downstairs to open the door, and she said, "You gotta help me because the cake is in the trunk." I thought, *It's in the trunk? What's the cake doing in the trunk?* We went outside and she opened the trunk, and there it was: a full-size birthday party cake, for like 50 people. She had purchased it at Costco. It was absolutely beautiful. But I was stunned; I thought, *What am I gonna do with this thing? It's way too big!* I love chocolate cake but I figured I'd be eating on this thing for two weeks or more. The rest of my life maybe!

We brought it up to my apartment. It was heavy, it seemed like it weighed 25 pounds. It said, "Happy Birthday Don." I figured I'd have to invite as many people as quickly as I could, for an impromptu party. Otherwise I didn't know what to do with it. Now all of a sudden I was stressed out because I had a party to put together. I definitely needed ice cream and a few other things. I called Frank, who was working downtown, and asked him to rescue me. He came over and we made a shopping list, and I went around to a few neighbors and told them about the party. I reserved the community room, and told people to invite whoever else they could find. Somehow I forgot to be stressed out and got into a party mood.

Frank got ice cream and plates and forks, and we set the cake out in the community room. At two o'clock, people started showing up. I was really happy that it all came together. One guy was surprised by how old I am. I was stunned that I could have so much fun planning and having a party, knowing it was my *last* birthday party! I can imagine a lot of people would rather just crawl under the bed and forget about it. But I embraced it. Today I learned that you can still get excited like a little kid about a birthday and a cake, and the people that surround you at a time like that, even when you know it's your last time. It was a wonderful little party and I'm just delighted that it all came together the way it did.

## DAY 73 – SUNDAY JUNE 2, 2013

I woke up exhausted this morning. I didn't really get a good night's sleep. I woke up at my regular time this morning, eight o'clock. I wanted to go to church today. I could've easily skipped it and slept a couple more hours, but I love to be there on Sundays and be part of the service. I look forward to Communion, and to visiting with friends there.

I had breakfast and went to church, and then I decided to take a nice walk in the sunshine. Out on the street, I encountered somebody that I've known for a long time. He's disabled, a paraplegic, and he gets around using a scooter. It's a very difficult life for him, but today he was all excited. He operates a non-profit organization which works with mentally challenged young people. They work as reporters, covering events around Portland: sporting events, music events, any kind of event where he can get free tickets. The young people who work as reporters interview the artist or the athlete or whoever. They record the interviews and post them on their website.

One event that his organization covered was the recent grand re-opening of the Green-Wyatt Federal Building here in Portland. One of his ace reporters was there, who apparently tends to ask a lot of difficult questions. He's a young man with a real interest in politics, but his questions are really outside the box and he tends to throw people off and confuse them. Before conducting the interview, this young man used one of the restrooms in the Federal Building, and found that they weren't very user-friendly. He has a physical disability as well as a mental disability, and he was disgusted. He was interviewing the general manager of the building, so he called him on it. He asked, "How do you get *in* the restroom door? Show me how to get through the restroom door." Apparently the guy being interviewed was really caught off-guard and didn't know how to answer.

Then my friend who operates the non-profit asked me how I was doing and I explained my circumstances. He shared with me that both of his parents had been cancer patients and had struggled with it for a long time before their deaths. He said that they had both prolonged their lives considerably by drinking shark liver oil. He explained the statistics concerning shark livers and the fact that sharks as a species never have cancer; their bodies are resistant to any kind of cancerous cells. He urged me to get a bottle of shark liver oil and to start using it immediately! He was adamant about it.

I thanked him, of course. You have to at least give some thought to people's suggestions. I mean, what if shark liver oil really *could* suppress cancer? That's something you automatically think about; you seize on it – for about a minute. It didn't take me long to realize that shark liver oil is *not* what I'm looking for right now. But it's funny how every time somebody tells you something like that, you think, *Wow, could that work? Is that possible?* But if it really worked, a lot more people would know about it. Besides, we have enough trouble with people killing sharks just to make shark fin soup; we don't need shark liver pirates killing more sharks for stupid reasons.

Basically it's been a really relaxing day. I went through all my birthday cards from yesterday and someone gave me a $50 Starbucks gift card! But I really don't have anything else to say about today.

**DAY 74 – MONDAY JUNE 3, 2013**

Before I got out of bed this morning, I felt incredibly good. I had had a tremendous night's rest. I did my usual test: I stepped on the floor, and stood up and moved around. Everything was working well and I wasn't dizzy. I felt incredibly rested and it was amazing. I got my breakfast ready, made my cup of coffee, and worked on my blog for about an hour and a half. It was a really productive morning.

Around 11:30 my hospice nurse, Susan, came over. We had a nice conversation. She asked me, "How are you doing overall?" I told her, "I've been feeling a lot better over the last few days. The main reason is that I've started taking really nice, hot, soaking baths at night, which really relaxes me. The heat and the steam are helping me to detox." I believe that as my liver fails, it will start producing more toxins, and it's good to get as many of those toxins out of my system as I can. She said, "You're absolutely right; I agree with you 100% on the baths. But I thought you were having trouble with the hot water."

I explained that I had found a solution to that problem. "I boil several gallons of water and add it to my bath, so I get a hot bath."

She asked, "You're boiling your own water?"

I said, "Yes, it's just like they used to do in the Old West! Boil the water and pour it in the tub."

She said, "I get it, but that's a lotta work!"

I replied, "I don't care how much work it is; I get to have a hot bath!"

The conversation escalated from there. Susan got more and more upset about it. She agreed that it's wrong, in a newly-remodeled building, that people can't get adequate hot water for a bath. I explained that there's nothing that I can really do about it. Even if I get a letter from my doctor, building management will drag their feet for a while. Apparently they *have* a solution, but it costs money. Plus no one knows how much time I've got left here. So I'll just continue to boil my bath water.

Finally she said, "Well, I'm gonna call your doctor and get an order to provide adequate hot water for you. Hot baths are extremely beneficial for you, for getting rid of toxins, and for relaxation." I said, "If you wanna take that on, I'm happy to go along with it." We talked for a while longer after that, and went over my exercise plan: I'll continue taking walks and climbing stairs, and stay on my feet for as long as I can. She agreed that all of that will be beneficial to me; I'll feel better longer as this thing progresses. When she left, she seemed adamant about taking care of the water heater business.

Later on I climbed the five sets of stairs to the top floor, and I noticed that the door to the roof was propped open. That door is a big old heavy thing and I'd never seen it open before. I decided to go up there and check it out. This building has what's called a "green roof." There are plants and grass on the whole surface. But it looked yucky; the grass was all brown and full of weeds. I thought, *That's no "green" roof; there's no ecological benefit here!* Of course nobody ever sees it, since the residents aren't allowed up here.

I decided to be adventurous and explore the roof. It has a four-foot railing all the way around it so you can't fall off. On the back side of the building, some guy was rappelling down the side with some tools, to fix something. He was all the way down to the third or fourth floor. I figured he'd be down there for a while so I had time to wander around. What an incredible view from up there; you can see the city in all directions. It was amazing! I could see the Willamette River and Mount Hood too. I hung out up there for about 30 minutes, and took some pictures. It was a really fun adventure.

After that I had to sit down at my computer to do my monthly bills, which I pay online. I breezed through most of them, and didn't make any mistakes until I got to the last one. Somehow I couldn't figure it out. I ended up having to reset my password a couple of times. I knew I was doing something wrong, but I couldn't figure out exactly what. So I just kept cycling through it over and over again. I finally *did* sort it out and got it paid, but that one bill took me about an hour. By then I felt really anxious and dizzy. That's how the disease is affecting me. I don't understand why I can't figure things out that used to be so simple. In those situations I should probably stop, take a deep breath, lie down, get some rest, and relax. But I kept thinking, *I'm just a couple of clicks away from getting it done!* Next time I do my bills, I'm gonna have a friend come over and sit through it with me. I could just call my son and have him take over my accounts and pay the bills, but I wanna do it for as long as I possibly can.

I was still reeling around from that when I got a call back from Susan. She had already contacted my doctor for authorization and had sent a letter on hospice letterhead to building management about resolving the water heater issue. I've heard that there's another guy in the building who sent in a similar letter from his doctor, but the building manager has been stalling him for a month. So it's not like they're gonna do anything tomorrow, and they might never do anything by the time I'm gone! So we'll see where it goes from there.

Parts of today were difficult, but there were also a few really rewarding moments that I was very excited about. So on balance, I'd have to say it was a good day, but I'm exhausted and worn out right now.

## DAY 75 – TUESDAY JUNE 4, 2013

I had a really good night's rest last night, and woke up feeling ready to get started on my day. After breakfast, I enjoyed looking for space photographs for my John in Cyberspace blog. The Hubble photograph archives are just amazing. Many of them are copyrighted so I can't use them on my blog, but I can use the ones that are copyright-free, as long as I credit them properly. I'm a stickler about copyrights! I wanna be sure I don't violate copyright laws. Ha! I wish I could say that that was 100% true throughout my life, but I know that over the years I probably violated a lot of people's copyrights. Not intentionally – more by not searching too deeply for what was actually copyrighted and what wasn't. Sometimes when you're working in the middle of the night putting a publication together, you end up bending the rules a little bit because you don't wanna stay up all night long.

I took a very long walk today. The weather was absolutely spectacular. I ran into two guys that I know, whom I hadn't seen for a few days. They know about my situation. They walked up to me as I was walking along with my walker, and one of them said, "How come you're out here in this bright sunlight without an umbrella?" I looked at 'em and replied, "Because I'm not worried about skin cancer." They both just cracked up; they thought it was absolutely hilarious. I didn't really think it was so hilarious myself. But they got a big laugh out of it, which was kinda funny.

Today I finally tracked down an old friend that I'd been trying to contact for several weeks. It turns out that I'd been calling the wrong telephone number. When I set up my new phone, I entered his number incorrectly. So I've left multiple messages at this wrong number that has one of those stupid answering things that doesn't say the name of the person that you're calling, it just lists the telephone number. You can call that number for ten years without finding out that it's the *wrong* number; there's no way to know! My friend hadn't gotten my messages, obviously, but then his wife contacted me through Facebook and gave me the right number. So I finally called and talked to my friend. He's gonna come up and visit, hopefully soon. That was important because he was a big checkmark on the box of people whom I need to talk to.

Later I had my weekly coffee session with Ellen, over at Fred Meyer's. If I ask her to go to the Fred Meyer's Starbucks, not only do I buy her a coffee, but I get some shopping done that I can't do at Safeway around the corner. A clever ploy on my part! We had an enjoyable conversation. I've had to put a rule in place with several people, that we're not going to talk about my physical condition. I don't want to be probed about my medical condition, how I feel, what my doctor says, what medications I'm taking, and all those things. That conversation is off-limits. My medical conversations right now are with my doctor and nurse, and with Karen and my son, and that's it. No one else needs to be privy to that. If they ask me questions about it, I'll just say, "Yeah, I don't wanna talk about my medical condition." I'd rather talk about other things.

Anyway, I've still got a couple hours here so I'm gonna go out in the sunshine and take my last walk for the day. It was a pretty productive day, and overall I'm feeling pretty good.

26

SETBACKS AND EXHAUSTION

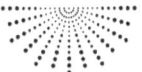

**DAY 76 – WEDNESDAY JUNE 5, 2013**

When I woke up this morning, I realized that things were different. Usually I go along for a while, doing well and feeling about the same every day, and then all of a sudden, something happens and I suffer what I call a big setback. Kind of a milestone day, where things aren't the same as yesterday. Sometimes it's temporary because I'm just overtired, but when I got up today and did my little stand-up test and started walking around, I realized I wasn't walking around the same as I had the day before. It just seemed a lot different.

I remembered that my hospice volunteer was scheduled to come over at ten o'clock. I hustled around to get ready for her but I felt like calling and canceling her visit. I felt sad. It just felt like all of a sudden I had taken a big step back. But I decided to push through it and I didn't cancel, although I was tired when she arrived, much more tired than usual. I asked her to help with the laundry. Normally I just do that myself, but I didn't feel like it today. She also did some dusting around the apartment; I hadn't gotten to it for a while. We had a nice two hours together. When she left, a little after twelve o'clock, I was still feeling really, really out-of-sorts. Later I worked on my blog, and things just weren't quite right. I had trouble putting sentences together as I was typing.

This afternoon I had a daytime dream. It was pretty vivid. It felt like I was asleep and in a dream, but I wasn't actually asleep. In most dreams, you experience something from the back of your mind as you sleep. I think what happens to me is that my brain performs the same function but I'm not really sleeping. The dream is there, happening around me, yet it's not – I'm awake; I'm standing around or doing something. It's the weirdest sensation and it's really confusing. I've experienced this several times in the past few weeks. I used to think it was a déjà-vu, where all of a sudden you think you're experiencing something that has happened before, but it's not the same.

This evening I took a hot bath. At one point I was looking down at the drain where the water runs out. I just sat there staring at it. As the water goes out of the tub and finally most of it is gone, there's always this last little whirlpool above the drain. I was mesmerized by the water, and all of a sudden I had this sensation that that was my life, just going *whoossshhh*, right down the drain like a little whirlpool. It was sad.

I was relieved to see the whole *day* go down the drain, because it was a tough day of feeling like nothing's ever gonna be the same again.

## DAY 77 – THURSDAY JUNE 6, 2013

I woke up this morning feeling better than yesterday, which was great because I thought that I had taken a huge step backwards yesterday and that everything was gonna be really different from now on. I'd had a great night's sleep. After breakfast, I was very excited to get to work on my blog. I've been putting up a new post every day. I find something in the book of John that inspires me, and I add a space photo. It's really fun to find the photos and do all the work. It inspires me to get out of bed in the morning.

I took a couple of walks today. When I got back to the building after my first walk, I saw a guy who lives on the same floor as me. I hadn't yet told him about my cancer, but I know that he is a cancer survivor; he had it a few years ago. Today was the first time he'd seen me with a walker. His apartment is right across from the elevator, and his door opened just as I came out of the elevator with my walker. He looked down at it and asked, "What's up with *this?*" I said, "Well, my cancer came back." He gave me a very unusual look and he said, *"Shit!"* Then he turned around abruptly, went back into his apartment, and slammed the door.

I was in shock. That's the strangest reaction I've experienced yet! I mean, how bizarre. But I kinda blew it off and left. Then, coincidentally, this afternoon, I bumped into him again downstairs by the mailboxes in the lobby. He always used to stop and say hello or hi or something like that. But today he came up to me was facing right at me, and he just blew right by and didn't say one word. I was blown away by the whole thing. I didn't understand his reaction; I was like, *What exactly is going on here?*

Anyway, I got a few more things done and had my dinner, and now I'm ready to wind down my day, have a nice hot bath, and get some sleep.

## DAY 78 – FRIDAY JUNE 7, 2013

I was really excited when I woke up this morning. I was very anxious to work on my blog. The whole purpose of the blog is to make it my testimony on the internet, something that I hope will be out there for years and years and years to come It's exciting to leave something, a legacy of some sort, even if it's just something you scratched on a rock someplace. The point is to leave something on this earth that makes sense to at least a few people. I use Blogger, which is owned by Google, which has a stipulation that if somebody passes away, their blog can stay online in perpetuity, for time immemorial. Until Google disappears! It's kind of exciting that it would be there in cyberspace. That's a lot different from having a bunch of papers or a file that nobody would ever look at. I think it's a great idea, because people have blogs that they want to leave as a reminder to others, that they once existed on this earth.

Around 10 o'clock I decided to take a walk. It was the most beautiful, sun-shiny, wonderful Portland day that you can possibly imagine, and I took about a one-mile walk.

In the afternoon I decided to get some rest because Karen was going to come over later with two friends of ours. I wanted to conserve my energy so I could be ready for that visit. Talking with people and being conversational has become very tiring for me; it wears my brain down really fast. I planned to sleep for an hour and a half.

I had just laid down when my telephone rang; it was my friend Lester. I had left him a voice message just yesterday about coming by to see me on Monday, so I wasn't really expecting to hear from him. I answered the phone and he said, "Hi it's Lester, I'm at the front door of your building."

I said, "What? Why are you at the front door of my building?"

He said, "Because I said I was gonna see you today!"

I said, "I'm really happy that you're here, but I don't know *why* you're here because I was under the impression I was gonna see you on Monday." Somehow our communication must've gotten fouled up; maybe he didn't get my message.

Either way, I got up and headed downstairs to let him in. By this time it was almost two o'clock and I realized this visit was really gonna upset my apple cart because I wouldn't have a chance to get any rest. But I really wanted to see him.

By the time Lester left, it was at least four o'clock. Again I tried to get some rest, but two or three more people called me, wanting to know when I could get together with them. I did my best to deal with all of that, and then Karen called me and said she'd be there in about half an hour. After that, I just couldn't manage to fall asleep.

Karen and her friends arrived around 5:30. Despite my lack of rest, the four of us had a really pleasant conversation; everyone handled the situation nicely. In circumstances like mine, what people want more than anything else is to be treated normally. Friends know the situation is difficult. But we wanna have as good a conversation and as enjoyable a time as possible, without bringing up all the difficult stuff. That stuff ruins the conversation and causes more stress and anxiety. Just relax and be pleasant and have a good conversation; *spend time together*. People who can do that are really helpful; they make it all much nicer. Most of the people in my building have handled it that way. They treat me like I'm the same guy today that I've been all along. I like that! I think the most beneficial thing for someone with a terminal illness is spending time with the people they care about. Real, genuine time. I can't speak for everyone in my situation, but I don't wanna be handled like someone who's dying.

In spite of being exhausting, today was a success. I got some work done and I spent time with several people whom I enjoy being with.

# 27
# PORTLAND, OREGON

## DAY 79 – SATURDAY JUNE 8, 2013

I felt very rested this morning, as though I'd had an incredibly good night's sleep. I think that was because I was so tired yesterday evening. Talking with people wears me out as much as physical activity. This had never really registered with me before now. My brain fatigues very easily in the condition that it's in, and I've realized that talking is just as tiring as climbing stairs. I wasn't up for very long when all of a sudden the energy that I had when I woke up left me in a big hurry, and I felt extremely tired. I thought, *Uh-oh, maybe I've had another setback.*

Today we had the Grand Floral Parade in Portland, which is the official kickoff of the annual Rose Festival. I've seen this parade every year since I first came back to Oregon in the 90's. In the beginning, I used to get really excited about it. Over the last ten years or so, I haven't been as interested. It seems to me like it's always the same groups of people and the same bands from the same high schools. Having lived in Los Angeles all those years, I went to several rose festivals in Pasadena, and nothing compares to a Pasadena rose festival float because they are absolutely spectacular. After Pasadena, you can go to any other city in the United States and if they have a rose parade, it's just not gonna be the same.

But I think Portlanders embrace this event. They come downtown and shop and line up on the sidewalks for hours. It's a huge thing here. I wasn't sure I wanted to go, since I've seen it so many times, but after I had breakfast and worked on my blog, I decided to take a break and go see if the parade had started yet. I live three blocks from an intersection where you can get a very good view.

I walked down there at about 11:30. On my way, I thought, *Uh-oh, this isn't right; I don't have any energy today.* Usually I take about a one-mile walk in the morning, but today I felt like I couldn't have gone more than those three blocks to see the parade. When I got there, somebody told me it'd probably be another half an hour before the parade came through. I didn't feel like sticking around so I headed back home. But then around noon, I thought I might like to see at least a part of it. There's always this great band called the *One More Time Around Marching Band*, which has about 500 members. They're all people who played in a high school or college band at some point. Many of them are in their sixties, and it gives them an opportunity to keep playing in a big giant marching band. It's very entertaining. They always play "Louie Louie," which is their signature song. It's really exciting if you get to hear that one. With 500 people in the band, it's a big sound – it might not be the *greatest* sound, but it's a *big* sound, that's for sure!

So I thought, *It'd be worth going down there to see that band, 'cause after all, this is undoubtedly my last Rose Parade. I'll give it one more time around!* I walked back down to the parade route and found a nice spot. There was a hole in the crowd so I could see really well. The parade hadn't arrived yet; it was about 15 minutes late. It's always late!

I sat there in the sunshine. It was one of the most beautiful days I've seen in Portland in I-don't-know-how-long; absolutely spectacular. A clear, blue sky, just the perfect temperature and the right amount of breeze. Anyone who has gone to all these Rose Parades has sat through some really miserable parades in the *rain*. I mean, pouring rain. Sometimes it has been driving rain. So you can't imagine what it's like for people to be out there in their tank tops.

I waited patiently, sitting on my walker seat, which is so cool. Pretty soon I heard the first part of the parade coming through. The police department always leads the parade with about ten cars. They like to show right away that they're in charge. Shortly thereafter there's the grand marshal, and then a couple floats come through. Portland Rose Festival floats always look really flimsy to me. They bounce a lot, and look like they're gonna fall apart. But I was trying to be upbeat about it.

Pretty soon I heard the band coming, the *One More Time Around Marching Band*. They weren't playing a song yet, but I could hear the drums rumbling. It's exciting to hear that. The band has cheerleaders, and some of them are in their 50's and 60's, wearing their cheerleader outfits from high school. To me, that band is the most fun thing in the whole parade. Just as they got to my intersection, they fired up old "Louie Louie" right on cue, and as they walked by where I was sitting, they just about played the whole song. That pretty much made the whole parade for *me*, right there.

---

## A LAST TIME FOR EVERYTHING

*I was sitting in the sunshine, watching the parade go by, and all of a sudden I just felt incredibly sad. I guess it was the realization that this was truly my last Rose Parade, and it just really choked me up. My eyes actually teared up a bit. I think there's something in all of us, there's this little kid in all of us, to whom a parade is something very special – even if it's a crummy parade! It takes us right back to our childhood. Back then we would sit there and get so excited to see the parade come along; it wouldn't matter what was in the parade. So I became very melancholy about the whole thing.*

Then I looked up and saw the beautiful, beautiful sky. When you get weather like this in Portland, Oregon in early June, it's amazing and so special. We all wait for summer here, the 21$^{st}$ of June, which kicks off great weather for about 8, 9, or 10 weeks. It's a magical time, to be outdoors and not have to worry about rain. When I first heard about my terminal condition, I thought I had a really good chance of making it through the whole summer. But the way I'm feeling right now, I'm almost positive that that's not going to be possible. Not many things have upset me as far as not being able to finish something, or not being able to see it or be part of it again. But the idea of missing summer disturbs me. Thinking about that, I felt like crying.

Eventually the bright, beautiful day cheered me up again and I got back into the swing of things. I watched a lot more of the parade than I ever would've watched before, probably because I knew it was my last time. I thought, *If I give it this last chance, maybe this time they'll pull off something that's a little bit different.* Ha!

I guess the parade had had kind of a magical effect on me over the years which I hadn't realized. It turned out to be the highlight of my day.

## DAY 80 – SUNDAY JUNE 9, 2013

When I woke up this morning, I felt pretty good. I wasn't as run down and tired as I was yesterday. Yesterday it seemed like I had taken a huge step backwards, but this morning it felt like maybe it'd only been a little step. That was encouraging.

I wanted to mention a couple other things from yesterday. First of all, yesterday afternoon I was in Safeway, one of my daily stops. I saw a woman there who used to live in my building. I was diagnosed with cancer after she moved to another building up the street. When I've seen her outside, she has always been really encouraging, saying stuff like, "You're gonna get through this; you're gonna make it; you look great!" We've talked a number of times in the past couple-o' three months, but I hadn't told her about my relapse. It's not necessary to tell everybody.

I was rolling around the store with Johnnie Walker when I bumped into her. Walking toward her, I could see that she was looking right at me. She saw me with that walker and got a stunned look on her face, then she just turned abruptly and walked away. I could tell she'd realized immediately that I've suffered a huge relapse, and she wasn't able to deal with it so she just left. I was kinda shocked, but the funny part of it was that I also felt relieved. I thought, *Now I don't have to explain this! I don't have to go into any detail with her because it's pretty obvious.*

Then there was something else that happened last night. Late in the evening I heard a lot of screaming out on the street outside of my apartment. I live on the 5th floor. I went out on the deck, and to my shock and disbelief, I saw nude bike riders pedaling down my street, SW 12th Avenue. I'm not talking about just a couple of people. Today I heard on the news that there were over 4000 of them. 4000 nude bike riders! I'd never seen anything like that. At one point I saw four or five people standing on the sidewalk, nude, *without bikes*. Ha! Maybe they live nearby and decided to come out and stand there in support of the nude bike riders. I thought the whole thing would be over fairly quickly – how many nude bike riders can there be in one city? Think about it. A hundred or two? No, more and more of them just kept coming down the street. It wasn't just five or ten dribbling along; no, the street was *full* of people. Nude! On bicycles! I couldn't believe my eyes. I'd heard about Portland's Naked Bike Ride before but until you see it yourself from the balcony of your own apartment building, you can't imagine it. I was just flabbergasted.

This morning after church, I stopped by Safeway and had a coffee at Starbucks. A few weeks ago when I was in there, I ran into a guy I know, and when I told him about my situation, he quoted a verse from the Bible to me which I really liked. He had quoted it off the top of his head and wasn't sure exactly where it was in the Bible. Since then, Karen asked a pastor whom she knows, who's very familiar with the Bible and a few of its translations; she told Karen that it was Psalm 116, verse 15. Today I saw that guy again, who first mentioned it to me, and he had tracked it down as well. It says, "Precious in the sight of the Lord is the death of his saints." That strikes me as very beautiful, absolutely beautiful. God is talking about his people, and it's incredibly comforting to me to hear that. It provides reassurance of being loved by God, that he will notice that my life has ended, and will welcome me. The Bible is an amazing book, the most amazing book in the world as far as I'm concerned. It's stunning when you find one verse that has such an impact.

**DAY 81 – MONDAY JUNE 10, 2013**

I woke up this morning to a bright, sun-shiny day in Portland. It's unbelievable; I think this has been the 10$^{th}$ sunny day in a row in the middle of June. That's truly unheard of here! It's always great to wake up to a sun-shiny day no matter what your situation is.

This morning was pretty good. I got an excellent night's sleep and didn't have any pain during the night. I haven't had any pain at all yet, other than a few little twinges here and there. This morning I took a fairly long walk, maybe a mile or a mile and a half, up and down SW 12$^{th}$ almost all the way to Burnside. Next I worked on my John in Cyberspace blog, which has been getting a fair number of views. It's averaging 25, 30 hits a day! I feel good that people are looking at it and paying attention.

Today I had to pay a bunch of bills. It just took ages to get it done. I had trouble with the calculator. It takes me a long time to figure out if I'm gonna add or subtract or whatever. I have to keep reminding myself of what I'm doing, and think through every single, solitary function before I do it. I finally got it done, but I talked to my son today and told him that bill-paying is just getting too complicated for me. He's signatory on my checking account, and we pretty much decided that for next month, I'll have my online banking set up so that he can do it. After today, I just don't see how I'm gonna be able to figure all that out. Well, I can figure it out but it just takes too long! And the longer it takes, the more I feel pressured and anxious and I start getting a headache, so it's just not worth it for me to do those kinds of activities. I'd be much better off taking a walk or relaxing.

I had to do a really sad thing today. I struggled with it for quite a while, but I finally decided to permanently close down my Square People blog. I'm not deleting it from the internet; it'll still be on there for years to come. But I'm not doing any more posts. It was really sad because that's where I first met Karen, the very first time that I took pictures for that blog, three years ago. Karen was the first person that I photographed for the blog, and the pictures that I took of her recently at the Festival of Flowers are in my very last post. The blog has had almost 14,000 page views. It's something I definitely have to let go of, emotionally. I'm sentimental about it.

The way I got started doing the Square People blog in 2010 began with my decision to buy a new camera, that I didn't wanna buy on credit. I figured it'd cost around seven hundred to a thousand dollars for a Nikon. I saw a Help Wanted ad for the 2010 census. I had worked on the 2000 census, so I had experience. I figured that if I did that again, I could use the money for a new camera. I went down to the library and applied for the job.

You have to take a test to work for the Census. Around the time I took the test, I was having a lotta trouble with my right eye: I needed cataract surgery, and I could hardly focus on anything closer than 18 inches. It was hard to read the test and it took me longer than everybody else, but I managed to work my way through all the questions. It's not an easy test to begin with; college graduates fail this thing. But I managed to pass it; I have no idea how.

So I was hired. The next step was to attend a one-week training session. My eye surgery was scheduled to happen three days before the training week, and I thought, *Oh no, right after having eye surgery I'll have to get up early and take a bus who-knows-how-far-away to take the training.* I was pretty worried. Finally I got a telephone call from the woman who was coordinating the training. She told me, "The training will be at 1500 SW 12th Avenue in Portland, Oregon."

I said, "No, I think you have that wrong. *I* live at 1500 SW 12th Avenue. That's *my* address."

She replied, "Well I don't know anything about *your* address, but the training will be at 1500 SW 12th Avenue."

I said, "Well, that's impossible, that's where *I* live!"

She said, "That's not *my* problem! All I can tell you is that that's where the training will be."

I couldn't believe that; it didn't make any sense. I asked, "Could you please look again just to make sure, because what you're giving me is my own address. That's the building I live in!" She repeated it one more time, and I just hung up the phone, totally perplexed. I just knew she was wrong.

Later I headed downstairs to the manager's office and asked him, "Is the Census Bureau scheduled to have a training session in our community room next week?" The manager confirmed it. I said, "What?!? Are you kidding me?" I couldn't believe it! All I had to do was get up in the morning, eat my cereal, and head downstairs. So that's how it worked out. When the training started, I'd just had my eye surgery and I was still having trouble seeing because it wasn't fully healed yet. But I got through the training, then went out and worked for the Census for several weeks. I made the money I wanted, and bought the camera that I wanted. Without that camera, there wouldn't have been a blog, and I wouldn't have met Karen.

The two really big events for me today were realizing that I'm not gonna be able to handle my finances in the very near future, and saying goodbye to my blog. Tomorrow I will probably have forgotten about Square People, and may never really give it much more thought. But it was a lot of fun for three years.

# SECTION 5: DAILY ROUTINES AND WORSENING SYMPTOMS

I ended the call with Larry by saying, "Hey, keep in touch, alright? We'll check out the football season as it comes along." I absolutely don't believe I'll see any of it, but that was the only way I could end the conversation. There was nothing else to talk about. The living go on, and people who are dying come to an abrupt end.

## 28

## A NEED TO RE-BUILD BRIDGES

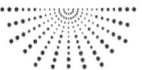

**DAY 82 – TUESDAY JUNE 11, 2013**

When I woke up this morning, I was really missing Karen. She has been traveling for work for a couple-a three days. We only live about six miles apart, so it was difficult to think of her being far away, unable to come over right away if I needed her.

I got a good night's rest. When I sleep well, I think it's about 50% because I take a quarter pill of trazadone at bed-time, and 50% because of my hot baths at night. Those hot baths are incredibly beneficial. I position the shower curtain so the steam can't escape quickly, so it's like a little steam room. It helps to detox my body, but it also has psychological benefits. It's *so* relaxing, and all the tensions of the day just seem to melt away. To anyone who's in pain or taking a lot of medications, I would recommend regular hot baths. That way you can count on having a period of time each day to do something relaxing and beneficial to your health, especially if you turn it into a little steam room. I've definitely felt much better every day since I started doing it. When I wake up in the morning, I feel refreshed and relaxed, and ready to go!

On many mornings, for a little while like maybe an hour, I start out feeling as though the disease is gone. It's like I could get up and have a normal day. But then, once I'm up and about and preparing my breakfast, I start to feel run down. I start to sense a loss of mobility, and feel more tired than I was the day before. Then within another hour my anxiety level starts to build up because I'm not sure what the coming day will bring or what kinda situations I'll be involved in.

Working on my new blog just after I get up in the morning has become my usual daily routine. I'd recommend that type of thing to anyone facing similar circumstances: find something to do, some project or activity that's really important to you, for a portion of each day. For me, it's that John in Cyberspace blog. It's exciting to me to put something out on the internet, which will be there for years after I'm gone. And I enjoy working on it because it involves scripture and creativity. My other project that's really important right now is talking with Karen every night about what I'm experiencing. Aside from my faith, those two things are helping me through this more than anything else: the blog in the morning and my recap of the day's events every night. Those activities give me something to think about and be concerned about, and I hope that through those projects I can somehow help other people facing a similar situation.

I had coffee with Ellen today. We've been getting together once a week, and she often brings me treats. Today it was a half-gallon of very expensive ice cream, with chocolate swirls and other things going on.

It's really gratifying that we've remained friends this long. When we first got divorced, things weren't very friendly, but over the years we've gotten past that. Now that I'm in this time of trouble, she has stepped up and been a really good friend, and it's truly comforting to have her in my life.

After seeing Ellen though, my stomach felt really acidic because of the coffee. I've been noticing that more and more often over the past two or three days. I love having my two cups of coffee a day; it's another one of my daily routines. The first cup in the morning is usually solitary, while I'm working on my blog, but my afternoon coffee generally involves visiting with somebody. So I'd be really disappointed if I have to get rid of coffee.

For a few weeks now, my son has made a point of calling me every day. Our conversations have gotten deeper and deeper, in the sense that we're starting to discuss things we've never really discussed before. It's very rewarding to have those kinds of conversations right now. There's more emotion there than before. He asked me recently, "How's Karen dealing with this?" He has asked the same question about a couple other people as well. I think he's wondering how other people are dealing with it, because he's struggling with how to deal with it himself.

Karen asked me whether I told my son that she often cries about it. I *did* tell him, because I think sadness is a normal, healthy emotion. And I think tears can be incredibly healing. They're a wonderful built-in mechanism in our bodies, for dealing with things that we wouldn't otherwise be able to deal with. Crying gives you a cleansing feeling; it gets difficult emotions out of your system. Some people don't shed tears, or they find it extremely difficult; I would not wanna be one of those people. Anyway, I really look forward to my daily conversations with Allen.

That's pretty much it for today. Things are definitely getting worse. It's harder to get around, and my walks have gotten shorter. My body is running down. Every night when I take my bath now, I watch the water run out. It has become a ritual: watching the drain flow until it forms a little spiral, and then *whoosh* it's gone. That's my life! I can just see it running out.

## DAY 83 – WEDNESDAY JUNE 12, 2013

First things first. It's so bizarre to wake up and feel like a normal person for about an hour before everything goes south. I sleep well and wake up thinking, *Wow, I could go out and do something really significant today!* But within an hour or so, that energy dissipates and I don't feel like I can do much of anything.

I've added a section on my blog, a sort of history of my career in publishing. Desktop publishing was a hugely significant development during those years, when now you could use a MacIntosh computer to completely compose a newspaper page. That was back in 1985, 1986. The computer screen was about eight inches wide, and the MacIntosh cost two thousand dollars, which was a lot of money in 1985. The software was another thousand to fifteen hundred, but you needed it to do page production. PhotoShop was first introduced in 1990. To buy the computer and all the software you needed, you were looking at an investment of over three thousand dollars.

In 1985 I bought a program called Aldus PageMaker. Back then, you'd install software off of around 16 floppy disks. But PageMaker was phenomenal because it was written by real, honest-to-goodness printing professionals who transferred all of their printing knowledge to digital type and photos, and digital page composition. Adobe eventually bought the program from Aldus, and somewhere towards the late 90's they dumped it and came out with a new product called InDesign. InDesign is the page-making program of choice for just about all graphic designers in the United States, except for me! I still have PageMaker.

I've been having more dizzy spells lately. It's hard to explain. I *don't* feel like I'm gonna fall down, but I feel like the world is spinning and my brain is just kinda free-wheeling out of control. I don't get sick to my stomach, but I feel like I just can't go anywhere unless I hang on to something. Those episodes have been getting more frequent, and stronger. They used to last for about a minute, but now they last three to four minutes, and I have to find my way to a place where I can sit down. If I'm out walking, I sit on my walker. I know it's all part of the progression of the disease. The question is, how do I keep going, and how can I fight the disease and stay on my feet as long as I possibly can?

**DAY 84 – THURSDAY JUNE 13, 2013**

Today is really about only one thing, and that's pretty much all I'm gonna talk about. Today I saw somebody that I haven't seen or communicated with for over twenty years: my second ex-wife, Catherine. We had an initial conversation a week ago, and then she decided to visit me.

Catherine and I met in the 1980's in Los Angeles. I was working for a publishing company and she was just starting out as a lawyer. She was involved in corporate law and she felt that it was a dog-eat-dog world in which she had to represent a lot of greedy people. It seemed like she found it unsatisfying, her clients' constant battles over money. We started seeing each other and after about a year or so we got married. We were only married for a few years and didn't have any children.

In many ways we had a fantastic relationship, but we faced many difficult times. At first my adopted mother was still alive, and for three years she lived with Elizabeth and me, with aides coming in daily to help her. I wanted to keep her from ending up in a nursing facility. Meanwhile Catherine was struggling with her law career. Eventually my mother died but it took a year or two to put all that behind us.

Over time, Catherine transitioned to a different area of the law. She got involved in child abuse cases, which was sometimes extremely gratifying and other times really horrifying. Eventually I decided to leave the company that I'd been with for five years, because I'd basically worked myself out of a job. I'd been the general manager for a while and there weren't any new challenges left there. All that was left was to continue doing the same thing over and over, and I wanted a new challenge. We decided to move to San Diego. I had a couple of business plans that I was working on and I thought I could work on those down there, all the while enjoying the beautiful southern California weather.

Catherine was able to transition successfully from L.A. to San Diego, handling more and more child abuse cases. Looking back, that move was a mistake for *me* because I felt that I had put all my connections behind me and now I was like a fish out of water. L.A. had been my home for so long that everybody I knew seemed to be about a block away there. In San Diego, everybody that I knew was over a hundred miles away. So it was a difficult time, and ultimately our marriage didn't work out.

After the divorce, I decided to come back to Oregon and re-establish myself here, and she of course wanted to stay in San Diego because she had successfully re-established her career there. There wasn't any opportunity to see each other, so we drifted apart fairly quickly. I was always gonna call, but I never did. Time went on and on and on and on and on! Then to my surprise, I hadn't seen her for 23 years.

Last year when Karen arranged a surprise party for my 75th birthday, she wrote to Catherine because I still had her contact information in my files. They had a telephone conversation, and Karen explained to her that I was dealing with a serious illness. Catherine emailed me but I didn't wanna be in touch with her at that point. Then about a month ago I emailed her back and last week we ended up talking. I called her and she was really delighted to hear my voice. I explained that I had terminal cancer and didn't know how much time I had left. I really felt it was absolutely necessary to contact her since we had been in love at one time. I knew it was gonna be difficult, but she was very responsive, and definitely wanted to talk and catch up as best we could.

She came up with the idea of coming to visit. At first I wasn't sure it was a good idea, but the more I thought about it, the more I thought I would really like to see her too so that we could have whatever kind of closure we needed. To be honest, I was totally blown away by the whole idea, after all these years. She arrived here at 3:30 this afternoon. It seemed pretty obvious to me, after talking for a few minutes, that we both *did* need some closure on the marriage that we'd had.

I feel that *everyone* needs to do that: find the people that you have open issues with. Pile those issues together and bring 'em to the forefront. One of the steps in Alcoholics Anonymous is to find people that you've harmed in any way, and make amends to them. *Everybody* needs to do that if at all possible. Although it's a key AA principle, one of the twelve steps, it's really good to do it even if you're not involved in AA. Find the people in your life that you may have issues with, where some healing needs to take place. Do it while you still can. If you wait too long and the person passes away, you'll lose the chance.

Our conversation today was all over the place. We talked for about two and a half hours. We're gonna get together again tomorrow morning and finish our conversation and then she'll head to the airport to fly back to California.

That has basically been my day. Seeing and talking with Catherine again was an unbelievably major event in my life. I mean, unless you've been through something like that, it'd be really hard to understand the ramifications. At one time in my life, I loved her and was going to spend the rest of my life with her; now I haven't seen her for 23 years and I get the opportunity to speak with her as I'm dying. That was overwhelming.

## DAY 85 – FRIDAY JUNE 14, 2013

When I woke up today, I was still extremely tired from my visit with Catherine yesterday. She arrived here just after ten o'clock this morning, and I felt that today's visit would be more difficult than yesterday's. But I thought it was incredibly important for us to have this conversation and I hoped it would result in healing for each of us.

I sensed that she really did have a lot mourning to do, about our relationship and the loss of our marriage. She wanted to discuss it in quite a bit of detail. For some reason she felt that she had wronged me or hurt me – I think she used the word "wounded" a couple-a three times – and she was here to make amends for that, to say that she was sorry. She felt really disturbed that she may have hurt me, and wanted to get it all out in the open.

I told her, "I don't feel that you wronged me. I think our marriage ended because of philosophical differences, not because of how we felt about each other." I believe that we loved each other. I still love her, in a totally different way now because of how much time has passed; I still think she's an amazing woman, and that's why it was so difficult to go through these conversations with her. That would be difficult under *any* circumstances. When somebody is dying, it's even *more* difficult. But I wouldn't have traded the experience for anything.

I hugged her and said "Please don't ever feel as though you harmed me. Go forward into the rest of your life knowing that I have nothing but the best feelings for you. I don't feel that you harmed me." I think there was a lot of healing for both of us in a very short period of time, and I couldn't be happier about that. She still has a lot of life to live; I don't want her to carry any guilt about me. Also she's married to a very nice guy who allowed her to make this trip. A man has to be pretty comfortable with himself to say, "Yes, go ahead and spend two days visiting your ex-husband who's dying." I told her, "Please thank him, from the bottom of my heart, that we had the opportunity to have these conversations." We ended by saying a prayer together. We have different mindsets as far as faith is concerned, so we said prayers in our own way for each other.

Overall it was a real opportunity for healing. I didn't think I *needed* healing in this situation, but I found that I did. It's incredible – I didn't talk to her for all those years, then Karen decided to contact her. Then, a year later, in a terminal illness situation, I finally felt that I needed to call her, and all of a sudden she chose to come here – it's all pretty amazing how it came about. She thinks Karen is an angel for initiating the whole thing and helping her figure out which days would be best to come and visit; I couldn't have figured that out myself at this point.

I just wanna say again, that it's so important to take the time now to look back through your connections with people. If there's anything that needs to be resolved with anyone, take care of it while you still have the opportunity.

29

# BOUNCE-BACKS, BEARS AND BARBERSHOPS

**DAY 86 – SATURDAY JUNE 15, 2013**

Today I had another major setback, physically. These setbacks come along every few days. All of a sudden things are simply worse and they never get better again. I suddenly realize I've reached another plateau in the progression of the disease in my body. The past two days, where I saw my ex-wife whom I hadn't seen in over twenty years, were extremely emotional, difficult, and mentally exhausting. I had hoped that after that experience, I would have a bounce-back today. It happens sometimes, where I'm really tired one day and then I bounce back the next day. But when I got up this morning I realized that not only did I *not* have a bounce-back, I was definitely worse: the kind of "worse" where I know it's not gonna get better; it's another plateau.

My body feels disconnected, like my arms are going one way and my eyes are going someplace else; it's very confusing. Also I'm experiencing something else a lot more – I don't like to use the term dizziness, because it's not that. I can stand up straight without feeling like I'm gonna fall over. But when I walk around, I have trouble with my eyes and motion and things like that. And I've been feeling pressure on the left side of my head. I'm also losing my appetite. I have to remind myself that it's time to fix something to eat. In the past, I didn't have to think about it; I would just get hungry and go eat at regular intervals. Now I'm pretty sure I could go all day long without really eating. But at least I'm not feeling any pain.

Since I've been ill, I've seen that my loyal friends are the ones who don't give up on me. They keep coming back for more – ha! – and they check on me constantly to see how I'm doing. That's just a handful of people. *Most* people don't know how to handle it, and they're not interested in finding out. They do their best and then hurry to get out of it. But some people call me consistently and wanna know how I'm doing. They don't pressure me for details; they just ask about my overall wellbeing. That's incredibly helpful for someone in my position. I don't need sympathy and people crying and all that. I need people who care, who just want an update.

One friend called me today, who lives several hours away and can't get here to visit. She got upset and started crying. She feels guilty about not being able to see me. I told her, "Please don't worry about that. All I need from you is to keep in touch. You give me all the comfort I could possibly need, simply by caring sincerely." Also we share the same faith so it's always really gratifying to talk with her about that. It's not that I want people to come here or to do anything in particular for me. What someone in my circumstances needs is for people to be courageous: don't be afraid of the disease and the consequences, just call and let them know that you care.

### Blessing #27

*I'm really blessed because I have a few people in my life who follow through on a regular basis and want to know how I'm doing. The key word here is 'courage'. These friends have the courage to step up; they're not afraid of the illness and they don't project it onto their own situation. They have the courage to reach out consistently when somebody else is really in trouble. I would strongly urge people to do that for anyone who's in a difficult situation. Be courageous, pick up the* telephone, and say hello. I truly appreciate the people who do that for me. I love all of them and I want to acknowledge that today.

## DAY 87 – SUNDAY JUNE 16, 2013

I had a couple of unusual episodes last night while I was sleeping. The first thing that happened was that I woke up somewhere around two o'clock in the morning with a pretty severe pain in my head. It was on the left side, above my ear and down the side of my head. I've felt pressure there before, so I assume that that's from a tumor. The pain didn't last very long, maybe about ten minutes. But I guess this means that more pain is on the way.

The second thing that happened last night was that I had an amazingly vivid dream, in which I heard something growling and pounding on the door to my apartment. It wasn't *this* apartment, but I was in a room somewhat like this. My white recliner chair was there. I heard this scratching and growling, and I peeked out the door. There was a giant bear, like a grizzly, trying to push the door open. I was able to push the door back and secure it. Then I went and got the recliner, and pressed it up against the door like a big door stop. And I *sat* in the recliner, to add extra weight, and extended my feet straight out to push back against the door. The bear kept trying to force its way in. It was ferocious! I was absolutely terrified. The confrontation went on for a while. Nobody knows how long dreams actually last, but this one seemed to last a long time. I finally woke up in a sweat. It was intense, my battle with the bear.

Looking at that dream, I think the bear represented death. It was trying to force its way in and end my life. I was trying to keep the bear out by pushing back at the door. In this particular case, the bear lost, because I woke up and the bear was gone. I'm not a big dream-analyst guy, but I think that's a reasonable interpretation. It was a life and death struggle! Even though I have faith and I feel confident that there's a life after this one, I know that nobody *wants* to die. Nobody wants to leave the things that they know and love. So that was a really unique way for my mind to manifest that struggle.

I started the day with those two things on my mind: pain is on the way, and the bear is at the door, trying to get in. Over the past couple days, I've really felt that the end is getting close. I can't make any predictions; I just know where I am, physically.

**Blessing #28**

*I really had to struggle to get up and go to church this morning. I was tired and I just wanted to stay in bed; another hour of sleep would've been great. But it was very important to me to go and participate in Communion today. My only focus with regards to attending church wasn't the sermon and learning how to live the Christian life and love your fellow man; it was to be in the presence of the Lord and take Communion. That was what got me out of bed and pushed me forward. It was a struggle but I did it. I was very happy and appreciative of the opportunity to go down front one more time in my life and take Communion in church; it was a huge blessing.*

After church, Karen came over to help me with a couple of errands. I wanted to have my hair cut today. I've thought about quite a few "last" things that I've been experiencing, for instance how this might be the *last* time I get a haircut. When I was a small child, my first memories of getting a haircut were going into a barbershop surrounded by a bunch of big people, being the only kid in there and being very afraid. In those days barbershops had barber chairs, which are much different from the chairs that they have today. Barbers also had those red and white-striped poles that spun around and around and around.

There was something mysterious about a barbershop, for a child. All those big people talking about big people stuff. And there I was, just this little person, too small to sit right on the barber chair like everyone else. I got boosted up onto a board that they put across the armrests of chair so I'd be high up enough for the barber to cut my hair. I would almost always be the only child in there, with all these grown-ups around, talking about things I didn't understand. It was almost like a rite of passage – I was growing up and getting a *real* haircut at a barbershop, instead of my mom just putting a bowl over my head and cutting the loose ends with scissors.

---

**A LAST TIME FOR EVERYTHING**

*Getting my hair cut today just led me to reminiscing about what a fantastic experience it was to get a haircut as a child. Thinking of my appointment today as probably my last haircut brought up very powerful feelings, I don't know why. I was just tremendously moved by it. It was very emotional.*

---

So that was my day. Now I'm tired, and I wanna go to sleep and see if the bear comes back again tonight!

## DAY 88 – MONDAY JUNE 17, 2013

It was another difficult day; I think I did a bit too much yesterday. It's hard for me to gage how much energy I'll have available to spend in a day. I don't seem to judge that very well. I think I'm feeling OK, or I really push myself even if I don't feel great, and I do way more than I should. Then I wake up the next morning pretty tired, even if I've had a good night's sleep. That's how I felt this morning, that I pushed myself too far yesterday.

When I got out of bed, I started worrying about the hospice nurse coming by later. It's been almost two weeks since I last saw Susan. I started worrying because she always wants specific answers about *everything*. That's her job, of course. When I talk to *most* people about my condition, I can kinda leave some things out, gloss over some stuff and not be too specific. They get bits and pieces of information and I can kinda spin it the way I want; they won't know the difference. It would be kinda stupid to do that with my nurse, because she's the one who can prescribe medications and do things to keep me comfortable. So I have to be specific with her; I can't tell her I've been feeling better each day. Obviously each day gets progressively worse. When I haven't seen her in a while, it's hard to explain everything that has happened. So I started worrying about it as soon as I got up today.

The other thing that's upsetting about my hospice nurse, I think, is that she's a reality check. She wants to know where I am now, as opposed to where I was a week or two ago. Going over it in detail puts me face-to-face with how much I've deteriorated in that period of time.

I told Susan about my dream about the bear at the door, and she found that really intriguing. She recognized right away what the whole thing was about, and we ended up having a really interesting conversation about dreams.

She said I was doing a great job, and doing everything that I *should* be doing. That gave me a lot of confidence. She's a very caring woman. She was an oncology nurse for a long time before switching to hospice. You couldn't have a better person involved in this particular line of work.

Today I also had a long talk with Catherine, my *other* ex-wife. Ha! She called me as sort of a follow-up on her visit last week, and we had a really nice talk. Plus I had a long call with my son; we talked for about an hour. It was a beautiful day so I went for a walk to help keep my anxiety level down. I overdid it again; I walked clear down to Burnside Street and back. I ran into two or three different people I knew, and had brief conversations with them. So it was a very full, sociable day.

## DAY 89 – TUESDAY JUNE 18, 2013

Last night I had an excellent night's sleep. The bear hasn't come back so it was a peaceful, quiet night.

I'm starting to have problems with my stomach, due to pressure building up which is causing pain. It has reached the point of being uncomfortable most of the time. The other problem with my stomach is that I don't really feel like eating. I think, *Well, I could eat breakfast now, but no, I don't wanna get a stomach-ache. I'll just skip it this one time and avoid the aggravation.* I have to push myself through my meals because I want to continue eating as much as I can, to get proper nutrition.

I got through my breakfast and decided to take a nice walk since it was beautiful outside. I picked a route that had sunshine on both sides of the street. I think I walked a mile overall, and came back feeling pretty good except that I was quite tired. I'm having to stop two or three times along the way and rest, which is a new experience. I used to be able to walk a lot farther without resting at all. But I'm not complaining, because that walker is a marvelous thing and without it I wouldn't be walking anywhere. Also, walking helps to alleviate some of my stomach pain.

Ellen came by in the afternoon to go out for coffee. She has learned not to push me too much with medical questions, but today, when I came out the door and headed for her car, I was *really* wobbly. I have trouble navigating and I've become very unsteady and unsure of myself, and of course she immediately picked up on that because it's a visual sign that something's wrong. I got into the car and she wanted to know all about that. I said, "Hey, you know that things are getting worse, not better, and there's nothing I can do about it. Let's just go get some coffee."

We went to Starbucks, and she did something that I really didn't like. The Starbucks that we go to has a very small parking lot and sometimes it's totally jammed up. We pulled in, and the whole place was full. Then Ellen said, "Wait a minute, I have a handicap placard that we can use." She'd had an injury that entitled her to a temporary handicap placard, and she pulled it out and hung it from the rearview mirror. We pulled into the handicap spot. I don't like doing that. I've dealt with people with disabilities and it's really tough when people take that parking spot when they don't need it.

But then I realized that under the circumstances, I certainly qualify to use that spot! I was feeling very wobbly, and there's no question that if I had a car, I would be entitled to park there. I thought, *Well, on that basis, I'm OK with this.* So we got our spot and went inside.

During our conversation, Ellen became more and more concerned about my situation. She said, "You should be telling your son how you really feel," and things like that. I told her that Allen and I have that discussion every day. So she said, "Then I need to take your picture and send it to him, because he thinks you feel terrible, and actually you look great!" We both laughed at that, and I agreed to let her take a picture and send it to him.

Later I talked with Allen, and he seemed a little more at ease about me. I explained again what it means to be in hospice care: my life is *ending.* He asked a lot of questions that he has never asked before, and I think he really did come away with a much better understanding. In fact, he was very complimentary of the way I'm trying to handle everything. So it was a good conversation, really the best conversation we've had since all of this started. We're getting closer and he understands the reality of the situation. He's going to lose his father, which is very unpleasant for him. It's also very unpleasant for me; I don't wanna lose my son. But that is the reality here.

# 30
# MORE REACTIONS TO SAD NEWS

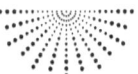

**DAY 90 – WEDNESDAY JUNE 19, 2013**

Last night I had an incredible night's sleep again. I went to bed about 10:30 and as soon as I put my head on the pillow I was *out* like a light. That's because I did a lot yesterday. There were important telephone calls, and a long walk, and when I went to bed, I just went right to sleep. I usually text Karen every night to let her know that I'm OK, but last night I didn't even think about it; I was just out. Then I woke up feeling really good.

I've been noticing that even though I wake up feeling well rested, my energy level starts to drop almost instantly. A few weeks ago, I would be up for an hour-and-a-half to two hours before I noticed my energy level starting to fall off. Now after I'm up for about three minutes, it seems like it's fallen off considerably. It's just a daily thing; I have less and less energy every day. It's also taking me longer to have breakfast, shower, and get dressed. These are all indications that my body is slowly but surely running down, running out of gas.

The hospice volunteer, Edith, was scheduled for 10 a.m. today. Whenever somebody's scheduled to spend time here, I get nervous because I think I have to do a bunch of things to prepare for them. And I'm not used to people helping me with chores and stuff; that makes me anxious. I start thinking, *I don't wanna do this; it'll be be a lot of work and maybe I oughtta cancel her visit this week.* But I knew I needed her help because there were several things that I wanted to get done and I didn't have the energy to do them myself.

Edith mopped the kitchen and bathroom floors, cleaned the kitchen countertops, and vacuumed the apartment. She did a really good job; the place looks great. I helped as much as I could, but I spent most of the time working on my computer. I figured, *I'm the boss, and I'm just gonna hang out and delegate.* Ha!

Later I took my first walk of the day, which is usually about a one-mile circuit. I can still walk that far, but not without resting a couple-a three times. On my way home, a strange thing happened, which was kind of irritating. There's a guy who lives in the building. Our communication is horrible. He's originally from Russia, but he's been in the United States for about 50 years. In the time that he's been here, he has barely learned any English. I hate to say it and I don't mean to be judgmental, but that annoys me. If somebody has been in the U.S. for like five years and their English isn't perfect because they're still learning, that doesn't upset me. But 50 years is a long time to barely be able to communicate.

He's actually an interesting guy. When I first met him, he showed me newspaper clippings and photographs from when he was an Olympic gymnast on the Russian team as a young man. Apparently he had been quite good at his sport, and he was very proud of himself. It was extremely interesting, but having a conversation with him has always been really hard. He *wanted* to tell me about it, but we couldn't really talk!

After my surgery last year, I lost a lot of weight. My shoulders had always been strong and broad, but not anymore. Several months ago the Russian guy came up to me one day. He started patting my arms and shoulders, saying, "What happened? What happened?", indicating my muscles. He could see that something had happened to my strength. I replied that I would explain it if we could communicate. How do you explain cancer surgery using hand signals? I finally said, "Never mind," and walked away.

So today, we walked in the building at the same time and he got onto the elevator with me. I don't think he had seen me with my walker before. He looked at the walker and waved his hand past it with a look of disgust, as if to say, "What is *this*? You should be *strong*; what are you doing with *this* thing?" I just looked at him and shrugged my shoulders. There was no use trying to explain it to him because he wouldn't have understood. I figured that would be the end of it, but then he did something that *really* annoyed me.

He went to the corner of the elevator where the two rails come together, the rails to support yourself in the elevator. He put his hands on the rails, and did a series of about ten or twelve pushups on the rails, to show how strong and powerful he is. I just stared at him. I really wanted to punch him! I didn't need somebody showing me how strong they are and how they've taken great care of themselves. I felt really inadequate and hurt by his actions; I was really upset. That's a really rude, hurtful thing to do, making a deliberate show of your superior strength when somebody else is losing their strength. I'm not in this condition because I didn't take care of myself! It was a very, very difficult experience. When the elevator door opened, I just walked out and didn't say anything more to him.

Later this afternoon I ran into my next-door neighbor, Faye. She mentioned that she had heard a noise from my apartment during the night and she was concerned. What had actually happened was that I had just dropped something and it made a loud sound, so everything was fine. But she had been worried about me. Back in my apartment, I thought about that for a while and then I decided to go talk with her because I don't want her to be concerned and worried about me.

I knocked on Faye's door and asked her to come over so we could talk about my situation. I said, "You've been a wonderful neighbor for the past three years, and I thank you for that. But I want to clarify where I'm at right now in case you have any questions. I don't want you to worry about me. If I need help in the middle of the night, I have someone I can call." I explained that once you're in hospice, your life is going to end soon, and you no longer worry about certain things. If something happens to me and I pass away in the middle of the night, it's not something to be upset about. No one should think, "Oh, if I'd only done something, he'd still be alive!" I don't want people to have those kinds of feelings, like, if they had only done certain things, the situation could've been prevented. It *can't* be prevented. In fact, the sooner this all happens, the better it'll be for everybody concerned.

Faye and I ended up having a fabulous conversation, and she was very grateful. She said she learned a lot about hospice from speaking with me. Also, I think that what I said gave her permission to not worry about me. If anything happens, that's what's supposed to happen; no one should blame themselves. I believe it's important to be straightforward and tell people what's on your mind. Karen told me this evening that that's something she admires about me. If it's possible to be straightforward with people, that can clear the air with somebody and make things a lot easier.

The day was really balanced out – on the negative side with the Russian guy out-muscling me, and on the positive side with the nice conversation I had with Faye. Things are getting more difficult, but I just wanna thank God for another basically pain-free day and the ability to do the things I needed to do.

## DAY 91 – THURSDAY JUNE 20, 2013

Today was a miserable day, from the standpoint of frustration and anxiety and all the things that I try to avoid. The morning started out beautiful. I woke up feeling like I'd never been sick! It was a marvelous feeling. In fact, I felt like I *wasn't* sick at all. Then it started to sink in and I thought, *Wait a minute...* Ha! It was difficult to let the realization finally set in. So I got up and got dressed. I've been trying new alternatives for breakfast, because my usual oatmeal and berries have started upsetting my stomach a little bit. That's where my frustration started today: I don't really wanna change my breakfast.

After breakfast, I took a short walk and then worked on my blog. My John in Cyberspace blog had a lotta hits yesterday, almost 70 views. It always makes me feel good to know that people see my message of hope. I hope they enjoy the Bible verses and space photos. It gives me a real sense of purpose, which I love, and a way to be productive in the morning hours. I don't know how my day would start off if I didn't have that to look forward to.

After that, I thought that I had an appointment at noon with Karen and the hospice social worker, Rome. Obviously there was some confusion, because it got to be about 1:30 and they still weren't here. I could've picked up the phone, but I chose to just sit here and stew about it rather than calling to find out what was going on. In the meantime I called Multnomah County Aging, Disability and Veterans Services to set up an intake call to determine whether I can have any benefits through their agency. I finally called Karen, and then she and Rome arrived soon after that.

We discussed various scenarios of what might happen to me as my condition deteriorates, specifically when I can't quite take care of myself anymore. I could end up in a foster-care home where you have 24-7 assisted care. I said the same thing that I've said from the beginning, that I don't wanna leave this apartment. I like it here. This apartment has everything I need; it's set up for disabled people, with grabbars everywhere. It's very safe and I couldn't be in a better place, if I can find a little extra help. We all agreed that this is definitely the best place for me, and now it's just a matter of staffing it. What kind of help will I need, and when, and who will provide it? How much will that cost?

I got the sense that Rome will consider what I want in this situation, and that's very important to me. He's not gonna call the sheriff and tell them that I'm endangering myself, or anything like that. I've gotten rid of just about everything I own, so there's plenty of space in my apartment. If it became necessary, we could set up another twin bed in here for somebody to come and spend the night. But basically I found out that if I wanna spend the night by myself and I'm capable of doing it, even if it's a struggle, nobody's gonna prevent me from doing that. That was really what I wanted to hear. As far as what happens when I'm no longer capable, well, that's still absolutely terrifying.

I still remember the look on my mother's face, during the last three years of her life when she couldn't talk anymore after having a stroke. She lived in the home I shared with Catherine, and we managed the people who came in to care for her. I remember seeing actual terror in her eyes – not about her condition, but about what was gonna happen next. Who was going to come and take care of her? Who would handle this or that? Every once in a while I'd have to hire a new health-care worker. I would tell her about it in advance. She understood me but she couldn't speak; instead she would write little notes. When I told her that I had to hire somebody new, she'd have an absolute look of terror – she didn't have to say a word because I'd see it in her eyes. Who will this new person be? How will they treat me?

I'd always assure her that it was going to be alright. Catherine and I would monitor the situation very carefully to make sure the new person took good care of her. We would get references from past employers. But the look in her eyes didn't go away until she had proof, by being under that new person's care for a while and seeing how she was treated.

A couple of times I came home from work and I could tell from my mother's face that things hadn't gone well that day with a new aide. I didn't have to ask; her eyes said it all. She would look at me and then look over at the aide; I would always have the person there so I could see my mother's reaction. I would ask, "OK, what happened?" The aide might answer, "Well, we had a bad time with this, that or the other thing." If the aide lied, my mother would shake her head to say "no"; that was the determining factor as to what actually happened. The aide would always have to come clean.

I had to fire one person. We never did find out what happened; my mother was unable to tell us, and the woman swore up and down that nothing had happened. But I had no choice; I could tell from my mother's eyes that I wasn't getting the whole story. It made no difference whether my mother was right or wrong; I had to dismiss the person. When you can only rely on a person's eyes, it's amazing what you can see. You don't look at anyone's eyes that intently unless you're relying on them for the truth.

Those thoughts have been going through my head ever since the discussion this afternoon. What's it like to be unable to do anything or to speak, if someone is doing something you're unhappy with? What was it like for my mother? I never thought I'd find myself in that situation. I'm not *in* that situation right now, but it's a possibility as my brain deteriorates.

Later in the afternoon I received a phone call from the intake person at Aging, Disability and Veterans Services. They start with an intake call, then send someone out to evaluate the situation and determine the type and cost of care that can be provided. My intake call was a nightmare because the person was reading off a list of requirements and she had no clue as to what I was talking about. I told her, "I can't give you a 60-day outline of what I'm going to need. It's impossible for me to predict that." But she kept demanding, "We have to know what you're gonna need for the first 30 days and the next 60 days and so on." I replied, "I can't do that. I have a brain condition. I could have an aneurysm tonight, and I would never need to call you again." We kept going back and forth over the same scenario. I finally asked, "Are you going to order an intake visit for me or not? This conversation is driving me crazy; it's like a broken record and I can't take it anymore." She said, "I'm *going* to order the intake right now", and that was the end of the conversation.

I think about the hundreds of thousands of people who are facing the prospect of finding the care they need and being afraid. Nobody wants to go through that – wondering who will take care of you and how they're gonna treat you. It's a terrifying thing. I didn't want the radiation treatments that I received for this cancer. I asked my oncologist and radiologist whether it was possible for me to skip that treatment. I was told, "No, no, this is an insurance policy. We need to do this, to improve your chances by… some percentage." Well, thirty days of radiation treatment cost the government eighty-nine thousand dollars. I have to say that I would *much* rather have had that $89,000 to take care of myself for thirty days *now*, than to have had that radiation treatment. I would take that trade any day! *Any* day. If I'd been given that option. Our healthcare system is broken; it can't just go on like this forever.

One last thing happened today. I called my old friend Gene. When he called me several weeks ago, he had sounded really anxious to come and visit me. He lives about a hundred and fifty miles away, and he has his own health problems, so I had said that a visit wasn't necessary. He insisted that it was important and he'd come visit within two weeks, but several weeks went by and I didn't hear any more from him. So I decided to call him on the telephone.

Again he talked about coming to visit, but I said it wasn't worth it for him to drive that far just to spend two hours together; we could just keep in touch on the phone. Then he said that a couple weeks ago, his tongue got really swollen. It sounded like he'd had an extreme allergic reaction. Just like that, he jumped from my situation to his swollen tongue. He could've asked, "So how are you doing?" Or, "Since I'm not coming to visit, what's going on?" Really, *any* kind of a question about my situation. But he just wanted me to be sympathetic about the swollen tongue! Which I *was*; I asked questions and said I hoped it was just a one-time thing.

I'm just stunned when this kind of thing happens. I'm not judging anyone for their actions, like the guy who abruptly turned away from me and slammed his door when I told him I was terminally ill. But it *is* stunning to me. If somebody told *me* they were terminally ill, I would wanna be somewhat sympathetic and find out a little more about it, and have the courtesy of showing the person that I care. It's just that simple courtesy. For Gene to just blow it off and say "Well, I'll give you a call sometime," was stunning to me.

But I know what it is: deep down inside, people don't wanna hear it and don't wanna know about it. It's a reminder of their own mortality. People can be so concerned about their own situation and what *might* happen to them*selves*. Many are very uncomfortable around people who are disabled or terminally ill. They wanna stick their heads in the sand and say, "I don't want that to happen to me, and I don't wanna be around anybody who's in that situation."

Overall it was a dreadful day and I'm happy to let it sink beneath the waves. But I *do* wanna thank God for another day, and for the opportunity to start the process of making a plan for my final days or weeks; I'm thankful for that.

# 31
# NO ROADMAP FOR WHAT LIES AHEAD

**DAY 92 – FRIDAY JUNE 21, 2013**

Today was just a hectic mess, and I have got to make an effort to stop talking to too many people on the same day. I've also got to stay focused on planning for my care once I'm incapacitated. I need to just get a plan in place for that timeframe, and be done with all these conversations with caregivers and people from the county and my social worker and my son and everybody else. The situation is what it is and it'll all be over soon, so never mind all the drama that goes along with it.

Today it all started with a call from my son. He sounded very alarmed and upset because every day I say to him, "I'm not feeling any better today; I feel worse." He's worried about how I'm doing and what kind of care I'm receiving, while he's 3000 miles away. So we've been considering having him come out and stay here for a while to help me, but he has a business to run and a family in Georgia. He *could* deal with work from a distance. But then there's the question of when he should come out, and whether he should stay for the duration until I'm gone, or visit more than once.

That phone call sent me on a downward spiral. I started thinking that maybe I'd be eligible for more in-home care if I wasn't in hospice. I could do that until things get much worse. Then Allen wouldn't have to worry so much. My son picked up on that idea and said, "Well yeah, maybe you *should* get out of the hospice program! You should talk to somebody about that." I told him I'd make some calls and sort it out and we'd talk later. From there, I got totally off-track because I forgot about what *hospice* is. That was totally my fault.

I initiated a round of telephone calls. I called the hospice social worker and said that I was thinking about getting out of the program because I figured I would have more benefits and a higher level of care with my old health insurance. Rome disagreed with me, so I said I'd call him back later. Next I called my doctor's office but he was busy so I spoke with his nurse. Then another call to my son.

Somewhere along the line, I finally woke up to what was actually happening. I had started worrying about being taken care of long-term. Outside of hospice, maybe I'd be eligible for life support and all of that if something happened to me. People wouldn't have to worry so much because I'd be taken care of. But I don't *want* life support; that's the whole point of having an Advance Directive! If I become unconscious, I do not want to be kept alive through a feeding tube. I'm terminally ill, and when it's my time, I will die. Just thinking about what hospice really is, I realized it would be stupid to back out, because I've already stated my wishes and that kind of advanced care is not gonna happen! Once I realized that, I thought, *I don't need to be wasting my time having all of these conversations.* All I did was cause myself an enormous amount of confusion, along with all the other people that I got involved in it.

I want my life to end peacefully and with dignity. My mother had three or four strokes, and she would've died each time had they not put her on a life support system, with IVs and all sorts of things to keep her going until her condition stabilized. A hundred years ago if someone had a stroke, they either died or they didn't, but they didn't have IVs and feeding tubes. In my case, I don't want to be brought back from a stroke or anything else, only to die later anyway from the cancer.

So I called everybody back and explained that I had just gotten completely off-track. It was extremely frustrating and I must not get myself into that box ever again: calling all those people and asking questions and trying to make sense of it all, and then calling them all back and saying, "Never mind."

I lost a whole day of enjoying the nice weather and possibly having some quality conversations with friends. I lost many hours of my precious time, trying to figure out how to avoid scenarios that will never happen. It was awful. But I *am* thankful for the day. I had an opportunity to learn something, and perhaps the days that I have left will be more peaceful.

## DAY 93 – SATURDAY JUNE 22, 2013

When I woke up this morning, I felt well-rested but I had some pain as well, in my stomach and up to my shoulder. Based on that, I didn't expect to have a very good day. Frank was supposed to come over at noon but I called him to cancel. I realized that I needed a day off from the stress and strain of people calling and visiting; maybe a day off could help me to rebound a bit. I didn't like cancelling on Frank since it gives me a good feeling to interact with people every day. It was very beautiful outside so after breakfast I went for a walk. That usually helps reduce anxiety and stomach pain.

I headed down 12th Avenue to Burnside, but when I turned around to come back, I didn't have any energy. So I sat on my nifty little Johnnie Walker-chair in the sunshine and watched the people go by. I felt kind of sad. It was a lovely Saturday morning in downtown Portland, with people going in and out of coffee shops, heading to the zoo or wherever. Folks looked happy – families and couples, enjoying a beautiful day. Meanwhile I'm sitting there in my walker, knowing that I'm dying. My days of going for long walks or the zoo or anything like that are over.

Today's the first day of summer. When I started this journey, I thought I didn't wanna die in the summertime. I know it sounds ridiculous, but now I think I would *rather* die in the summer because I can get outdoors. For whatever days I have left, I can enjoy the sunshine. It's been ninety-something days since I decided not to do chemo or any further radiation, and I've enjoyed the weather on most of those days. I couldn't have done that in the winter; I would've been trapped indoors for the last few months of my life.

In the afternoon, I *started* to go to the store. About halfway there, I realized I didn't have the energy so I headed back home to rest instead. That felt like another big setback. It's been a day of diminished returns: everything seems more difficult, from walking to working on my blog, and my stomach was upset so most of the day I didn't feel like eating. I'm going to talk to the nutritionist on Monday, to figure out what I can eat that'll be easy to digest. I don't really care about nutrition so much anymore; I need to eat foods that are easy to digest so I'll be comfortable. Nutrition is out, comfort is in. I may have to start eating baby food!

It was a hard day, having so little energy and seeing all those other people enjoying the day. But I'm also thankful for the things I did accomplish, and for the opportunity to do my best for another day.

## DAY 94 – SUNDAY JUNE 23, 2013

There's always that moment, first thing in the morning when I have no pain and I've had a very sound sleep, and I wake up thinking, *Do I feel better or worse?* At that moment, I don't know yet; all I know is that I've been sleeping comfortably. Then I get outta bed and start moving around. Today it only took me about 30 seconds to realize that I felt worse. That was a major setback. Until now, after taking a day off from visits and phone calls, and cutting back on my walking, I'd bounce back a bit the next day. But not this morning. It's depressing. Summer has arrived and I'd love to get out and enjoy it!

I decided to stick to a liquid diet today to see if that would calm my stomach down somewhat. Is it food or anxiety that's causing the most trouble? If it's food, I can alter my diet. If it's anxiety, it doesn't make any difference *what* I eat. By the end of the day, my stomach actually did feel a little better by sticking to liquids.

Either way, I believe my liver is enlarging because of the cancer. It's pushing against other organs, and that also makes my stomach uncomfortable. Meanwhile I believe I have cancer in my brain as well. It's not causing pain but I can tell that it's getting worse. So the race is on, to take my life. Who's gonna win, my liver or my brain?

I picked up a new anti-anxiety medication at the drugstore today. The pharmacist warned me about becoming addicted to it; he was adamant about that. He said that I'd have serious side effects if I just stop taking it for any reason. I got a good laugh. He was just doing his job and I didn't say anything about it, but I'm really not worried about addiction at this point!

I saw Emma this afternoon. I almost cancelled her visit because I felt so tired. But she came over and we had a really nice conversation. She's going through a lot right now in her personal life, and I tried to console her. It's getting harder to do that because I'm so focused on my own problems, but I do wanna continue to help people with their personal lives until the last day of my life, if I can. You can't *not* be concerned about the people you love; it's part of living. That concern causes a lot of anxiety when your life is ending. When my father was dying of pneumonia, I saw the anxiety in his face. He was afraid of what would happen to his wife; he was deeply concerned about her.

I'm appreciative for this day, and I thank God even though it was difficult.

## DAY 95 – MONDAY JUNE 24, 2013

I feel that I've lost even more of my mobility and the capabilities that I had yesterday. It's difficult, recognizing what's happening. I went for a walk this morning, but all I could do was four blocks. I went to the store, but I just got a coffee and then came back. I didn't have the energy to do any shopping.

### *Blessing #29*

*Pastor Phillip came by today. We did a lot of reminiscing about the days when I used to attend his church; we had a wonderful, heartwarming conversation. We prayed together before he left. He was here for almost two hours. I'm extremely blessed to have him as a friend, someone that I can count on. Having people like that in my life at such a time is an amazing thing.*

## DAY 96 – TUESDAY JUNE 25, 2013

When I woke up this morning, it seemed like a fairly promising day. I had slept well; I felt good and had more energy than yesterday.

After breakfast I worked on my blog. I struggled with figuring out which characters I was typing, and getting the words in the right order.

Then Allen called me. Once again he wanted to review the procedure in case something happens to me: what will hospice do and what *won't* they do. We've been over it multiple times now. I get weary and frustrated trying to deal with the details of events that we don't know anything about yet. Hospice care includes helping me with pain and discomfort, and *maybe* taking me someplace else if absolutely necessary for my last few days on this earth. It's difficult to try repeatedly to figure out and explain how it'll work, because we don't yet know what'll happen. All we know is that I've got cancer in my liver and probably my brain, and maybe in other areas.

My doctor told me that most cancer patients don't die from the cancer itself but from some side effect like pneumonia, an infection, a stroke, a seizure, or an aneurysm. Nobody knows what it'll be. Basically you go to sleep at night, and if you wake up in the morning, you have another day. If you don't wake up, your life has ended. I was reminded of the little childhood prayer: "Now I lay me down to sleep, I pray the Lord my soul to keep. If I die before I wake, I pray the Lord my soul to take." When I was a kid, I would get down by the side of my bed at night and say that little prayer. Suddenly it seems very appropriate again.

Later I had another intake phone call with someone from Multnomah County Aging, Disability and Veterans Services. It went just like the call last week. They asked me to predict how much help I'm gonna need in the near future. On a sliding-scale basis, I can pay to have someone help clean the apartment, provide aid with bathing, and help with other simple chores. They want to know how many hours I'll require, and what I can afford to pay. I asked, 'How can I possibly begin to venture a guess at how much help I'm going to need?" She asked, "How much did you require *last* month?" I didn't require *any* aid last month. It just went back and forth like that. At any rate, she'll come by in a couple days to do a more thorough intake, and my social worker will be here too to help with that.

My hospice nurse arrived around two o'clock. We reviewed all the scenarios again, regarding what I should do if I'm in pain: whom to call, what can be done, which meds I can take. It's really, really exhausting to go over these things again and again.

Then Janine called and wanted to have a really long conversation. I need to remember that it's OK for me to say, "I can't talk any more; that's enough for today." But it's hard to do. Later I tackled a couple loads of laundry. I really ended up doing too much today, and now I'm just frazzled. It was all I could do to get through the day.

I did get one really good piece of news today; it came in the mail. An express loan certificate from One Main Financial. I was really excited because it said, "Use this certificate to get four thousand dollars *today*. You're pre-approved; all you need to do is apply." It also says that I wouldn't have to make any payments for three months. Ha! These guys are not playing it too smart. I want to call them and say, "You really oughtta screen your applicants a little bit better! Maybe request a note from a doctor before handing out four thousand dollars in cash; make sure the applicant is gonna live long enough to pay it back."

## DAY 97 – WEDNESDAY JUNE 26, 2013

This morning I felt the residual effects of overdoing everything yesterday. And I didn't feel like having breakfast, which is very unusual for me. I did eat, but right away I started having a lot of pain in my stomach. At some point I experienced this unbelievable wave of neurological mumbo-jumbo spreading through my head. My body felt really heavy and felt as though it was inflating. It's stunning how quickly a strange feeling like that can engulf you. I really didn't have a clue what was going on; I suddenly wanted to get off my feet as quickly as possible because everything was going haywire.

The hospice nurses know what'll happen as a result of the cancer in my liver; they've seen the effects of liver cancer many times. But with the brain, there's no roadmap. We don't know which part of my brain is affected so we can't predict what might happen. One time recently I saw a green blob for a day, but only with one of my eyes. It's unpredictable. Sometimes I feel like I'm in a dream even though I'm awake. This time I felt like my body was being filled up with hydrogen gas, and my head was going to explode. It's really hard to explain the sensation! So I just went back to bed; I couldn't deal with it.

After an hour I decided to go outside to see if I could take a walk. I hadn't been out since Monday, and I felt like a caged tiger. When I lived in San Diego, I would sometimes go to the zoo. I'd look at the beautiful animals and think, *This is a tragedy, putting these magnificent creatures in a compound where all they can do is pace around.* If you watch those big cats, that's all they do: pace and pace and pace. And here I was pacing around my apartment this morning, feeling like I didn't have the confidence to go outside. I stopped liking zoos because it seems so unfair for a beautiful, powerful animal like that to be trapped. When I don't have the energy to go outside, I feel trapped too. But I finally went out and walked two blocks. I had to stop several times to rest, but I went out.

## 32
## FEAR, FRIENDS, FATIGUE, FAITH

**DAY 98 – THURSDAY JUNE 27, 2013**

I'm having more and more trouble navigating and my head has been doing really strange things. This morning I had – I'll call it another episode. A strange feeling came over me like a wave. It wasn't quite dizziness. I had to blink my eyes repeatedly in order to focus. I'm usually standing up or walking around when it happens, and I have to reach out and grab something to steady myself. These episodes are getting more intense and they're happening more frequently, sometimes twice a day. They last for a few minutes. It's really upsetting because I don't know what it is or what will happen next. I usually have to go sit down.

This afternoon I had an appointment with Rome and Karen and a representative from Multnomah County Aging, Disability and Veterans Services. A lot of questions were asked, including whether I'd be willing – if necessary – to go to an adult foster care home if I became unable to care for myself. The County wouldn't be able to provide 24-hour care here in my apartment so I'd have to have someplace else to go. That would most likely be for the last few days of my life; that's where my life would end. The whole conversation was cordial and friendly but it was also upsetting: more discussion of when that might happen, even though we can't predict anything. Only the Lord knows when my time is gonna come, and he isn't going to let me know.

**DAY 99 – FRIDAY JUNE 28, 2013**

Last night I didn't have the nice restful sleep that I normally have. I was very distressed about everything we discussed yesterday, especially the thought of being taken out of my home and going to a foster facility. My freedom would be gone at that point. I know that I wouldn't be going there unless I was absolutely ready and *wanted* to go, but the idea is looming on the horizon and last night I couldn't shut it out of my mind. So it was difficult to sleep, and this morning I'm still anxious about it.

I know I'm going to die, and my faith in Jesus will carry me through that. But my faith doesn't reassure me about the actual process of dying. It's stressful to lose a little more of my abilities each day. I had a couple of really serious episodes today where I couldn't coordinate my body with my head; twice I had to just sit down and wait for the confusion to pass. It's frightening to think about where I'm headed.

Frank helped me with something today. Most people only have a few really good friends in life. I've known Frank for over twenty years, and I don't think I've ever called him with a problem, where he didn't respond and try to help immediately. He has *always* been there when things are really important. I have an air-conditioning unit, and temperatures are supposed to be up in the 90's for the next few days. It used to be a 15-minute job for me to get that AC set up, but today I realized I could no longer lift it. I called Frank and asked if he'd have time today or tomorrow to help me with it, and he insisted on coming over right away. He got it taken care of in a matter of minutes. It was a tremendous relief to be able to count on him. Not only is Frank a great friend; he's very competent, honest and punctual. I'm incredibly lucky to have him as a friend. It's important, going through life, to spend enough time on your closest friendships so that you can always be there for them and they can always be there for you; it's an incredible treasure to have people like that in your life.

## DAY 100 – SATURDAY JUNE 29, 2013

It's the hundredth day of my journey. That certainly sounds like a milestone! I awoke feeling really good this morning, which was great because the past week really wound me down. Not long after I got up, though, I started to feel pretty weak.

Today my friend Larry called, whom I still haven't told about the cancer. I hesitated to answer, but Larry has called me twice recently and I figured I couldn't avoid his call a third time. We always talk about the Washington State Cougars and the Oregon Ducks. But today I figured I had to tell him about my situation or else I'd be deceiving him in a way. I don't know how many more times I'll have to start that conversation but it's not getting any easier. He called me expecting to have a fun conversation about college football teams, and I had to stop him. "Larry, I need to let you know that my cancer has returned, and it's untreatable." There was a huge pause. I thought, *What do I say next? Offer more details? I don't know!*

He finally said, "That's too bad, I'm really sorry to hear it." I started to explain a little more but I could tell pretty quickly that he didn't want details. OK, I guess I didn't need to go into it. Then he dropped the whole subject and launched back into our usual topics: sports, football, and so on. He just picked up where we had left off, and the whole cancer thing drifted off into the sunset. I was OK with that until he started projecting about how the coming fall season might go. With that subject, I started to feel really agitated. It's shattering to realize that I won't see the Ducks this fall, which I've always looked forward to every year. It feels awful to be excluded from that conversation!

That has happened to me over and over and over again, because people don't have a clue as to what to talk about with a terminally ill person. Most people are rarely in that situation. They might speak with someone who has a heart condition or diabetes or a broken leg, but they figure that person has some time left, so there's no problem with discussing something they'll both experience in the future. But cancer is a death sentence, at a certain stage. It doesn't make sense to discuss the future with someone who's dying of cancer, especially any subject that the person is passionate about, because then they feel left out.

I ended the call with Larry by saying, "Hey, keep in touch, alright? We'll check out the football season as it comes along." I absolutely don't believe I'll see any of it, but that was the only way I could end it. The living go on, and people who are dying come to an abrupt end. There was nothing else to talk about.

What *does* a terminally ill person wanna talk about? What do they wanna say or hear? I think that if someone tells you they're terminally ill, first they wanna know that you care and you're sorry to hear it. Then ask, "Is there anything I can do for you, to make it easier?" Just those two things can set the right tone. *Don't* start projecting into the future. The exception would be if a friend calls, who has the same faith as I do, and we start talking about a future based in that faith. That's entirely different because it's a future that we both believe in, where we'll be transformed into something else. Last, keep the call short. It's important to call often to show you care, but it doesn't have to be a long conversation.

## DAY 101 – SUNDAY JUNE 30, 2013

The days are getting more difficult. I don't have the same anticipation every morning that I had a few weeks ago. And the list of things to accomplish in my remaining time is getting shorter and shorter. So it's getting more difficult to get out of bed and start the day. I've had a lot of stomach discomfort this week, which also gets in the way of doing anything productive.

Today I didn't have enough energy to get to church. I worked on my blog instead. In the book of John, Jesus specifically says, over and over again, who he is and why he's here. That's the core of my faith. I feel that that book is the clearest and most encouraging book in the entire Bible. So I have fun working on the blog, and it gives me a tremendous sense of accomplishment. I hope that people who read it are encouraged and that it gives them faith and hope, especially if they're in similar circumstances.

As a Christian, *my* view is that people either believe in Jesus as their savior or they don't; there's no in-between. Faith in Jesus is either the most incredible thing that could happen to a person, or it means absolutely nothing; it's one or the other. What Jesus is *not*, is "moderately important". He's either the *most* important person that ever walked on this earth, or he's totally unimportant, but he's not somewhere in the middle. I realize that plenty of people disagree with me, but when someone says that Jesus was just a great teacher or whatever, to *me*, that misses the whole point. In the book of John, Jesus says that he came from the father, he's part of the trinity, and he's going back to the father. He says it a dozen times in different ways. So for me, that's why that's the most important book right now, as my life ends. Through my faith in Jesus, I will be with God after I die, and nothing could be more reassuring.

But today was difficult. Every day my energy level drops a little bit, and it seems that I give up some more of my life. The feeling of well-being that I usually wake up with doesn't last long. At first I feel like I'm gonna have a spectacular day, but all of a sudden I'm running outta juice. Years ago I used to get up at six o'clock in the morning, and go until 11 at night!

Today Karen took me out to do some errands and then we sat in the sunshine at a nice park. I noticed that it's really difficult for me to observe people walking by who, I believe, don't take good care of their bodies. Everyone has the free will and ability to manage their life any way they want to. But some people seem to abuse what they were given and they truly roll the dice with their own health, with cigarettes or drugs or drinking too much alcohol. If I feel hurt or jealous, or feel like my situation is unfair, it's when I see people who haven't made the healthiest choices yet they seem to be doing fine. Sometimes

I think, *Why me? I took good care of myself, eating the right foods and exercising, and all those things are supposed to help!* But none of that helps with cancer. Five-year-olds can get cancer. You can be any age and take great care of yourself and get a terrible tumor. It's not your fault, but it shows up to end your life. That's sad, and it really bothers me.

33

# SEEKING AND ACCEPTING HELP

**DAY 102 – MONDAY JULY 1, 2013**

*T*oday was a mixed bag. I woke up earlier than usual, probably because the sun was shining so brightly outside. I had a little bit of something to eat, and decided to tackle my first project of the day, my blog. I found a really nice photograph of Saturn for my blog post, and I got that done in less than an hour – that's really fast for me! I also went through all of my financial stuff for the first of the month, which I didn't think I'd be able to do any more by this point.

By late morning, I was experiencing some pain on my right side, just under my ribcage. Up to this point I've been reluctant to think much about pain, but the pain in my side has been getting more and more persistent. It's becoming the really big gorilla in the room that I haven't wanted to think about. But I know it's not going away. It's cancer pain, not gas or a pulled muscle. I'd certainly like to imagine that it's something else.

In the past I never worried too much about pain. If I had an injury or something, I worked my way through it and took very few pain pills, maybe just an aspirin once in a while. Any time a doctor sent me home with heavy-duty pain medication, like Vicodin or other major pain pills, I wouldn't take them. Those types of meds scared me so I just stuck with aspirin or ibuprofen. Today I got out my heating pad and cranked it up to full bore, and I lay on it for half an hour. The pain subsided. Since that helped, I believe I've got a little more time before I have to get involved in pain drugs. I'm really relieved about that. But I'm sure that worse pain is coming.

I went out for coffee twice today, and both times I noticed a group of young people. They would commonly be known as "panhandlers" in Portland, a term I don't like because it's *not* complimentary. But if you're sitting around on the sidewalk begging for money, that's what you are! There's no politically-correct word for *sitting on the sidewalk and begging*, especially when you're like 20 years old.

I watched them for a while, and I couldn't help feeling really sad. They've chosen to lose the best part of their lives, sitting there staring at the sidewalk and begging for money. I wanted to walk over and offer them another perspective. I felt like saying, "If you were to find yourself in *my* shoes, you would really take a long, hard look at what you're doing right now because it's a real tragedy." It's one thing to walk by someone like that and say, "Sorry, I don't have any money for you." It's another thing entirely to sit there and watch 'em, when you're dying, seeing *their* lives evaporating before your eyes! Tragic.

## DAY 103 – TUESDAY JULY 2, 2013

Today was very difficult. I didn't sleep well last night because it was too hot in the room. Plus I overdid it yesterday: I had too many things on my plate, got all fired up to get things done, worked hard, and wore myself down. But I'm not going to beat up on myself about it. When I have energy, I have to use it to the best of my ability. If I'm wiped out the next day, so be it. I can't mete out my energy and say, "I'm only gonna use this much of it today and save this much for tomorrow," because I don't know how many tomorrows I have! I have to do what I can when I can. But then I have to pay the price, too, and wake up really tired, feeling like I'm not ready for the day.

This morning I looked at Yahoo news, and there was this horrible story about Pierce Brosnan losing his 41-year-old daughter to ovarian cancer. Not only that, his first wife died of ovarian cancer years earlier! I like Pierce Brosnan; I've seen him in a number of movies. My heart just went out to him; I can't imagine how anybody could endure losing two family members to cancer. It's one thing for *me* to die, at my age. It's another thing for a 41-year-old woman to die. So that story just set my day off on a very bad note. I felt devastated even though I certainly don't know Pierce Brosnan personally.

The day went downhill from there. I went to the store and got my morning coffee, which I drank outside on the sidewalk in the shade. After that, I didn't have enough energy to go back in the store to get anything. I started walking home, and I had to stop after about half a block. I couldn't go any further. Half a block! Two weeks ago I could walk 13 blocks. That was a devastating setback. Setbacks are difficult to take, even though I know where I'm ultimately headed. It's human nature to want to feel *better* every day.

Frank came over for lunch today. I have a chair in my apartment, a leather recliner, which I call my guest chair. Any time somebody comes to visit, I offer them the guest chair and I sit on my office chair. But when Frank arrived, I said, "I'm keeping the guest chair today." It's the first time I've ever done that. That's a huge change for me! It doesn't sound like much but it is. When Frank left, he shook my hand and said, "I'm really proud of you. You are really fighting this thing." That made me feel good.

## DAY 104 – WEDNESDAY JULY 3, 2013

I was very relieved this morning when I woke up feeling considerably better than yesterday. I started looking at what I had planned for the day, meaning my very limited agenda. Ha! Most people set up a big, long to-do list. I've got maybe three things on mine, and that looks overwhelming and daunting. But it turned out to be an excellent day.

**Blessing #30**

> *The weather was absolutely delightful. The temperature had gone down about ten degrees from yesterday. I think that gave me a fresh burst of energy that I hadn't felt for days. I went outside and I was able to walk upright, just pushing my walker along with one finger instead of leaning on it. I was just kinda cruisin' along and it felt amazing. I ordered my coffee at the Starbucks inside the grocery store, and found a spot to sit outside under a tree, and it was the most fabulous half hour that I've had in weeks. Everything just came together: no pain, a beautiful sun-shiny day, a really nice, hot cup of coffee, and a beautiful view. I thought,* Wow, you struggle along day after day, and just one day like this makes a huge difference, makes it all seem worthwhile. *For that 30 minutes, I was really happy to be alive.*

My hospice volunteer, Edith, was here today. We worked together for about two hours, mostly on laundry. I was pretty much the taskmaster-type person, pushing hard to get the work done. Well, what I *really* mean is that I didn't accomplish all that much; she did most of the work. She was really, really helpful. It obviously takes a special kind of person to go into the home of someone who's dying, and help them with their chores. Her visits are really a joy. It's not just that the work she does really helps me; it's nice to have the companionship for a couple hours a week.

I've never been comfortable accepting help from people; accepting help has always bothered me. It's pretty late in my life to suddenly decide that it's actually kinda nice to have people take the time and help out. It's a new thing and it feels good, because this is something that Edith wants to do. She volunteered for it, right? I say that that makes her a hero.

This afternoon I went out for another cup of coffee, and ran into a most objectionable person. I know the guy but I've never considered him a friend. I wanted to sit under the shade tree and enjoy my coffee and watch the world go by. All of a sudden this guy rolls up on his scooter, and starts in on me about bed bugs: how obnoxious they are, and how he's gonna sue the building, and he's gonna sue *this* guy and he's gonna sue *that* guy. Some people are very opinionated and they have this attitude, a chip on their shoulder. I felt bad about his situation but I didn't wanna deal with him. I said, "Well I hope you get that bed bug thing resolved." Then he launched into another half dozen problems that all involved lawsuits and this, that and the other thing. I finally said, "I hope you're able to work all that stuff out. I'll pray for you, but I gotta go now."

I literally had to leave. I took the rest of my coffee and went back inside the store to finish it. I'd help the guy if I could, but he's not gonna listen to me! People like that don't care what anybody else has to say; they just wanna *complain*. I wanted to tell him, "I appreciate what you're saying, but I only have a couple months to live and I can't spend any more time on this."

## DAY 105 – THURSDAY JULY 4, 2013

When I woke up this morning, I was excited because it's the Fourth of July! The Fourth of July is one of my favorite holidays; I love everything about it. Since childhood I enjoyed the fireworks and the picnics and the parades. It's the birthday of our nation, and I have an extremely high regard for the United States and our history. The people who signed the Declaration of Independence were signing their executions if they failed, and to me, that's pretty heroic. I know this country has a lot of faults but we've also done a lot of good around the world.

---

## A LAST TIME FOR EVERYTHING

*I've had some great Fourths of July over the years, and I was looking forward to one last Fourth, which I was going to spend with Karen. At the same time it was kinda sad because it's another one of those 'lasts' that I talk about. Karen and I made a drive out to Mount Hood, up to Timberline Lodge. We walked a little ways along a trail, but I got tired out really fast. Then we sat in the car for a while just looking up toward the summit, and I reminisced a bit about the times that I've hiked up there. It was an absolutely beautiful day, which the Fourth of July usually is. I enjoyed being on Mt. Hood but it was bittersweet. I have so many wonderful memories of it but I'm not gonna be able to go back there again.*

---

## DAY 106 – FRIDAY JULY 5, 2013

I was very, very tired when I woke up this morning. Really tired from the trip yesterday. It didn't seem like it should be that big of a deal, but the long drive plus getting out on a trail for a quarter-mile *was* a big deal. I was reminded of why I loved hiking so much. Hiking works a lot more muscles than when you're just walking down the street; it's much more strenuous. But I don't have the energy to hike anymore. It took a huge toll on me and I felt it this morning. Then again, I also felt very relaxed after working all those different muscles, and because I so enjoyed being out there; that counteracted my tiredness.

Today was the day for the culmination of the water heater battle, which has been going on for over five months. Back in March when I spoke to the building manager, I was told, "Well, we'll have to try different things and look at different solutions." I pointed out that the solution was obvious: a larger water heater. Instead they raised the temperature of my current water heater by ten degrees. The water was hotter, but that didn't increase the amount of water. I asked about it a few weeks later and the building manager said, "We'll let you know." After another month, I was told that if I got a doctor's authorization, management would be able to look at it from a different viewpoint. In the meantime I've been heating up extra water myself in pots on the stove. I know it sounds ridiculous, but every night I carry these two-gallon pots of boiling water from the kitchen to the bathroom and dump them in the tub. My hospice nurse, Susan, was alarmed when I told her about that. She worries that I could burn myself, which is definitely a valid concern! She requested a note from my doctor, who issued a letter stating that I need 15 gallons of hot water for my daily bath – so *do* something about it.

Building management is required to make reasonable accommodations for residents with health issues. For example, people can request grab bars. Or they can request that the carpet be taken out if they have severe allergies. They just need doctors' orders. Susan took care of that several weeks ago, but no one told *me* that I still had to fill out some more paperwork. I finally went down to the office to ask if anything was going to happen soon, and I was told that not all the paperwork had been filled out yet. I just said, "Oh, no," and walked out; I was so tired of it all. I figured I had my own solution so forget about getting any outside help!

The next time Susan was here, she asked me, "How's the hot water situation going?" I told her about the extra paperwork that I just didn't have the energy to fill out. She said not to worry; she'd take care of it. She marched down to the office, got the form, filled the whole thing out meticulously, had me sign it, and brought it back down there. Then she kept bugging them every day until they took action.

Last Friday they finally told me that a plumber would be here *today* to install a brand-new water heater, a larger one that isn't energy-efficient. At last, I won. The big day finally came. He arrived this morning and told me he had set aside the entire day for this project. He had no idea how long it would take because he had never replaced a water heater before. That seemed odd since he was a plumber. So I was worried and anxious, but five hours later, he was done. It was installed.

A couple hours after that, it was time to test it. How much hot water would it produce? With the previous heater, I had used a tape measure and found that it produced three and a half inches of hot water in the tub. With the new one today, when it got to three and a half inches, the water was still running really hot. It got to four inches, then five inches. When it finally started to cool down, it was six and a half inches of water, which is *double* what I had before. I really had won the battle! And cleaned a lot of gunk out of the system; there was a lot of dirt in the tub. But now I *have* enough hot water. It was a tremendous feeling of victory, after that five-and-a-half month battle to get a decent bath. Thank God!

## SECTION 6: TO DIE IN THE SUMMERTIME

Today I've been thinking about life choices some more. We start very young, making choices: who our friends will be, how we're gonna treat people. Some of our choices have profound effects on our lives, while of course most of them are just day-to-day decisions like what to wear or what to eat. This past week I think I made my final big choice.

34

# MEMORIES: ONE JOY THAT CANCER HASN'T STOLEN

**DAY 107 – SATURDAY JULY 6, 2013**

---

### A LAST TIME FOR EVERYTHING

*When I woke up this morning, I felt pretty anxious and it took me a little while to figure out why: it was my son's birthday. I was distressed because this was the last time I'd be around for his birthday. The day my son was born was probably the most amazing day of my life. Recognizing that today was the last time I'd have a birthday with him was really hard for me.*

---

On July 4th the year Allen was born, I hoped all day long that he'd be born that day. He was due any day so I figured he *could've* been born on the 4th, which, as I've said, is one of my favorite holidays. At the time, I thought that would've been amazing.

Ellen and I lived in Playa del Rey, which is six miles south of Santa

Monica. Allen's birth was planned for the Santa Monica hospital, so our holiday plans weren't far from home, just in case. From breakfast time on, I kept asking Ellen, "How do you feel? Are you OK? Do we need to go to the hospital?" She'd say, "No, leave me alone, I don't need to go to the hospital."

An hour later I'd ask her again. "Are you having any labor pains? Should I get the car ready?" She'd say, "No, leave me alone! I'm *not* going to have a baby right now." All day long I was thinking, *Oh no, time is running out here; we've only got until midnight!*

In the afternoon we had a barbecue with some of our neighbors. You could see the ocean from our apartment building, and there was a big park right out front, so it was a great place to hang out with people. I kept bothering my wife all day long. In the afternoon I asked her, "Should you really be eating or drinking that? What if we have to go to the hospital?" It got to the point where she couldn't stand to be around me because I kept pestering her.

We had planned to go to the fireworks at Santa Monica Pier, but I asked Ellen, "Should we even go to the fireworks? There'll be a big crowd down there, jam-packed with all kinds of people. What would happen if we needed to go to the hospital?" She replied, "We're *not going* to the hospital; stop talking about it. I haven't had *any* indication that the baby is coming."

As we got ready to head to the fireworks, I said, "Maybe we should put your suitcase in the car. It'd be crazy to come all the way home and then back to Santa Monica if we need to go to the hospital. Let's put the suitcase in the trunk just in case, since it's already packed." She agreed to bringing the suitcase since I insisted on it, but she reassured me that we wouldn't need it that night. I said, "You never know; labor pains can start any time!" I thought, *Uh-oh, by the time we get there, it'll be almost nine p.m.; only three hours left of the 4th of July!*

The fireworks started at sunset. It was incredibly beautiful watching them from the beach. Also I knew we were only a mile or two from the hospital, so we'd be able to get there in a hurry if we needed to. It was absolutely perfect – and I was absolutely confident that something would happen. The fireworks lasted about an hour, and as we were walking back to the the car, I asked Ellen again how she felt. She said, "I feel *fine* and I wanna go home." I persisted, "Are you sure about that?" She told me I was driving her crazy. I reluctantly got in the car and asked, "What about all the traffic? What if we have to come back through that? Should we wait awhile just to be on the safe side?" She stopped answering me! So I drove home.

By then it was about 10:30 at night, and I felt dejected: our baby wouldn't be born on the 4th of July. As it turned out, he wasn't born until July 6th, two days later. But I had held our hope until the last minute. I realized there was a point of no return; even if we got to the hospital before midnight, the delivery would have to happen really fast to take place on the 4th. So by 10:30 I knew it wasn't meant to be.

I've been reflecting on those memories a lot today. In the end I couldn't have cared less that he *wasn't* born on the Fourth of July!

## DAY 108 – SUNDAY JULY 7, 2013

This was the last day of a holiday weekend that was difficult for me. I've felt quite anxious over the past few days and I've been alone a lot. The trip to Mt. Hood with Karen on the Fourth was fantastic, but Friday and Saturday I was alone quite a bit because I wasn't feeling well. I didn't have the energy to go out and interact with anybody. Physically I feel like my condition is dropping off faster than I expected. When I go for my walks, it's a very short period of time before I have to sit down and rest. That's very upsetting because I love to walk. It's like everything in my life is slowly but surely being taken away. I know that that's what's supposed to happen, but I certainly don't enjoy it. For instance I love the Fourth of July and all the events that go along with it, but I wasn't really able to participate in any of those events.

Everybody feels anxious sometimes, but with a terminal illness, everything has extra emotion attached to it. I get overloaded with emotions over just the simplest things. A radio broadcast about people I don't know personally can get me all worked up. I've always hated taking medications for anything, but now I'm taking a pill for anxiety and another one to help me sleep. I feel a little less anxious because of those pills, but every medication has side effects, and I think those meds make me feel more tired. So I'm not as anxious as I would otherwise be, but I have less energy.

For the third week in a row, I haven't been able to go to church. I can get up in the morning and get ready, but I don't have the strength and the energy to go there and sit through the entire service. I thought about maybe going for half an hour, but I don't have the energy to do even that much. And I don't see myself having more energy *next* Sunday. Maybe I'll ask the pastor to come and talk with me once a week, to have some kinda connection. Or maybe that hospice pastor could be a source of spirituality for me right now.

**DAY 109 – MONDAY JULY 8, 2013**

When I woke up this morning, I felt pretty good. I'd had a great night's sleep and I thought I might be able to have a really good day. I got up, had breakfast and worked on my blog for maybe an hour and a half. I happened to check my Facebook page and someone who liked my John in Cyberspace blog had commented, "God bless you Don McCall, I'll see you in eternity." I thought that was really cool; it made my day.

Things are progressing and getting worse, and I have to plan for the next steps, whatever they might be. I don't think I'll be able to do my food shopping for much longer. Even now it's a problem because I get confused. Finding everything I need, standing in line at the checkout, using my debit card – it's exhausting and confusing.

Ellen recently said that she wants to help somehow. I tried to tell her, "You don't have enough time; you've got pets and your daughters and grandchildren. I feel like it would be an imposition on you." She sounded upset and insisted, "It's *not* an imposition, I *do* have time. I want to help and be part of the team." I thought about it. Ellen is a fabulous cook. Maybe she could help with shopping and food prep. She called me today and I made that suggestion, and she said she'd definitely help out. She said once a week she could get groceries, prepare the food, and organize stuff in baggies in the refrigerator so that all I'd have to do is pull it out of the fridge and heat it up. I told her that'd be a *huge* help.

This evening I went out for my second walk of the day, and it went pretty well. I stopped and sat in the sunshine a bunch of times. With the pressure that I've been feeling in my head, I often have this sense of dread that it could be my last walk. It's unnerving because I truly love walking. I always loved riding my bike and hiking, but now I'll settle for walking, as a last resort. I know that my walks are gonna go away too at some point so I have to enjoy every minute. I love being outside, watching the sunset, watching the people – it's a perfect time of year for all of that. I have to cherish every moment and see how far I can go.

## DAY 110 – TUESDAY JULY 9, 2013

I didn't wanna get up today; I could've slept another two hours. But I know that I can't just give up and stop trying. I have to get the most that I can out of every day, and accomplish as much as I can. The prospect of working on my blog is what gets me out of bed in the morning; it certainly was the motivating factor today.

Late morning I decided to go to the grocery store. I know just yesterday I spoke with Ellen about getting my groceries, but I felt like I wanted to get out and do it. I started off up the street, and about halfway there, I suddenly felt incredibly tired. It's two and a half blocks from here to the store, but I only got a block and a half when I had to stop and rest. That was the first time I ever didn't have enough energy to make it all the way to the store without a break. After a rest, I managed to get going again. At the store, I picked up a prescription and a few items, but I was feeling really wobbly so I needed to sit down and rest again. That's never happened before either, while I was *in* the store.

Eventually I got all my items and headed to the check-out counter. There was a new check-out person working; I had never seen her before. She was agitated and upset, and she was dealing with a couple of difficult customers ahead of me. Every once in a while you go to the store and there's somebody in there acting like they came in to refinance their house instead of buying groceries. They have all this paperwork and coupons and all kinds of questions like, "How do I get a Safeway card? How do I do this? How do I get that?" I had to put my food on the conveyor belt and sit down to rest again. I sat there looking at the people in line behind me, unable to get up and go until it was my turn.

The new clerk finally got through my stuff, and then I had to go to the customer service desk to get quarters for the laundry. There again, there was one guy ahead of me, with a whole wad of paperwork: money orders, questions, and all kinds-a stuff. I had to sit down again! By the time I got outta the store, I was exhausted. I thought, *I don't ever wanna go back in that store again.* I had to stop and rest again on the walk back to my apartment. Once I made it home and put my groceries away, I just laid down flat on my bed for an hour before I could even get up again.

Everything else that I did today – paying bills, making phone calls, taking a short afternoon walk, setting up my google calendar for the rest of the week – I had to lie down and rest afterwards before I could do anything else. I was so tired. Maybe that was partly because it was a hot day. But that's what it has come down to: riding my bike along the waterfront eight weeks ago, to really struggling now to get around within a few blocks of my apartment on foot. How many more days do I have left, where I can get around with Johnnie Walker?

That's what this disease does. I understand that but I'm getting tired of it. My priorities right now are just getting up and surviving the day: trying to stay on my feet and battle this disease.

## DAY 111 – WEDNESDAY JULY 10, 2013

This morning I woke up feeling some pain. I thought, *Why am I doing this? Why bother getting up?* It was really hard to find the motivation to get up and get going. The weather looked beautiful, but I thought about how I wouldn't really have the energy to go out and enjoy it. Then I focused on the idea of working on my blog. It took me a while to get up and make some breakfast, but I was motivated to get over to my computer and tackle my next blog post.

Today's big event was meeting with Ellen, who has become my unofficial hospice volunteer. She'll be helping me with grocery shopping and cooking. Before she showed up, I wanted to put together a typical shopping list as a template. That task showed me how much my brain has deteriorated: I have been using the PageMaker program on my computer for years and years. I've designed literally thousands of pages using that program: publications, advertisements, graphics projects. I could knock out a fairly complex page in 30 minutes. Today, just putting together a simple grocery list took me close to two hours. I've actually forgotten many of the commands that I've always known. It used to be nearly automatic, to hit a key and get the computer to make some text boldface or change the font size. Now I look through all the menus, thinking, *Wait a minute now, how do I do that?* It's very frustrating!

I finally got the list together, and Ellen came over and we had our meeting to figure out how to coordinate everything. I look forward to working with her on it. I'm sure it'll all turn out well. If not, I'll go on a hunger strike! Ha! No, it really is a big relief, a big stress-reducer. I'll just be able to reach in the refrigerator, pull out a pot, put it on the stove and heat up some soup. Without having to go to the store and figure out what to buy, then waiting in line, and all of that. I really appreciate what Ellen will be doing.

## DAY 112 – THURSDAY JULY 11, 2013

When I woke up this morning, I felt better than I have over the past few days. I wasn't in pain, my stomach felt good, and I had quite a bit of energy. I was really pleased! I felt like I was gonna have a great day.

I ate breakfast and worked on my blog, and then I had about half an hour before Susan was scheduled to visit. Suddenly I started to feel anxious. I go through that interview with Susan every week to ten days, and it is very extensive. She asks all sorts of questions to prepare her report. It's just routine stuff, but I've reached a point where I no longer care about all of it. I don't care what my blood pressure is. She measured my biceps today and they're about 30 percent smaller than they were the last time she measured. I don't really need that information. *Nothing* can be done about my condition; all it does is upset me to go through all the details and numbers regarding how I feel. I can tell by my own body where I'm at; I don't need a checklist.

Karen asked me whether it's OK to tell Susan that I don't wanna go through that assessment every time. Maybe next time around I'll ask if she can make it as short as possible, blow through it in a casual conversation and call it a day. I know she has to go through the drill; it's her job. But I don't need someone *else* to tell me that I'm worse off than I was a week ago; I *know* I have less energy, less appetite, and I'm losing weight. I don't need medical confirmation.

After Susan left, I had a plan. I pass by the library on my daily walks. I figured I could go in and borrow a handful of CDs to listen to. I could experiment with some new music for free. I got over to the library with no trouble, and took the elevator to the third floor. But I discovered that my walker didn't fit easily through the aisles. I kept having to say "excuse me" to people but there still was barely enough space to get through. Then I got to the CD section and I felt overwhelmed by all the different categories – popular and Latin and gospel and so on. I got so confused and felt so upset that I just sat down in the middle of the aisle and felt like crying. I looked at a few CDs but I couldn't make up my mind on any of them. It didn't occur to me to just grab a random handful and go; if I brought one home that I didn't like, I'd just bring it back. But I didn't think of that while I was there. I left, extremely upset because I ended up with nothing and I couldn't figure out why. I was just confused. The day was going downhill, fast. I started walking home – which, by the way, was all uphill.

I was about a block away from my apartment, feeling totally dejected. My library mission had been a failure. Suddenly I heard someone call my name. I turned around and realized that it was

Lauren, someone I really wanted to see. She used to be the director at the Loaves and Fishes, or Meals on Wheels center near my apartment. Because she doesn't work there anymore, I didn't know when I'd get a chance to see her again, but there she suddenly was, walking down the street.

We had a wonderful conversation. I volunteered at the Meals on Wheels center for several years and really enjoyed working with Lauren. We did things like put on a Super Bowl Sunday for people in the neighborhood – we sold tickets, rented a projection screen, had door prizes. We organized a couple of portrait days, where we did portraits of more than 70 people. Lauren knows about my condition. It was wonderful to see her, and we talked for about 45 minutes.

**Blessing #31**

*Lauren knew exactly what to say and what not to say; she's one of those people who just knows how to navigate that kind of a conversation. I think it's from all of her experience working with people who are a little older in life and have had problems and so on. It made my day to run into her just then; it was very special. I don't know if I'll ever see her again, but I'm so thankful to have had the opportunity to spend that time with her.*

## DAY 113 – FRIDAY JULY 12, 2013

When I woke up this morning, I realized I had made a gigantic blunder. Yesterday evening after talking with Karen, I decided to go outside for another walk. I know that my body is deteriorating and there's nothing I can do to stop it, but I wanted to prove to myself that that's *not* happening.

Normally I walk eight to ten blocks twice a day with frequent stops to rest. Last night I decided to take a longer walk, and to go as far as I could without stopping. It was my competitive side saying that it's all just a big mistake, that I'm *not* losing strength and muscle mass. I picked out a twelve-block route and started walking. I got past the first block, the fourth block, the eighth block – and I hadn't stopped yet. I thought, *I can do the whole thing without stopping. I have as much strength as I've always had. The cancer has all been some kind of illusion.*

I kept going and I finished the walk without a break. Based on how I've felt over the past few weeks, I shouldn't have been able to do it; I got home feeling really, really dizzy and unsteady. To my competitive mind, I was a winner. But the fact was, I had really run myself down, energy-wise. So when I woke up this morning, I didn't wanna get out of bed. I was exhausted despite a good night's sleep.

I eventually got up, had breakfast and worked on my blog. Early afternoon, I decided to go for a walk. I only lasted about four blocks, and I really struggled to get back home. After that I had to lie down again. So the afternoon and evening were a mighty struggle, just doing my regular chores and making some phone calls.

## DAY 114 – SATURDAY JULY 13, 2013

This has been a frustrating day. I had one of those episodes where I was reeling around and unsteady and very confused. I used to only have those every few days, but for the past few days, it has happened every day. It feels like something is squeezing my head, like a little vice. In those moments when it squeezes a little harder, my eyes start rolling around and I can't focus. I'll be looking at something, then all of a sudden the whole thing goes outta focus. I blink a lot and look at it again, and it finally comes back into focus.

This is another step in the progression since this all started. First I couldn't ride my bike anymore, which was disappointing and disheartening. I could still take walks, but then it was only with my walker; I lost the ability to go around independently. Then I could no longer walk long distances without stopping; I had to stop every block. Now I've almost reached the point where I don't wanna go outdoors because I worry that I'll have one of these brain episodes and have to call somebody to take me home. You reach a point where you say, "OK, I'm not gonna do *that* anymore; it's just not comfortable." I think I'm quickly reaching the point where I'll be confined to my building. I guess that's OK because I have my own little deck where I can sit in the sunshine, and I can walk up and down the hallways here 'til I'm blue in the face.

**Blessing #32**

> One really nice thing about this building is that one side of each hallway is lined with windows instead of having apartments on both sides. This is the only building I've ever been in, where you look out on a cityscape along the entire length of the hallway. It's really amazing. From the tenth floor I can see all of downtown. So I don't feel trapped here, which is how I would feel if the hallways were totally enclosed. Plus if I ever fell down in the building, there are a lot of neighbors around; everybody knows me. I don't feel vulnerable the way I do out on the street. And if I get tired of walking, I can just take the elevator back to my floor. I can stop when I want to; I'm in control. I'm very blessed to be living here.

Ellen came over today. She told me that her other ex-husband, Jeffrey, has been bugging her to bring him over to visit me. She discouraged him; she told him I get confused and exhausted by having too many visitors. Hanging out with him *can* be challenging. So he insisted on being able to do something to help me.

They came up with the idea that he could supply me with those little Via instant coffee packets from Starbucks, since he buys them for himself already anyway. It's a great idea – I love those Via packets! They make a perfect cup of coffee. Just heat up exactly eight ounces of water, cut open a packet, and never mind the coffee maker and all the utensils that go along with that. I've decided that Via is my product until I pass away. I'm ending my life on Via coffee packets. Karen agreed with me that that would make a great advertising campaign: "Don McCall ended his life drinking Via." Ha! Anyway, if Jeffrey wants to buy me coffee, I'm really excited about that. It's funny; one ex-husband supplying another ex-husband with coffee.

35

# FINDING WAYS TO STAY POSITIVE

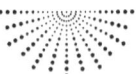

**DAY 115 – SUNDAY JULY 14, 2013**

*I* awoke this morning with a high degree of energy, and got up to work on my blog. I'm glad the blog will still be out there on the web even after I'm gone. People can continue to just bounce in and get something out of it, even if they only read one Bible verse; I'd be delighted with that. I don't know how God can work with it, but I'm sure he can. It's simple for God to positively affect people's lives with something like this, when it's plastered all over the internet. I'm sure God knows about social media. Social media is a powerful force for good and evil. Everything still comes down to that struggle between good and evil, and these days the battlefield is the internet.

**Blessing #33**

*I feel incredibly blessed to have my blog and my daily conversations with Karen to help keep my mind occupied. It would be really easy to just sit around all day and fixate on my illness. Instead, every day I have to think about what I want to say about my day: what I liked and what I didn't like, what was important. Sometimes as I'm talking with Karen, I'll mention some problem I'm having. Then later in the evening, I end up thinking about it some more and I come up with potential solutions. Then the next day I can try to do something about that problem. So our conversations help me focus on problems in a constructive way, instead of letting those problems drag me down. That way I'm fighting the disease. That's a huge blessing!*

Up 'til now I've always felt like taking a walk after working at my computer in the morning. Now I'd rather just go back to bed and rest. But I can still get something done at that time. I have a really positive sense of accomplishment after putting together a blog post, so that's a good time to catch up on telephone calls. Sometimes those calls get really emotional, which is tiring. Today I had long conversations with Geraldine and my son and Emma. Afterwards I started to get outta bed but I was absolutely, totally wiped out. My brain was mush. So I stayed there and rested some more.

Later on, Karen came over. We did an audio recording in which I told the story of one year of my life, when my family lived at the MacKenzie River. It was really strenuous to tell that whole story. The process turned my brain inside-out! I don't understand how using my mind can be so exhausting. It's a perplexing, neurological mystery.

My brain is under incredible stress. Sometimes I'm standing up, washing dishes or whatever, and I find myself in a dream! An actual dream. I have to shake my head to realize that I'm *not* in a dream; I'm awake and standing. Somehow my mind can flip back and forth between reality and a dream. Or maybe it's more like I'm shifting between my current reality and the past, back and forth. It's very strange. Sometimes it's hard to distinguish between reality and the past.

## DAY 116 – MONDAY JULY 15, 2013

Today I had a lot of important phone calls including my social worker, my hospice volunteer, and so on. After that my mind was just scrambled. Then I had some chores around the house. Everything takes me twice as long as it used to because I literally have to lie down after every activity. If it takes me 15 minutes to wash the dishes, I have to go and lie down for 15 minutes afterwards to recover from it.

Today I went outside for the first time in two days. The idea of not going outside at all is unbelievable to me since I've always loved the outdoors! I figured I'd go out and see how I felt, whether I liked being out. Well, I walked a block and a half, and I'd had enough. I absolutely didn't wanna go any farther. It wasn't a matter of endurance. One of my eyes was seeing everything out of proportion and out of focus, which made it very confusing. I was wandering in a world that I didn't really know, an alien environment.

I didn't get any joy out of being outside. I just wanted to get back home where I felt safe. Later I sat out on the deck to enjoy the sun. I thought, *It's a new world now. I have this apartment building, and that's it.* I see the handwriting on the wall; this whole situation is moving downhill quickly, considering how uncomfortable I was outdoors, and having to rest nearly every ten minutes no matter what I'm doing.

## DAY 117 – TUESDAY JULY 16, 2013

Today was difficult. It took me four hours to do my blog post this morning. I was trying to add in a series of links, using a widget. I've done it before and it's easy to do, but today I couldn't figure it out. I even looked at links that I had set up previously, and I could see how I did it, but it didn't work the same way this time. I'm stunned by how I can't comprehend something that I've done before, which should be very simple for me. But at least my blog got about 70 views today; that was encouraging. Catherine told me that she checks it every day, so she'll know whether I'm still here.

From about the time I get up 'til mid-morning, I don't want anybody around; I don't want any distractions. At that time of day I really have to reach down deep inside and pull out some motivation to move forward because what I'd really like to do is just get back in bed and sleep. That's gotta be normal for someone in my situation, and I feel that I'd be totally justified if I did that. Working on my blog is *incredibly* helpful because it pulls me right into the word of God and gets me focused on something that I love and wanna do.

I'm trying to work out a plan for the next 30 days and the next 60 days. I know that my condition could change suddenly, which would blow up any kind of plan, but I can't live my life without *some* kind of a plan. I can't keep going day to day to day to day with no idea what would happen if I became unable to take care of myself.

I had a heated, frustrating discussion about that today with my hospice social worker. He'd prefer not to make a plan; he'd rather wait til something happens and then react to it. I totally disagree with that approach. Now I'm seriously considering making a request to have a different social worker. He's very competent and I respect him, and he certainly has a great knowledge of social work. But he hasn't been in Portland all that long so I don't think he has all the necessary local experience and connections. I think he's in a situation where he'll have to ask other people for help and information. I'd rather deal with somebody who's been here a longer time and knows all the places where I might go when the time comes, someone who knows the ins and outs of the whole system.

If I'm going to need an adult foster care situation, I want to already have a list of half a dozen recommended foster care homes. I'd like to have somebody I trust go and actually see those places to check 'em out. We could investigate and prioritize them. Then when the time comes, all we need to do is call the places on the list to find out if they have any openings. We'd already know about these places, all of their qualifications. If I had the energy, I would get on the internet and research this myself. Here's where my social worker is at a disadvantage, coming from another city; he doesn't know anything about the facilities in this area. When we talked today, he sort of shrugged off the idea of doing that research. Not knowing where they might send me is very frustrating!

## DAY 118 – WEDNESDAY JULY 17, 2013

When I woke up this morning, I didn't really wanna get up. It seemed like there was a lotta stuff to do and people to deal with and I thought, *Another hour of sleep would be good. Maybe two hours. Maybe three!* But I have this mental thing where I have to try to push off around 8 am, regardless of the circumstances.

My hospice volunteer was scheduled to be here for a couple hours this afternoon. Sometimes having people help me seems to take *more* energy than my doing it myself. But Edith helps me do things that I really can't do. I get super-dizzy putting clothes in the washer and dryer because they're front-loaders where you have to bend down to stick the clothes in. Sometimes I feel like I'm gonna pass out, so I need Edith's help and I've gotta learn to deal with that.

Karen was gonna take me to a haircut today, and another friend was scheduled to come by too. The idea of seeing all those people in one day seemed like an overwhelming amount of stress and activity. On top of that, a couple days ago I found out that it might be possible to receive home health care from the people who work on the second floor of my building, the aides who care for the disabled folks on that floor. That's an exciting prospect because those folks know the building and the neighborhood and they wouldn't need any additional training to help *me* out. And they're already in the building every day. I'm very anxious to find out whether that'll work. Between that anxiety and everything scheduled for the day, I felt like I'd been run over by a tractor or something! Overall, there weren't really *all* that many things scheduled, but even that much can be overwhelming.

A funny conversation happened today. I have an acquaintance in this building who is a little bit eccentric, but I do like the guy. We tend to kid each other a lot, kind of on the silly side. He knows I have cancer. He told me a few days ago that he's being checked for kidney cancer. I tried to cheer him up by telling him that my dad had cancer in one kidney, but after having it removed, he lived for another 35 years. In prior conversations I had mentioned hospice and today my friend asked me what hospice is. I told him that basically once you're in the hospice program, you don't really have any more medical bills, but you have to agree that you're going to die within six months.

His eyes got kinda big and I could see that he was shocked. He said, "Well I'm not interested in a plan like *that!*" I replied, "I don't blame you! It's not exactly the best health plan available if you wanna get well." We laughed a bit about that.

**DAY 119 – THURSDAY JULY 18, 2013**

It was another difficult day even though nothing new happened. My fatigue level is climbing tremendously, but I'm still not experiencing any significant pain, other than my stomach feeling strange in the mornings. Household chores get more difficult every day, especially in the kitchen. If I'm on my feet for any length of time, my head just starts to throb.

I'm waiting to hear whether I'll be able to have the home health providers in the building help me out, say for an hour a day. All the decision-makers have discussed it but nothing is definitive as of yet. I'm pretty nervous about the whole thing because it would be an ideal solution.

Other than that, Ellen came by with some groceries, which was a huge help.

**DAY 120 – FRIDAY JULY 19, 2013**

The big word for the day, again, is fatigue. I don't know why I get more fatigued every day, but I guess that's the way it's gonna be. It must be the tumors at work.

On the other hand, I did have enough energy to go outside for a walk. I guess I'm not totally confined to the building just yet! I started by going four blocks but it was so beautiful out that I added a couple blocks to soak up more of the sunshine. I stopped quite a few times along the way. When I got to within a block of home, I really ran outta gas. I just hit the wall at this little restaurant where they have tables outside, so I sat there until I was able to work up the energy to make it home. Near the building I saw one of my neighbors coming down the street struggling with two gallon-bottles of milk. I offered to wheel them along on my walker so he wouldn't drop them. He was relieved and I was psyched that I could help to haul his stuff home for him on my walker.

Today I got a telephone call from one of the most interesting people I know. Afterwards I realized that I really regret not spending more time with him when I could have. He owned an art gallery in San Francisco for 25 years. He's retired now, but he's always got some kind of project that he's excited about. For instance, there's an annual homeless fair in downtown Portland, where all sorts of people offer their skills for free to help the homeless, such as barbers giving free haircuts or people administering simple medical help. My friend noticed that a lot of children attend this homeless event, and he felt that there needs to be something for them. He found Biblical coloring books and crayons at Dollar Tree, so he bought a bunch of 'em to hand out to the children at the fair. He also sang me a song. He'd heard it at church and all week he'd been thinking of singing it to me. His voice is a little better than mine. So we had a thoroughly enjoyable conversation.

I had a very positive and productive day with the people that I encountered and talked to. I got to thinking about how much different it would be if I were on chemo, trying to battle that stuff. I'd be lying in bed, feeling sick. This day reinforced my choice *not* to go forward with more chemo, since it wouldn't have been a total cure anyway.

## DAY 121 – SATURDAY JULY 20, 2013

First thing in the morning I'm kinda reluctant to stand up because I'm usually wondering whether I've lost any more ground during the night. Will today be tougher than yesterday? It's a psychological barrier. This morning I put my feet on the floor and started walking around, and I was OK. Nothing different or weird going on. I felt like I might be able to have a good day.

I usually pray in the morning before I get going, that I'll be able to get through the day without any major incidents. I also pray for my friends. One of the hardest things is to think about the people that I'm going to leave behind. I want the best for all of my friends, and I want them to succeed and be happy and have a good life. But I won't be there to see how their lives go forward; I won't be able to help if they need me.

My head feels like it's in a vice, and every day there's a little bit more pressure. As that pressure increases, my mobility decreases. For instance, my ability to sort things out in the kitchen. It's not to the extent that I'm gonna burn the place down, but I'm having more and more trouble with washing dishes. That has become a major chore. I wash some of them and then I have to lie down for ten minutes.

Although I haven't had a brain scan, I'm convinced that I have cancer in my brain and it's progressing much faster than the cancer in my liver. I've heard that as liver cancer progresses, your legs and midsection start to swell, but that's not happening to me. Occasionally I'll have a sharp, shooting pain in the area of my liver, which is happening a little more often.

Various friends want to visit but I've gotta limit it to one visit per day. Today, Christina and Aaron Lee came over with their baby, and I really enjoyed their visit. Later Ellen came by with groceries. When people come by, I get engaged in the conversation and I wanna be *sharp*. So I overextend myself mentally, and afterwards I'm exhausted. After the young family's visit and then seeing Ellen today, I felt like I'd been run over by a truck! Before my illness, I had no understanding of mental fatigue.

Today was an absolutely superior day. I enjoyed the people I interacted with today, and the weather was beautiful. I'm not a world traveler, but there's no place I'd rather be than Portland, Oregon on a sunny summer day, when temperatures are in the low 80's with a breeze blowing. I actually got outside for a walk in the early evening. None of what I did today would've been possible if I'd been on chemo right now. On chemo, I wouldn't have wanted to see anybody or go outside at all. Maybe my life has been shortened a few months by avoiding chemo, but I'll take days like today *any* time over what I would've gotten with chemo.

## DAY 122 – SUNDAY JULY 21, 2013

This morning I felt kinda discouraged because this is the fifth week in a row that I haven't been able to go to church and take Communion. Even if I could get to church, getting in and out of the building would be really tough, and then there's no way I could sit there for an hour and a half. It didn't feel good; I wanted to go but I knew that I couldn't. Working on my blog every morning is a spiritual endeavor now. At this point in my life I'm leaning and counting on the promises that Jesus makes in the book of John.

As of today, my John in Cyberspace blog has had two thousand page views. Many of those are from people whom I know. Sometimes I wonder if there are people out there that I don't know, watching my blog and saying, "Well when's this guy actually gonna die? How long do we have to wait? It's been 122 days; is this some kinda scam? Is he gonna start asking for money?" I can imagine some people thinking, "We better stop following this blog because he's gonna email us saying that he wants one last trip to Barbados or something like that." Ha!

**Blessing #34**

*Four o'clock in the afternoon has become my favorite time of day. That's when the sunshine hits my entire deck. I make a big sandwich and go sit out there for 15 or 20 minutes and let the sunshine beat down on me. There's nothing like sunshine for warming your body; it's absolutely phenomenal. When I sit there staring up at the blue sky, with warm sunlight encompassing my whole body, it's the only time of day when I feel like a normal person. It's like what I used to do on the beach in California: sit in the late afternoon sun, feeling the sea breeze blowing in. Nothing else in the world feels that marvelous. So four o'clock is my special hour. I'm grateful for what I have; I feel relatively good, from the standpoint of what I could be feeling.*

. . .

## DAY 123 – MONDAY JULY 22, 2013

Today has been an amazing day in a lotta ways. I did some things I hadn't done for a while and it was a really, really productive day. So I'm extremely tired tonight and I may have to pay the price tomorrow.

I've been anxious to find out whether I'll be able to get home health care and other household help from the aides who already work in this apartment building. I called the guy who had the final say on it, and he told me that it's going to work and an intake person will come by to figure out what I need and set up a schedule. I thanked him and said that I couldn't possibly express how much I appreciated it. After that call, I felt *much* better. It felt like a huge piece of the puzzle had been put into place.

Then I worked on my blog and did some cleaning, and had an appointment with my hospice nurse at noon. Susan and I had our weekly chat about how much I've deteriorated. Today I asked her to explain what's going on with my brain. She said, "A brain tumor sucks all the nutrients out of your system and causes fatigue. It makes you feel like you don't wanna eat. It feeds off the nutrients from your food, depriving your body of those nutrients." It's a tough situation. I have two tumors going on, and they're fighting each other for nutrients and not leaving me very much.

We had a frank discussion about what might happen, what some of the likely scenarios would be. She said, "One likely scenario, which happens quite often, is that someone just goes to sleep and doesn't wake up." I thought, *That's exactly what I want! That would be a miracle.* She said, "Another scenario is that the person just kinda wastes away, and then something else goes wrong and they succumb to that." She agreed with me that the brain tumor is probably progressing faster than the liver tumor, since I don't have many of the classic liver cancer symptoms yet. So it's the brain tumor that's actually working toward the final knockout punch.

Then I asked Susan, "The last time I saw my doctor was two and a half months ago. At that time he said I had about two months to go. *You've* worked in hospice a long time and you see me almost weekly. What would *your* assessment be?" She said, "It's really hard to say, but

I would think no more than one or two months." It felt good to just have that all out on the table.

During her last visit, she asked me so many questions and I was totally exhausted by it. This time I actually cut off the questioning and asked her to leave. I told her I needed to rest instead. She said, "OK, no problem," and picked up her stuff. She always gives me a hug before she goes; she hugged me and she left. I exercised my boundaries, and it was all good.

Then I decided to make a trip to the store. It would be my first trip there in almost two weeks. I've been really anxious about going to the store because somehow I could see myself just being swallowed up by it. Maybe ending up in some back room, forgotten behind a bunch of boxes or something, I don't know! I was getting overwhelmed by the thought of going there again: that big place with thousands of products, and people running all over the place. But I grabbed Johnnie Walker and went all the way to the store.

Right across the street there's a nice place to sit in the sun on my walker. I parked it there for about ten minutes until I worked up the courage to go in. I had five items on my shopping list and had to drop off a prescription. I sort of stumbled around for a while and found everything I needed. When I got to the checkout line, all the lines were long. I was afraid I'd start to feel really dizzy. Sure enough, the guy ahead of me seemed to be in the process of re-financing his house, with stuff all over the counter and lots of coupons. I was trapped because there were people in line behind me, and this guy just went on and on and on. I thought I was gonna pass out right there. He finally got it all together and left.

I got through and then I had to go to the customer service desk for quarters. Of course there was a guy buying five or six different varieties of lottery tickets, and one more guy who just wanted a pack of cigarettes. The woman behind the counter started looking for the cigarettes and they didn't have the right brand so that turned into a five-minute conversation to determine which brand would be the best substitute. My head was starting to spin and I thought I wasn't gonna make it, I was gonna have to leave. But it was finally my turn and I got my quarters and got outta there. I was really wobbly and felt like my head was spinning around.

I crossed the street to my safe place, sat down in the sun, and tried to get up enough energy to make it home. A guy whom I knew happened to pass by. I couldn't recall his name but I know I've taken his portrait. He asked, "What's going on? You still taking pictures?" I told him that I'd had to give that up. I couldn't even have stood up at that point, let alone take a picture! He said, "Well, I guess you're just kicking back and enjoying life now, right?" I replied, "Well I guess maybe you could say that!" He gave me a big thumbs-up and took off, and I thought, *Yeah, here I am, sitting in this walker, barely able to move, and I'm just kicking back and enjoying life. How do people reach that conclusion?*

36

# THE NEW NORMAL: AIDES AND BRAIN EPISODES

**DAY 124 – TUESDAY JULY 23, 2013**

Today was only about one thing – after finding out yesterday that I'll be able to receive home health services from the aides in the building, today we started working out the details. This is huge! If I need help in the middle of the night, they're only three floors away on an elevator. And I get to stay in my own apartment. We arranged for an aide to come up for two hours a day, five days a week, to help with food prep, household cleaning, laundry, and getting groceries. They'll also go for a walk with me if I wanna walk outside. That gives me an incredible feeling of peace. I wouldn't be able to hire outside help for just two hours a day, but these people are already in the building for the whole day so two hours with me works into their schedule just fine. I'm really excited that that finally all came together. The second floor residents are almost all totally disabled, and the aides work with them every day. So I know they're well qualified to help *me* out.

A nurse came over this afternoon and we spent over two hours working through stacks of intake paperwork. I was surprised that she didn't have a computer. Using a laptop, the name and address would've appeared automatically on every page. Without that, she had to write my name and contact info on every form she filled out. But we got through it. *She* did all the writing. I couldn't even hold my head up by the time we were done; it was the most grueling process I've ever experienced! I was absolutely exhausted. When she got up to leave, I feebly held out my hand to shake hands and thank her, and I sat there in my chair with my head hanging down. She said, "I'll let myself out. Don't worry, everything's fine and you did great." I sat there for another five or ten minutes then stumbled over to my bed and slept for an hour.

Anyway it's a done deal. It's a huge, huge blessing to be set up for these services.

## DAY 125 – WEDNESDAY JULY 24, 2013

When I woke up this morning, I did my usual test to see if my arms, legs and feet were working alright. Out in the kitchen, I was suddenly overwhelmed by a brain issue; I don't know what else to call it. Something snapped in my head and I started feeling woozy and I didn't know what to do next. I tried to get my breakfast together but I pulled out the cereal box upside-down and poured it all over the counter. I knew what I was trying to do, but I couldn't coordinate my actions. I finally gave up and went to sit on my bed for ten or fifteen minutes to let it pass. Eventually I felt a little bit better.

Ellen came over today to help out with meal planning. She cooked some items that I can heat up for dinner for the next several days, so that's a big help. My basic plan for dinners, going forward, is to have a clump of rice, a nice vegetable, and some kind of meat, like chicken strips or fish or ground beef. No more soup; I'm sick of it. If I see another bowl of soup I'm gonna throw up.

I also walked over to the store to pick up a prescription. Ellen came along for moral support. She was really worried that I wouldn't make it over there and back, but I was just going to the pharmacy counter, not wandering around the store and waiting in the check-out line, so everything went fine.

My hospice volunteer was here today too, for the last time. Since I'll be having aides from the building coming in, I won't need a volunteer. But I was sorry to see her go; I enjoyed her company and she was a tremendous help. The aides are going to start by the end of this week or next Monday; they just need to re-work their schedules a little bit to fit me in.

Anyway I accomplished a lot today but I feel like it knocked my brain completely sideways.

## DAY 126 – THURSDAY JULY 25, 2013

I've been having some weird sensations during the night so I've become very skeptical when I wake up in the morning. I hesitate to put both feet on the floor. Is anything missing, can I still move the way I want to? Has my brain stopped communicating with one of my arms or legs during the night? In my circumstances, anything could happen. I have that moment of hesitation, and it's absolutely the worst time of the day for me. Putting my feet on the floor, standing up, and taking those first few steps every morning, to see if things are the same as the day before, is not much fun. The last few mornings I've noticed that each day I'm a little less steady on my feet than I was the day before. I don't have the confidence that I used to have. So when I woke up today, I thought, *Well, I could just lie here another hour or so.* But really, in the back of my mind, I knew I was avoiding those test steps.

### Blessing #35

*Later in the morning, after working on my blog, I realized that I felt more relaxed today. It's probably because I'm set up to receive care from the aides downstairs. I feel more confident since I won't have to worry about where people are coming from or what to expect. Dealing with people from outside would've been an absolute nightmare! It's a huge relief for my son, too. This situation in the building is probably the biggest blessing I've had in the whole course of my illness, because*

> it's so convenient and it may allow me to stay in my apartment until my final days.

Sure enough, I got a call from the Adventist home health coordinator mid-morning, and she said that an aide would be up to see me at noon. So I didn't have to wait 'til next week. When the aide arrived, I was very pleased to see that she's someone I know. I've spoken with her down in the laundry room a few times; she's a friendly gal. She walked in and said, "Oh, it's *you!*" She recalled that I used to visit a guy named Kent on the 2nd floor, who died a few months ago. Right away we had a good rapport.

I gave her an update on my situation and we put together a list of what I need help with. She worked through the list pretty darn fast, so I'm thinking it may be hard to fill up a two-hour visit at this point. I know that'll change as time goes by. She'll be here two hours a day, three days a week, and then someone else will come on the other days, also someone whom I already know. That way I won't have to deal with different aides each time.

## DAY 127 – FRIDAY JULY 26, 2013

Today was a mixed bag kind of day. In the mornings I don't do much web surfing anymore; maybe check the baseball standings and that's about it. The Dodgers are red-hot right now and that's exciting. I check my calendar for the day, and it may only have four or five items, including phone calls, but even that much wears me out. I noticed that I had over 150 hits on my blog today! That's definitely a motivator to keep going with it. Frank came over today. I prepared a lunch for him, but when he showed up, he said he'd just eaten four donuts so he wasn't hungry. A new aide came by at two o'clock, not the gal who was here yesterday. It turns out that she has been working in the building about a month longer than I've been living here. So we hit it off really well. She reassured me that the aides in the building are capable of providing all kinds of heavy-duty care, and they'll be able to increase my hours as needed.

There was one downside to the day. I had a huge brain episode. I was walking through the lobby downstairs, and all of a sudden everything just started to go outta control. I was reeling, absolutely reeling. I had to come back and lie down for about a half hour. The only way I can describe these episodes is that I just feel overwhelmed and feel like I might fall. It affects my vision somewhat. I *don't* actually feel dizzy or like I'm floating. I feel detached from my surroundings and I have to reach out and touch the wall to reconnect with where I am. My feet are usually touching the floor so I feel connected there, but the rest of my body is basically out there, wobbling around. I don't have to *lean* on the wall to feel connected, but I do have to *touch* it; that gives me stability. I usually know when these episodes start; I can feel it coming on and that's enough warning to turn around and sit down. It's kinda like an earthquake – there's a little bit of shaking and then all of a sudden – pow! – it really hits hard. I go and sit down or lie down, and after ten or fifteen minutes, it goes away.

**DAY 128 – SATURDAY JULY 27, 2013**

When I got up this morning, I was having another one of those episodes. It was weird because I've never had one first thing in the morning. There was extra pressure in my head, too, that I hadn't felt before. I started working on my blog, and it felt like I was wearing a tight helmet; it was really strange. It lasted over an hour. Later I was in the kitchen and I realized that I had to keep touching things in order to have a point of contact to stabilize myself – especially before and after turning to face a different direction. For example, if I wanted to pick something up off the counter, I'd have to touch the counter and lift the object at the same time in order to feel stable. I thought, *Is it gonna be like this all the time from now on?*

Ellen came over today to help with meal prep and planning. We had our regular food conference to decide what to buy and cook. I'm still trying to figure out a combination of foods that won't upset my stomach and will give me some energy throughout the day. Also, foods that I won't get bored with, day after day.

After we finished with that, I remembered that I had to take a pill. I only take four pills a day, and I keep them in a pill caddy, separated by the type of pill. Two pills that I take are white, one is blueish, and one is bright pink. I needed to take a bright pink one, so I opened the pink pill section of the caddy. The pills were all white! That didn't look right. Did I put them in the wrong section? I opened the section with the white pills. They were blue! That was weird. Every day I get my pink pill out of one section, my white pill from the other section, and so on, so I knew something wasn't right.

I showed Ellen the pink pill and said, "This pill is pink." She agreed. Then I said, "But it's *not* pink; it's white." She said, "It looks pink to me. Take it out and lay it on your sock." I was wearing white socks. I tried her suggestion and even there, the pink pill was still white. Then I tried one of the pills that looked blue, which was supposed to be white. She agreed that the pill was white, but even against my sock it looked blue. I was completely flabbergasted. The sock looked white to me, as it was supposed to look. But two of my pills looked to me like the wrong color. I took the pill that I needed to take, and decided to let it go.

An hour and a half later, I thought, *What do those pills look like now?* I went back and opened the caddy. The pink pills were pink again! And the white pills looked white again. All my clothes looked to me to be the right colors. So why did these two pills suddenly look completely different? I was astounded. The brain is an *un*believable organ. We take it for granted until it starts acting strange.

Now the question is, are these anomalies temporary, or will they keep happening? I've had some weird brain experiences that really messed me up for a day, but then the next day they were gone, for the most part. I'll have to wait to see what happens tomorrow.

I've started taking short walks outside just before going to bed. The weather has been incredible and the sun sets late at this time of year, around nine o'clock or so. The warmth from the sun when it's low in the sky – it's a sensation that can't be duplicated. It's just right, not too hot.

I didn't feel like leaving my apartment all day because of the strange feeling in my head, so I was worried about my evening walk. I didn't know if I had enough energy, and my legs ached, but I was determined. Late in the evening, Johnnie Walker and I headed out. Using the walker is just like touching the wall or a cabinet or the stove; it gives me stability. The feeling that it's there sends a signal to the brain, connecting me with my surroundings. I don't have to lean on the walker very much. In fact, I can stand upright and push the walker in front of me. Without it, I'd feel too disconnected to walk; I'd be outta control.

---

## A LAST TIME FOR EVERYTHING

*This evening I stopped to rest as the sun sank behind the west hills. It went down slowly, and right before it disappeared there was this little flare – tchoo! – and then it was gone. Given how I felt all day, I thought, I don't know if I'm gonna make it through the night; was this my last sunset? I thought about how every day on this planet is precious, every single, solitary day. When we don't take the time to fully experience life and be kind to other people and lead civilized lives, that's an incredible waste of an opportunity. Could I have done better and used my time more wisely? I think I did the best I could, and I don't really have any regrets. But I'd say it's a good idea to enjoy as many sunsets as possible, and take those moments to resolve to make tomorrow a better day and appreciate this beautiful place.*

---

## DAY 129 – SUNDAY JULY 28, 2013

Susan told me recently that as tumors develop, they devour the nutrients from the food you eat. If you eat a lot of healthy fruits and vegetables, normally your body would benefit from that. With cancer, the tumor gets the benefit. So now it almost seems pointless to eat anything other than high-carb or high-sugar food, which I can digest quickly for a burst of energy.

I was hoping the pressure in my head that I felt yesterday would subside today, but it hasn't. Maybe it's even a little worse. So this is a new plateau; it's the new "normal". Periodically I just have to accept a new "normal"; I can't protest that it's not fair that things have changed and that I can't have it the way it used to be. All I can do is keep the faith and accept it.

It's been a difficult day. I feel like calling it a day and going to bed. But I don't wanna give up just yet. This evening I plan to go out and take my nightly walk. I don't know how far I'll get; that's always a question-mark. At home, more and more I have to reach out and touch the walls or whatever's close by, so that my brain knows there's something that I can rely on to keep me upright. If I leave the apartment, my walker gives me the contact I need for stability and a feeling of well-being. That has gotten a lot worse in just the past two days, seriously impacting my mobility.

It's always hard when I realize I've descended to a new plateau. It's as if I'm climbing a mountain, and every time I stop to rest, suddenly I'm 20 feet lower. I'm climbing *down,* not up. It's backwards – when you go downhill you're supposed to coast, not climb. At the same time, I'm *OK*; I mean, I feel blessed to have had the life I've had, and I appreciate everything I've experienced. I've had so many blessings, and this illness doesn't take away from that for one minute.

Today I was sad that I can't go to church anymore. I may be able to walk that far, but then I'd be exhausted and immediately have to turn around and come home. The hospice pastor is coming by tomorrow and maybe he'll give me Communion, which would make me feel better. But not going to church is very difficult. This week I've got to work on finding a solution to that problem.

### Blessing #36

*Telling Karen about my day, every day, is extremely helpful to me. It keeps me focused and I look forward to it every evening; I'm really thankful for the opportunity to discuss my situation. I'm astounded by the fact that whatever's going on in my brain, it hasn't affected my memory or my ability to speak.*

## DAY 130 – MONDAY JULY 29, 2013

When I woke up this morning and started walking around, the way I felt once again confirmed that I've reached another plateau. I used to have isolated spells of feeling disoriented but that's happening all the time now. I can still walk on my own, but it's very uncomfortable unless I touch something. So that's what I've been doing as I've walked around my apartment all day today. Plus I still feel a lot of pressure at the back of my head. I think that actually felt worse today.

My aide was here today. We got along very well and got a tremendous amount of work accomplished. She took care of the laundry and went to the store. She cooked, and cleaned the kitchen. She mopped the kitchen floor. Her being here really lifted my spirits and helped me to make it through the day. I couldn't have done any of what she did, so I'm extremely glad this arrangement got worked out when it did, just in the nick of time. It would've been impossible for me to make it on my own another week.

The hospice pastor called this morning and he was going to come over today but I cancelled on that. I felt just too outta whack. Plus when my aide is here, it's like having someone over for a social visit for two hours. I don't have the energy after that to spend time with anyone else. Maybe from now on my social life will be limited to phone calls. That's simple and I can control it: when I want to call somebody, I pick up the phone, and I don't have to answer an incoming call if I don't feel like it. I guess that's just the way it's gonna be!

## DAY 131 – TUESDAY JULY 30, 2013

I'm struggling to accept the new "normal" that started a few days ago. I've been spending a lot more time just lying on my bed. I can still do some things, but not for very long. When I get my breakfast, by the time I grab a bowl, pour the cereal, add some fruit and pour milk into it, I'm tired and I have to sit down. This is such a huge setback. I used to go to the store every day: it was interesting to see people and wander around and have a cup of coffee, and sometimes I'd be out for two hours just wandering around. Now I don't even wanna walk over to the store, let alone do any shopping.

I tabulated how much time I spent resting yesterday, and it was something like 18 hours! That means I was only actually doing anything for about six hours. For me, that's an all-time minimum. I really have trouble accepting that reality. But when I'm resting, I *need* that rest. It's difficult to get back up and finish whatever chore I was doing. All day, over and over, I have to lie down and rest; it's crazy.

There's more pressure in my head today, and as that pressure increases, I know that there will be more and more things that I can no longer do.

## 37

## A RELIABLE, COMPETENT HEALTHCARE TEAM

**DAY 132 – WEDNESDAY JULY 31, 2013**

I've been hoping to have a bounce-back from the pressure that's been growing in my head for the past few days, but it looks like that's not gonna happen. It gets noticeably worse every day.

But I got a lot done today. I worked on my blog, got through some financial stuff, and spent time with my aide. If I didn't have these aides helping me out now, I'd really be in serious shape. So I'm *very* happy to have their help.

Yesterday evening I took a walk, and about halfway through, I realized it was gonna be a horrendous struggle to make it home. Getting exercise obviously isn't building up my strength and stamina at this point because anything I build up, the cancer takes away. So I don't know whether I'll even try to take a walk this evening.

I've been thinking again about being confined to the building for the rest of my days. This isn't a bad place to be confined to, and I could still go out on my deck and sit in the sun, but it would be another new "normal" in my journey that I'd have to get used to.

I met another one of the home health aides today. It has been hectic so far, meeting a different aide each day as they work on fitting me into their schedule. Once I've met all of them, I'll be able to gage what they do and how they do it. I'll get better at planning what I need done, and I'll be able to maximize their time here. The aide today has a cellphone similar to mine, and she quickly updated my phone with a bunch of telephone numbers that I needed. She also helped me get some envelopes ready for mailing. I felt really good about all of that.

As a result of our efforts to have these aides come up to help *me*, Adventist decided to offer in-home aid to *other* people in this building now too. My situation opened the door for others to get the same aid on a short-term basis. For instance a lady on the fourth floor just returned home after being hospitalized with a broken leg. She'll need quite a bit of help for several weeks, and they're gonna provide it. That's huge! It feels good to be part of a new trend in how things work around here.

I gotta say, I don't feel depressed, but I'm feeling a little down, seeing how my situation has taken another nasty turn for the worse. I've had to give up so many things. Now if I want to go somewhere, someone else has to pick me up and drive me there. That's hard, after decades of driving and bicycling. It all happened in such a short period of time.

**DAY 133 – THURSDAY AUGUST 1, 2013**

All day yesterday I didn't think I'd be able to take my evening walk, but when 7:30 rolled around, I got my walker and headed out. I walked a different route than on previous evenings, and I actually felt better once I was moving. I took a break at the end of each block, and tuned in to what was going on around me, watching people and looking at the buildings. I kept going, one block at a time, and made it back home. I actually really enjoyed it! When I got home I went to bed, and I slept for the longest stretch that I've slept in quite a long time, several hours straight, without waking up. I must've worn myself out on that walk. I woke up today feeling very well rested.

The aide who came here today told me that it was her first day on the job. So far I've seen a different aide each day, and that's stressful, so having someone brand-new to the job sent up an additional red flag. But I figured, there isn't anything that I need done – dishes, laundry, going to the store – that a gal in her early 20's can't handle. Even with the more experienced aides, every time it's someone new, I have to explain what I want done and how.

On the other hand, my apartment looks great. It's very clean. I have all the food that I need, and my dishes and laundry are all done and put away. At the end of my first week with these home health aides, I'd have to say that it has gone pretty well.

## DAY 134 – FRIDAY AUGUST 2, 2013

Today's the hundred and thirty-fourth day of my journey, since finding out that my cancer returned. Getting up this morning, I felt very unstable but I had a fair amount of energy – enough to tackle my daily blog post until I got tired an hour and a half later.

Yesterday evening it was cool and windy out, so I didn't go outside. It was a cloudy day so there wasn't any sunset to watch. I've lost so much weight through this illness that it felt cold when I stuck my head outside. So I walked the length of the hallway on every floor of the building instead. I took a break on each floor for a few minutes. Overall I felt very steady. I figured if I happened to fall or need help, there would be people around who could help me so I felt very safe.

Today my aide was scheduled to come up for a couple hours, plus Susan, the hospice nurse. Also Frank wanted to come by and have me take his picture to go with a job application he was working on. I was nervous because they were all going to arrive around the same time; it seemed like too much for me to handle. I couldn't believe Frank wanted me to take his picture. I thought, *I don't even know if I can still focus the camera, never mind download the photos and make adjustments in PhotoShop!*

Susan hadn't been here since the new situation with the home health aides had started, so she wasn't aware of all the players and my connection with Adventist. I got her lined up with the relevant telephone numbers so she could communicate with them. Susan is extremely competent. Of all the people I've dealt with in hospice, she's really the anchor, the one who holds it all together for me. Also she's always true to her word; it's amazing. When she says, "I'll do this", within a very short period of time you receive confirmation that she did it. It's extremely helpful and satisfying to have that kinda person on your team.

I told Susan that I've been thinking about trying the steroids again. I explained, "When I took 'em before, they wired me up and I was kinda bouncing off the walls. But now, you know, I can hardly *get* to the wall." She agreed that it might be a good idea, and said that she'd call my doctor to discuss it with him.

After my aide left, I closed the door and locked it up. I wanted to bolt it shut because I felt like I couldn't even *look* at anybody else today. Then I laid down for about an hour and a half because I was absolutely and totally exhausted. I thought about the possibility of taking steroids again. Maybe that could reduce the pressure in my head and I'd be more comfortable, more able to function. It seemed funny to me that that was *my* idea. I mean, who's in charge here? Why didn't my doctor or nurse think of it? Anyway, about an hour later the telephone rang, and I was told that Dr. Pine had enthusiastically endorsed the steroids prescription, and the medication would be delivered to my home tomorrow. That was another indicator of what a truly competent person Susan is, because the whole thing was all wrapped up in a matter of two hours. I'm incredibly grateful to be under her care.

It's difficult to find people whom you can *count* on, where you know that if you ask them to do something, they'll *do* it. I often ran into that problem during my career, with regards to hiring people. I'd tell 'em exactly, specifically what I needed, and they'd fall short. Once that happens a number of times, you lose confidence in that individual.

Overall I have to chalk it up as an incredibly productive day today, but also incredibly tiring. Let's just let this day sink beneath the waves.

**DAY 135 – SATURDAY AUGUST 3, 2013**

When I woke up today, I did my little test: can I stand up and walk? Can I *see*? Is there anything that I could do yesterday that I can't do now? Usually the answer is that I can still do what I did yesterday, but not as well.

This morning I worked on my blog and checked on a couple sports scores. I'd completely given up on sports a while ago, but the Dodgers are winning and they're in the top of the division so I'm hooked again. They're my team! So I always have to check them out. As for my plans for the day, Frank was coming over to pick up a disk with the photos from yesterday, Ellen was going to bring groceries and do some cooking, and someone was gonna deliver my new prescription.

The delivery person is usually really amped-up, running around delivering hundreds of these things all over the city. You never know when he's gonna show up. He'll ring the doorbell, 'I'm here with your delivery and I've only got two minutes!" If you don't happen to answer, he just takes off, and you can't predict when he'll come back. Dealing with that drives me crazy. I don't know when to expect him and when he does show up, he wants me to deal with him *immediately*, which is not always easy.

Before Frank showed up, I had to finish working on the pictures I took of him yesterday. He hadn't slept for about 24 hours when I took the photos, so he looked kinda haggard. I used PhotoShop to knock out some of the shadows under his eyes. But as much as I *love* using PhotoShop, cleaning up a bunch of photographs was an overwhelming project that I didn't need today. Frank was coming over at noon, Ellen was scheduled for two, and the impatient delivery guy was going to show up whenever. So as the morning went on, I felt more and more anxious.

Ellen arrived half an hour late. I got upset because she had said she would cook me a nice hamburger and I was getting hungrier by the minute. She finally got started, and I went out on the deck to sit in the sun and relax 'til the burger was ready. I was sitting out on the deck when I heard a knock at the door. I heard the guy say, "I've got a prescription to deliver. Can you accept it? I gotta go." Those delivery guys are like, "I'll give this thing to *anybody*! You got a dog? I'll leave it with the dog. *Somebody has to take this prescription off my hands!*" I'm sure they get paid by the number of deliveries and they have to rush around to all these places to make any money.

I heard him out there and thought, *Thank goodness I don't have to deal with him!* Ellen signed for the prescription and then, all of a sudden, the smoke alarm went off in the kitchen. The burger was just about done cooking when she got distracted by the guy at the door, and in that couple of minutes, it got burned and started to smoke. That set off the smoke alarm within the apartment, but I figured she'd get things under control. I was just starting to relax a little bit when I heard the building alarm go off. The alarm system for everyone. It makes this unbelievably bad announcement: "There's been an emergency reported on this floor! Please evacuate the building immediately! Disabled and handicapped persons, use your evacuation plan. Do not use the stairs or elevator." It repeats *over* and *over* and *over*, with a claxon horn every so often and strobe lights flashing. I knew it would go on until the fire department showed up.

As I listened to it, I knew that the building manager would see that *we* were the perpetrators. The system tells them exactly which apartment is responsible. So within a couple minutes, the manager showed up here, trying to figure out what was going on. Ellen explained what happened, and then he actually asked her whether she knew how to turn off the alarm! He works part-time on weekends and he's never been trained on how to turn off the alarm. I don't know how he expected Ellen to know; *she* doesn't live here!

Finally I heard the fire trucks approaching. They pulled up out front and soon a couple of firefighters came up to my apartment. By now the alarm had been going off for about twelve minutes. That alarm would work well as a torture device at Guantanamo Bay; play it over and over until the person *talks*. The firefighters asked what happened. Ellen said, "I got distracted and left the burger on too long and it set off the smoke alarm." They said, "Show me exactly what happened." This guy wanted to see the actual pan; he wanted to *examine* it. He asked her, "How did you put it out?" She explained what she did, and he gave her big kudos for reacting safely and knowing how to handle it. By the time he was done, the firefighters had examined the entire kitchen. Meanwhile I was still sitting on the deck, waiting for my burger!

After those guys got the building alarm shut off and the last fire truck pulled away, Ellen brought me my burger and I really enjoyed it. We chatted for quite a while afterwards, and she left around 4:30. Then I just caved in like a cheap card table. I laid down on my bed, pulled a blanket over me, and went to sleep for an hour. I was exhausted. It had been a hectic day.

## DAY 136 – SUNDAY AUGUST 4, 2013

I can see why a lot of people don't even get out of bed in the morning. Waking up is the most difficult part of the day. Just as I wake up, I'm well-rested and not in pain. But at that moment I know that as soon as I get out of bed and walk around, the dizziness and fatigue will start up again – everything that makes it difficult to get through the day. So I can see why a lot of people would rather just stay in bed. Get a big-screen TV and watch shows all day. But that isn't my nature; I can't do that.

Often I roll over and think, *Well, just 15 more minutes*. But no, if I give myself 15 minutes, it'll turn into half an hour. I roll over to the other side and I think, *OK, only five more minutes*. But I know where that leads; at that point it really is time to muster the stamina to start my day.

This morning I found out that the next season of *Breaking Bad* starts on August 11th. When I received my prognosis in the spring, I figured there was no way I'd live long enough to see the next season. But if it starts next week and I've still got maybe two months, I might be alive to see how it ends! I never would've pictured myself looking forward to something like that, but I am. I'm very excited about it. This coming season I think Walt is gonna die – or his family will be killed, whom he had initially set out to protect. In any case I expect there will be tragic deaths. Why should I care? I have other things that are far more of an incentive to stay alive. But I *do* care, so the race is on: whose life will end first, mine or Walt or one of his family members?

## DAY 137 – MONDAY AUGUST 5, 2013

Yesterday evening I was resting in bed and contemplating taking a walk outside. I stood up and looked at Johnnie Walker and thought, *There's no way I can do this.* Go outside and walk eight blocks? Impossible. I stood there awhile, looking at the walker. Then it occurred to me, *How do I know it's impossible until I try?* I could walk 25 or 30 feet and *then* quit, but it doesn't make much sense to quit before I even take one step. So I headed down the hall, took the elevator to the lobby, and peaked outside to see what the weather was like. Finally I worked up the courage to take off. As soon as I started walking, I started to feel a little bit better. I knew I could walk at least a couple blocks, which would be *so* much better than nothing at all.

So I walked two blocks, pushed the walker up against a wall, and sat in the sunshine. After about ten minutes I figured since I'd already walked two blocks, I could probably go another two blocks. So off I went, and after a couple more blocks I sat down and took another break in the sunshine. I was actually enjoying the evening! It's incredible though, how you can go from hiking up to twenty miles in the mountains, to where you can barely walk two blocks. But I felt better as I went, and once I'd gone four blocks out, I figured I could handle walking the four blocks back home.

When I stopped for breaks, a lot of people walked by. It was really nice out and they were all wearing shorts. Many were headed to see the Portland Thorns game, the new women's professional soccer team. Others were just enjoying the evening. As I sat there, watching them all walk by, I realized that nearly *no one* looked at me. Those who did, just quickly glanced at me out of the corner of their eye, as though they didn't want to risk interacting with me. I thought of the Bible story about the good Samaritan, where this guy got beat up and left for dead and people just walked right on by, until the good Samaritan came along and helped him. I started to feel as though I was on an alien planet somewhere. I wanted to reach out and touch or connect with somebody but there was nobody out there; they were all engrossed in other things. I was kinda stunned by the experience.

Anyway I finally finished my walk. I had started out super tired, and I ended up super tired. But I *did* have a tremendous feeling of elation and accomplishment, because I didn't give up; I got through my walk even though I hadn't felt like going at all.

Today I started taking steroid pills again. This time I'm taking half as much as before. My doctor said to take it with food, before 8 a.m. Throughout the day, I felt a little less pressure in my head, and I had a little more energy than I had yesterday. Also it seemed like I didn't get as confused when I worked on my blog post this morning. I rested awhile after my aide was here this afternoon, but I didn't have to rest as long as I have been lately. It might be the new pill, but it could also be the placebo effect. I'm expecting this new thing to help, and maybe that expectation is what's helping; I don't know. But overall the day was a shade better from the standpoint of fatigue and alertness, and I'm satisfied with that result. It'll probably take about a week to really see how this drug affects me.

## DAY 138 – TUESDAY AUGUST 6, 2013

I woke up feeling exhausted this morning. After taking a steroid pill yesterday, I got really wired throughout the day, and I overdid everything. When I have energy, I wanna use it right away; there's no way to dole it out piecemeal. So I was overly ambitious yesterday, and that made for a difficult day today because I continued to feel exhausted all day. I didn't get the same boost from the steroid today, so it'll be interesting to see how it affects me as I continue to take it.

*Blessing #37*

> *An interesting thing happened when I went outside for a walk last night. After Sunday evening where I felt like nobody saw me and I was an outsider in an alien world, Monday evening was dramatically*

*different. And I was equally stunned by it. Last night I stopped at my usual regular intervals. As always, I watched people as they walked by. I glance; I don't stare. Five or six people actually looked right at me, in the face, and nodded or smiled or made some little comment. A young woman walked by, smiled at me, and asked, "How are you?" A couple went by and they both smiled at me and said something. It was a stark contrast to what had happened the night before, almost like somebody was telling me, "Yes, there are people out there who actually do care, who have a heart and compassion." It was incredibly nice to get that new message!*

## DAY 139 – WEDNESDAY AUGUST 7, 2013

Today was a Day of Zero Energy. I knew as soon as I stood up this morning that it would be a rough day.

I worked on my blog, formatting the text of the Bible verses and selecting a space photograph to go with it. I'm continually amazed by the photos from the Hubble telescope. Prior to the Hubble, we only had land-based scopes, which were limited in range. Also it was difficult to find a completely dark place on the earth where there wasn't any light to affect the scope. Back in the 1980's I visited Mt. Palomar in California, and they said they wouldn't be able to use their telescope for deep space photographs after another 20 or 30 years because there would be too much interference from man-made light. The Hubble gets beautiful photographs of clouds and nebulas; they're just incredible.

This afternoon I had a meeting with the nurse who's in charge of my home health aides. She said that Susan had contacted her and they'd had a long discussion. So now the Providence hospice program is coordinating with Adventist home health care, and these two organizations will work to keep me in my home, hopefully until my last days. Maybe even 'til the very end, depending on how much pain I have to deal with at that point. Anyway I feel great that everybody's connected and they all know each other; it gives me a tremendous feeling of relief.

The nurse also checked my blood pressure, heart rate and oxygen level, and said they were all good. Sometimes I wonder: if all my vital signs are so great, why am I so sick? What's wrong with this picture? I'm glad my vital signs are all good, but I'd sure like to have more energy.

## 38
# YOUTH, CHOICES, MATURITY, APPRECIATION

**DAY 140 – THURSDAY AUGUST 8, 2013**

This morning I woke up feeling pretty good. I did my usual routine: blog, breakfast, and so on, but the good energy level that I woke up with was gone within 20 minutes and then I was really, really tired. That's gotta be a sign that my illness is progressing quickly, because I used to have at least a couple hours of energy before getting exhausted in the morning. At this point I'm not convinced that the steroids I started taking are giving me much of a boost.

This morning, I got a telephone call from Healthnet, calling to welcome me to their health plan as of August 1st. I'd been enrolled with Providence Medicare until now, and I'd never intentionally made any changes, so I was shocked! The woman tried to pump me for information: please confirm the address and the date of birth and all that. I told her I wouldn't provide any information because this was the first I'd heard about changing my health insurance. I said, "Send me something in the mail that says I'm on a new plan, and then you can have all the information you want." It was confusing and upsetting so I got off the phone as fast as I could.

I've found that as my cancer progresses, anything can throw me off-kilter. Any kind of a complication can knock me completely off the tracks. I called Providence and explained about the call from Healthnet. They looked up my records and confirmed that I was no longer on their plan as of August 1st. I asked, "Who called to make that change?" They said, "We don't know because that information is blocked by Medicare." That meant that the person calling from Healthnet was right; I *am* now on their plan, even though I never made that change. I was so confused.

Then all of a sudden, it dawned on me: what do I care? What difference does it make, which plan I'm on? No difference. It took me a while to calm down and see that perspective, but that's where I ended up. I had to figure that Medicare made the change, but it was frustrating that no one had bothered to notify me.

After that, the day went downhill. I had to deal with my aide, which went fine, but I was anxious about her visit because I had to figure out what I needed her to do. Then Ellen and one of her daughters were gonna come over but they were late. When people don't show up on time, it adds to my anxiety. Anything will trigger my anxiety, especially when people don't do what they say they're going to do. Also they had said they would only stay about 15 minutes, but they stayed much longer. It was just Anxiety City.

It doesn't matter what I talk about with people who visit. It's just the idea of engaging two people in conversation at the same time instead of just one. I try to respond to and address everything that's going on all at once, and I get frustrated. I'm no neurologist so I can't explain it, but it's really really painful.

Then a neighbor from down the hall came over to say that she's willing to go with me for my evening walks. She really wants to be helpful but I don't want anybody to walk with me and I had to tell her this five times before she backed down. My evening walk is *my* time, and I don't care if I fall down on the street and die, it's still *my* time.

By the time all those people had come and gone, I felt like my brain had been through the wringer. I need to take a vacation from all phone calls and visits tomorrow. Mental exhaustion leaves me so tired. I always knew that if I took a 15-mile hike, I would be physically exhausted and I'd get a great night's sleep. Then I'd wake up the next morning really refreshed because I'd been outdoors. I *knew* that. I *didn't* know that mental exhaustion does not work the same way. After a stressful day, you can lie awake half the night with insomnia because of some problem that you can't solve, and you feel wiped out instead of refreshed the next day. Mental stress is serious trouble. I can't take any kind of stress anymore!

## DAY 141 – FRIDAY AUGUST 9, 2013

This morning I woke up with shooting pains in my legs and chest, kind of like muscles that have been overworked or overtaxed. It feels like the muscle tissue can't sustain itself; it's painful and it doesn't have enough energy to work. I ended up feeling like that all day.

It was a very disturbing day. I hate having less energy every day. What am I gonna be able to do as this progresses? Just get up and walk around my apartment, get something to eat from the kitchen, go to the bathroom, and that's gonna be about *it*. It's difficult to face that. I got my blog post done today but then I spent most of the remainder of the day resting. I didn't have enough gas in the tank to do anything else.

The highlight of the day was that when my aide left, she said, "I just want you to know that coming here is a tremendous inspiration for me. Your attitude and the way you're handling this whole thing is really, really inspiring and helpful to me." She said that she feels the same way about a couple of her patients who are quadriplegics, who need help with everything they do. She said, "I can't tolerate it when people tell me how difficult their lives are. I tell them, 'If you think *your* life is difficult, spend a day at work with me and see what I see on a daily basis.'" It was a huge thing for me to hear all of that! It's not my goal to inspire people, but if I *do*, that's wonderful to know.

I already feel a strong bond with all of my home health aides. They're all committed to trying to keep me in this apartment until the very end; several have told me that. It's really wonderful to have people like that on my side. I know they don't get paid well; they do their job for a lot more than just the money. To me, that makes them heroes and I really appreciate what they do.

## DAY 142 – SATURDAY AUGUST 10, 2013

I was determined to go outside for a walk yesterday evening. My evening walk is the perfect way to gage my physical condition. Never mind my blood pressure, oxygen level, all the stuff that the nurses check on. I know how I'm doing based on how far I can walk. When I set out last night, I realized that I was walking much more slowly than before. I only walked a couple of blocks, then decided my usual eight blocks would be too far so I cut it short and headed back. I was thoroughly exhausted by the time I got home. Unless things change, my evening walk is now officially shorter, which I see as another milestone in this process.

It appears that not having any energy when I wake up in the morning is the new reality too. That and taking lots of breaks in whatever I'm doing, like working on my blog. I'll spend ten minutes at the computer and 20 minutes resting. Once I'm up in the morning, I get dressed and make the bed, so if I lie down, I just lie on top of the blankets. I've totally switched to wearing an all-sports look: gym shorts, gym socks, gym shirt, tennis shoes. Anyone who sees me wandering around would probably think I'm big into exercising and all that – a total physical fitness guy. My t-shirt says "Run" on it, with a Nike swoosh logo. My outfit really couldn't be more comfortable! But it probably seems a little odd to be terminally ill and walking around looking like a gym rat.

Ellen came over for a long visit today. I know she wants to be helpful, but I also think she just wants to talk. Maybe it's healing for her, after all the rocky times we've had over the years, during our marriage and afterwards in raising our son separately.

Ellen and I met in Eugene, Oregon when I was a junior in high school and she was a sophomore. She had moved to Eugene from Oak Ridge, a town about forty miles away. One night I went to a party and Ellen was there. I spotted her right away because she was very pretty.

I thought, *Wow, who's that?*, because I'd never seen her before. It was her first weekend in Eugene but she knew some of the kids because she had lived there years earlier.

I gravitated to her right away because she was new and she was pretty and I had a car and she might need a ride home later. Naturally I always tried to be helpful with providing rides home, especially if someone was really attractive and I wanted to spend time with them. We hit it off and definitely liked each other and talked about going on a date, but she got a ride home with some other friends that night.

The next day, I visited a friend. He and I were sitting in his front room, talking about – about the only thing we *ever* talked about, which was girls. I told him about meeting Ellen. "She's really pretty, and she's from Oak Ridge so she doesn't know many people here. I really like her and I'm planning to see her again," and so on. I was just going through that routine with him when we both looked out the window just as a girl was walking by the house. He said, "Oh wow, speaking of new girls, look at *her!*"

He explained, "She just moved here a couple weeks ago and she walks by every day. She's got the whole neighborhood worked up."

I said, "What? *Her?*"

He replied, "Yeah! That girl, right there, walking by!"

I said, "That's Ellen! That's who I've been telling you about!" His jaw dropped clear down, because apparently nobody had made a move to try to meet her. Meanwhile I'd already arranged with her that we would see each other again. He was flabbergasted.

### Blessing #38

*That's how I met Ellen. We went together for a really long time, through high school and afterwards; she was the classic high school sweetheart. We broke up a few times but always wanted to get back together. Eventually we got married and then later divorced. So we have a long history. The main thing that we have now is our son, and you can't avoid having a bond with somebody with whom you've had a child. We had many, many years of conflict, most of which we worked our way through. So now it's really nice to be able to look back at that, at the end of my life, and know that we're friends. It's a blessing to just sit and chat with Ellen about all of that.*

## DAY 143 – SUNDAY AUGUST 11, 2013

Yesterday evening I wanted to go out for a walk. I figured I'd be too exhausted to go more than a couple blocks, but I was amazed, when I got outside and started walking, how good I actually felt. I took my usual breaks along the way, certain buildings where I stop and sit and watch people go by. I don't go where I'll be overrun with people since I want a solitary walk.

I've mentioned how people react to me out there. If you see someone sitting on a walker with their head hanging down, you'd have to assume they're not doing all that great. There was that one night where a lotta people stopped and interacted with me and that was amazing, but that's pretty unusual. For the most part, people don't wanna see someone who's down and out. They avoid making eye contact and I think it's because they don't want to imagine themselves in that situation. They think, *Could that be me someday?* And they look elsewhere.

Last night when I reached my third rest spot along the walk, I glanced down the street and saw a group of four young guys with skateboards. I wondered whether they were homeless. One of them was walking about ten or fifteen feet ahead of the other three. As he walked by, he turned to look at me and made a face at me. He put his hands up behind his ears and made a weird sound with his mouth, like a baby babbling, "blebble-ebble-lebble-ebble," something like that. I was shocked; I had no idea why he would do that. He was ridiculing me! Then he stopped, turned away, and continued walking up the street. The other three were behind him and they just walked right by and didn't even look at me. It was the most bizarre thing that's happened to me out on a walk. I was stunned and disgusted by it.

As they walked away though, I started chuckling. I thought to myself, *There but for the grace of God goes my son.* Ha! I mean, that could've been *my* kid! Wow! I thought, *What a contrast, between my son Allen and someone who would behave like that.* I had no animosity toward that kid because I realized: here's someone who's had no background, no upbringing, no guidance, no *nothing*. No child would act like that if he'd had any kind of parenting at all. I realized what the circumstances were, and I felt that I handled it really well. Thank God that kid is not *my* son!

So I blew that off and headed on down the street, and ended up going the whole eight blocks. It felt like a huge accomplishment, since I hadn't thought I could even go *two* blocks.

Another thing happened last night. When I got home, I saw Lev, who lives in the building. He only has one leg because he had the other one amputated due to diabetes. He asked me how I was doing, which he asks me every time I see him. I've told him two or three times that I'm in hospice care, but he just sort of blows that off. So last night I said, "Y'know, Lev, we've talked about this a number of times. I'm in hospice care. Do you understand what that is?" I explained that the government covers your healthcare during your last few months – meaning you're supposed to die sooner or later. I tried, but he still didn't really seem to understand it. He constantly comes up with things that he thinks I should do, or drugs I should try, and I'm tired of it.

He started on a rant. "You can't give up, you can't just believe you're gonna die!" It got irritating pretty quickly and we had a heated discussion. I finally said, "If you don't understand my situation, please stop asking me how I'm doing, because I don't want to have this same conversation again and again." But he kept on going. "How can you give up like that?" I said, "I gotta go," and I walked away. He just doesn't understand; he keeps making suggestions and trying to make me hope for an improvement; maybe he figures that's possible as long as I'm still able to walk. It was a very annoying and frustrating conversation.

This morning I woke up with the most energy I've had in four or five days. It felt really good. I worked on my computer and I didn't have the usual confusion and fuzziness; mentally I was much sharper.

I got my blog post done and handled a couple-a telephone calls. I've come to realize that whether I want to spend time with someone depends an awful lot on how they view my situation and ask about it. If they *constantly* ask me detailed questions, it's just absolutely, totally annoying.

It was a bittersweet day. Karen took me out to visit my mother's grave at Mount Scott, and I realized that I can't go out on any more drives. Here I'm referring to my birth mother, Linda. The drive was really, really stressful. I was physically uncomfortable riding in the car, and very anxious. After Mount Scott, we drove past the house she used to live in, in outer Southeast Portland, where I stayed with her for a while when I first moved back to Portland. We also drove to Mount Tabor, where I've hiked many, many times.

I had mixed emotions about our drive. I enjoyed visiting my mother's grave for the last time, but driving past the house she used to live in brought up a lot of negative memories. She had a stepson living with her, whom I didn't get along with. So I went out for my last ride ever, and ended up seeing a place that I hate more than any place in Portland! Maybe we should've headed out to the Columbia River, to see something beautiful. There's nothing beautiful about that part of Southeast – there's misery, poverty, drugs, burglaries, crime, and a lot of hurting people. I hate that part of the city and it'll take some time to get that out of my head.

## DAY 144 – MONDAY AUGUST 12, 2013

Every evening when I want to head outside, at first I feel like I don't even have the energy to get out the front door. I wish I could express how exhausted I am at that moment, and how impossible a walk looks before I start out. But I head out down the hall, take the elevator downstairs and get out on the street, and somehow my adrenaline kicks in. I always feel like I really want to *do* this; I feel inspired. When I manage to complete my full eight-block walk, to me that's always a huge accomplishment, even if I stop to rest half a dozen times along the way.

After the trip to my mother's grave yesterday, the whole thing came home to me in a very powerful way, that I want to be buried, not cremated. And I don't want a formal funeral or anything like that, just a small, inexpensive graveside memorial service. I'm not gonna be there anyway! I want to be embalmed, and have the cheapest possible casket. Cheap, cheap, cheap embalming; cheap, cheap, cheap casket; cheap, cheap, cheap graveside service for family and friends. Also the cheapest possible marker, a flat stone in the ground, similar to what my mother has. Seeing my mother's grave was a big eye-opener for me.

So today was very hectic. Seems like Mondays always are. They usually start off with a barrage of phone calls, mostly medical people picking up where they left off last week. I had to sort out some confusion with my prescriptions this morning, but it got all straightened out.

Recently I've been thinking about how long people live, and why some have much shorter lives than others. Obviously some people make bad choices and do dumb things. And there are so many things that just happen to people, so they don't end up living a life like mine, seventy-six years. I would've like to reach 80, but I still feel incredibly blessed to have made it *this* far!

As a teenager, I had two or three incredibly close calls where I could've easily lost my life. It was always while riding in other people's cars. Today I thought about one particular incident that happened when I was 17. I still get chills when I think about it. My friend Pete and I went to a football game, University of Oregon versus Oregon State, in Corvallis. A home game for the Beavers, an away game for the Ducks. Back in the 50's, you could just drive to the game and buy a ticket that day, whereas nowadays, of course, you can't even get near the stadium if you haven't ordered a ticket online.

Pete borrowed his dad's car, a brand-new Pontiac. Back then a Pontiac was a fairly good-looking car but its main feature was the very powerful engine. If you put your foot down in one of those babies, you had 400 horse-power, something like that. It'd just blow you off the road. Usually in my group of friends I did all the driving because I was the only one who had a car. But on that particular night, I was a passenger. I don't recall who won the football game, but I was feeling pretty good on the way home so it must've been the Ducks. In those days the Beavers and Ducks both had terrible football teams.

After the game, we decided to try to get some beer. Our usual ploy was to stand around in front of a liquor store until somebody just a little bit older than us came by. If they were right around 22 years old, they'd still remember what a hassle it was to get beer before they were old enough. We'd say, "Hey, can you get us a six-pack?" Quite frequently, people would say, "Yeah, sure, I'll get you a six-pack, what do you want?" We got our beer and started back to Eugene.

Pete decided to punch it out a little bit, because the car *was* powerful and fun to drive. We were cruising down Highway 99. A few miles north of Eugene, there was a cut-off that connected with River Road which ran down to Eugene. The cut-off was a very straight, two-lane rural road with fields on both sides. We turned the corner, and my friend put his foot into it so we got goin' pretty good. We were maybe a mile from the railroad crossing when we saw a train coming from the left.

The train was coming down from the north, and we were heading east. It was still quite a ways down the tracks, and suddenly my friend decided to go for it. He just pushed it to the floorboard! We were probably going about 90. Plus we'd been drinking and it was dark out. At one point I looked over at him, and he looked back at me like he wasn't quite sure of himself. I figured he'd stop if he thought we wouldn't make it. He seemed to be playing a little game of chicken with me – wanting *me* to say, "Hey, don't do this!" before *he* chickened out. It was so foolish; neither of us wanted to be the one to admit to being afraid and slow it down. I was certainly calculating it: a train and a brand-new Pontiac flying toward each other at top speed; what's the trajectory gonna be? Who'll get there first?

It got scarier and scarier every second. It *looked* like we had the lead and maybe we'd make it, but we couldn't be sure. He just kept his foot on the floor, kept flyin' along. I was starting to doubt we could make it. Then I could hear the train engine and especially the horn, as the engineer picked up on the fact that we were racing it. I assume he was warning us to slow down. As the train engineer, if he was concerned about a collision, I think *he* would've started slowing down; he wasn't gonna play chicken with a car. We got closer and closer and I really couldn't tell who was gonna be there first.

And then we had no longer had a choice. We reached the 'point of no return', where it was too late to stop. I was getting really scared. Suddenly the track was right in front of us. We crossed it and the train was probably only a hundred feet away, maybe less. It was *that* close. We hit the track, which was kind of elevated because it was on a berm. We were *moving* and we went airborne. The car was like a bullet streaking through the air and he managed to keep it going straight. When we finally hit the road on the other side, the car hit so hard that it bottomed out. It sank clear to the ground and I was surprised we didn't break all the shocks. We bounced; we were airborne again before the car came down and bottomed out a second time. Then he was able to get it under control and he started driving normally again. We both realized we had just come within just a few feet of being killed. We looked at each other but didn't say anything. It all felt *very* strange. We just kept driving and we never talked about it after that.

For many years, I would sometimes wake up in a cold sweat, thinking about that incident and how close we came to just annihilating ourselves, for no reason whatsoever. Also I often felt that the life I had beyond that point was bonus time. I thought, *Hey, technically I shouldn't even be alive right now.*

So today I've been reflecting on several situations – close calls – that were almost as bad as that. My life could've ended, yet I was spared and here I am now, 76 years old. People really make some stupid choices. They have the free will to do that. Especially teenagers with fast cars and alcohol; I'm sure it happens every Saturday night throughout America.

# 39
# MOBILITY THROUGHOUT A LIFETIME

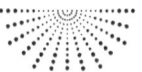

**DAY 145 – TUESDAY AUGUST 13, 2013**

Last night I was out for my walk and while I was stopping to rest, someone came up and said, "Hi Don! How are you?" I looked up; there was a lady whom I've photographed. It was really nice to see her! I bump into her occasionally. She has a very pretty face, but the first time I met her, based on her appearance, I thought she was homeless or very close to being homeless. She's very sweet but you can tell that she's had a difficult life.

When we did the portrait project at the Meals on Wheels center, we had the sign-ups about three weeks in advance. This lady signed up for it and she was very excited about it. I used to hang out at the center a lot, and she came up and asked me several times what to wear for the portrait and whether I thought she'd get a good picture. She told me she hadn't had her picture taken in about 35 years. I reassured her every time we talked, because she was obviously very concerned about it. She was grateful for the opportunity but also very apprehensive.

On the day of the portraits, she wore a nice shirt with a cowboy vest. She seemed very nervous, and kept going to check her appearance in the restroom mirror. But her picture came out really cute, and when she came back a week later to get her prints, she was just absolutely thrilled. Since then, each time I've seen her over the past couple years, I've noticed that she looks better – healthier, happier – and she has said that her living conditions have improved. But last night she was especially excited because she's been accepted into a HUD building, right across the street from the park, that was recently remodeled. She waited three years to get in there. Her appearance last night was 200 percent different from the first time I met her! It's so wonderful to witness a person transition like that. Seeing her and knowing that she finally has a steady place to live – that made my day.

That was the end of yesterday; now onto today. I was physically very tired today but I seemed to have a burst of mental energy and I got a lotta work done on my computer this morning. It was a productive morning. Later Ellen came by and brought groceries, and my aide was here and she did a great job getting chores done.

Throughout the day I was thinking about life choices, in general, and more specifically my personal choice to get involved in volunteerism about ten or fifteen years ago. Volunteering turned out to be highly rewarding, once I found the right situation. The Meals on Wheels center, right around the corner from me, was a great place for me to do a variety of volunteer projects, such as the portrait project that I've mentioned. Alisha, the wife of the pastor at church, is a professional photographer. She and I took all the portraits and then touched them up in PhotoShop. Seventy people participated! We printed one 8-by-10 photo for everyone, and I made up CDs for everyone with several of their best photos so they could take that to a photo printing place to get more copies. That was such a satisfying project.

**DAY 146 – WEDNESDAY AUGUST 14, 2013**

I woke up today feeling charged-up and ready to tackle the day, but physically having very little energy. It turned out to be an insane day in terms of dealing with people. I make appointments with people and put them on the calendar, but I still forget. I get confused on what time this person's coming over and what time that person is gonna call. Even when I'm right about what time someone's coming over, I get anxious waiting for them. If there's more than one person scheduled to visit, I get anxious because it feels like there's too much going on. So I can easily back myself into an incredibly small box of stress.

My aide was here and we had a lot of decisions to make regarding food prep and storage, to make things easier for me to put a quick lunch together. Then a nurse came from hospice, but it wasn't Susan because she's on vacation. So for 45 minutes I had to answer all kinds of questions from someone new. That's always tiring. As soon as she left, the phone rang and it was the county social worker who's coordinating my in-home care. He said we had an appointment to meet today and he was already in the building for other meetings anyway. I had completely forgotten about that, but he's a key player in my situation so of course I said to come on up. It was very nice to meet him. He's been involved with this building for about six years so he's on top of everything here. But he had a lot of questions, and by the time he was getting ready to leave, I couldn't even hold my head up anymore. My head was literally hanging down. He saw how tired I was and finally left me his business card and showed himself out.

After that I basically stumbled over to my bed and lay down on top of it. I didn't see how I could do *anything* else. But then of course, the phone rang. It was my son, making his daily call. I talked with him a little while but soon I had to tell him, "Son, I gotta go, I can't talk anymore." Not three minutes later the phone rang again! I was gonna let it go but it was somebody I really wanted to talk to so I answered. After that, I thought my head was gonna explode. I really did. I just lay there for about an hour and a half. I didn't wanna eat, or do anything on my computer, I was so exhausted. So it was a very difficult day. I'm gonna try to go outside for my walk later, but at the moment I have to say there's no chance I'll be able to do it.

## DAY 147 – THURSDAY AUGUST 15, 2013

Today felt like the most difficult day I've had since I became sick in the first place, because of fatigue. Yesterday I didn't have the energy to prep anything for today's blog post, so this morning I had to start from square one with that. I usually get my post done and then do some prep work for the next day's post, and finish by noon time. Today I didn't get done with this day's blog post until about six in the evening. I'd sit there and work on it until I ran out of energy, then lie down on my bed for a while, then get up and work on it some more. At one point I contemplated skipping it for the day, but I thought that would feel too much like a defeat so I stuck with it. It was extremely difficult to put the whole thing together.

In the evening I decided to try and take a walk, although at first I didn't think I'd even get out the door. I managed to get up enough energy to at least *try*, so I got downstairs and went outside. I got to the end of the first block, and I told myself, *If I can get to the end of the first block, I know I can get to the end of the second block.* It wasn't fun. It was drudgery. I felt the fatigue in my calf and hamstring muscles and it got worse every step I took; it felt like those muscles would just stop working altogether. It's disheartening because taking those walks is critically important to me.

**DAY 148 – FRIDAY AUGUST 16, 2013**

This morning I woke up feeling pretty energetic; I was amazed! I got up, had breakfast and worked on my blog. I had the whole blog post done by 9:30 a.m., and even did some prep work for tomorrow's post. Yesterday it took me 'til six o'clock; today it was 9:30. A huge difference. So I figured I'd use the day to catch up on some things around here that had gotten out of hand. There were piles of papers everywhere, things that I had to look through, odds and ends. I got my desktop cleared off and made telephone calls, and it was really a productive morning. I finally crashed about noon time; at that point I could feel that real fatigue coming back.

This afternoon my aide helped me get rid of stuff in my kitchen cabinets that I know I'm not gonna eat. It just confuses me when I open the cabinet and see, for instance, peanut butter and jam – because I can't eat that stuff anymore. When I open the fridge or the cabinets, I only wanna see stuff that I can eat.

After the aide left, I was as tired as usual, but I kept fighting it. I'd lie down for 15 minutes, then get up and get more stuff done at my desk for 10 or 15 minutes. Using that technique, I eventually got a lot done.

A funny thing happened today with my neighbor down the hall, who constantly wants to get involved in my care. On a number of occasions, I've said to her, "Hey, I'm handling this on my own here." But apparently she went down to the aide station on the second floor and had a nice little chat with them about me. She told them that they shouldn't be letting me go out for walks in the evening, all by myself. Of course the aides don't have any say in that, but she gave them a little lecture about it. Ha! It's kind of annoying when other people take it upon themselves to wander around the building and talk about my medical condition.

## DAY 149 – SATURDAY AUGUST 17, 2013

When I wake up in the morning, I have to stand up very carefully and see what's gonna happen next; I can't just jump outta bed and start walking around. I hesitate until I know what's working and what's not. My breakfast routine involves getting out the milk, a can of sliced pears, and cereal, and then pouring and mixing all those ingredients in a bowl. I was working on that this morning when all of a sudden I felt like I was gonna have a seizure. My head just felt really weird. It's the same experience I've had before but this was much more intense. I quickly set the cereal bowl down on the counter and stood there hanging onto the wall. I was able to clutch the walls, literally, all the way down the hall, to go and lie down. My head felt really strange, as though I couldn't hold it up. It was the worst episode of combined fatigue and balance trouble, or whatever it was, that I've had so far. I could hardly navigate at all.

Because of that, I've decided that my walk last night was definitely my last outside walk. Last night I went out and I felt very insecure, even with my walker. I mean, I *know* I'm going to die, but I don't wanna break my arm or something! That would cause me so much more grief in my final days, nursing a broken bone. Also I have to stop and rest every forty or fifty feet which hardly makes for a pleasurable walk. Having to battle just to get from point A to point B, instead of relaxing and enjoying the evening, is not pleasant. So it's just prudent that I knock it off. I can't do it anymore. It's the end of a long, long, long journey.

I think back to when I first started walking. As a toddler, around one year or so, I probably started running around on my feet. All of a sudden my parents said, "Uh-oh, he's walking, we gotta get 'im some shoes!" You start walking and your parents get you shoes because you could stub your toe or whatever. The whole process starts with that first little pair of baby shoes.

My next form of conveyance was a little toy pedal car that my parents bought me. I'd sit in it and pedal hard to drive it around. Not long after that, I got a tricycle. Around the age of six, I got my first two-wheel bicycle. I rode it around on the street right in front of the house. When I got my first full-size bicycle, around the age of nine, that gave me real mobility for the first time in my life. I could go from block to block and really start expanding my horizons with that bike.

Then of course at 16 years old, the big event happened – that's when I got my first automobile. I bought it with money I had saved from various part-time jobs. A 1949 Ford Victoria. And once I had my car, I could've driven all the way across the United States if I'd wanted to. That was the early progression of my mobility.

Over the years I owned many different cars. Then, back in 2007 I had a detached retina, which really cut down on my ability to drive. I just didn't feel comfortable behind the wheel anymore because I liked driving fast. I gave up my car and decided to rely on my bicycle, my Schwinn, and public transportation. Occasionally I'd rent a car if I really needed one. That's how it was up until a few months ago. Back in May I was still going on wonderful bike rides, until that one night in the emergency room when the doctors pretty much diagnosed that the cancer had entered my brain. That ended my biking. I hung the bike up out on the deck, and I just look at it with fondness now, realizing that I'll never ride it again.

When I lost my bike, I felt that I had lost the majority of my mobility because wherever I went, I would have to walk. A few months ago I could still walk a mile or two, but I've gone from that down to just a few blocks. Last night, struggling to walk outside, I realized that that was the final thing. I can't go outside and walk anymore. My whole life has gone from that first pair of baby shoes to my trike to owning cars, and back to bicycles, buses and trains, and just walking, to now essentially nothing. I'm not gonna do any of those things anymore. My very last means of transportation is my walker. I feel comfortable with it but I don't have the energy to go very far. The next thing will be that I won't be able to walk at all. It's a lot to lose in a very short period of time and I've felt sad about that today.

# 40
# PLANNING FOR THE END AND BEYOND

**DAY 150 – SUNDAY AUGUST 18, 2013**

When I woke up today I just had nothing, no energy at all. I sat on the edge of my bed for about five minutes before I could even stand up. But I was determined to maintain my usual routine, so I got started on my blog post and had my breakfast. After that, I had to lie down and rest.

Today I've been thinking about life choices some more. We start very young, making choices: who our friends will be, how we're gonna treat people. Some of our choices have profound effects on our lives, while of course most of them are just day-to-day decisions like what to wear or what to eat. This past week I think I made my final big choice.

When I first got sick, I made up some papers explaining what I wanted to happen if I were to die on the operating table. At that point I wanted to be cremated, because it seemed like the most economical and efficient choice. Expedite everything, get it done, get it over with. And I wanted my ashes thrown into the Columbia River, in Cascade Locks, Oregon. The thing is though, when other people have told me about cremation and throwing someone's ashes in the water or some other place, actually it has always turned me off. I wouldn't criticize anyone for doing it, but for *me*, traditionally Christians are buried, not cremated. Throughout history, a Christian burial has been a mainstay tradition of the church. I had always thought that when I died, that's what I'd want: a burial, a funeral at my grave, and then I'm off to the next dimension, whatever it is that Jesus has in store for me. I thought of cremation last year because I figured it'd be the easiest option to deal with, but it wasn't *really* what I wanted.

I started reconsidering the burial question about a week ago after Karen took me out for a drive and suggested visiting my birth mother's grave. It hadn't occurred to me to go and visit her grave before I die, and even at that moment I'd just wanted to go home because I was so tired. Karen asked if I wanted to visit my mother's grave and all of a sudden a light went on; *Why didn't I think of that?* So we went up to Mt. Scott National Cemetery. My mom was buried with her husband, who was a military veteran.

Old forgotten feelings flooded over me at the grave. For the first couple-three years after she died, I had so enjoyed going there. I went frequently, then just tapered off over time. Eventually I found myself up there once a year, walking around and talking to my mom. That was my routine. I thought maybe my mother could hear me, I don't know. Last week I suddenly remembered what a pleasant experience that had been. I had done that in California too, visiting my adopted parents' grave and talking to them. Obviously it wasn't like an actual conversation; it was more a matter of saying things that I wish I'd said before they died. All week I've been remembering visiting the graves of other people I've known and lost, for instance a friend who was killed when we were both in our 30's. So I have a pleasant feeling about graves; they're not morbid at all. You go to a person's grave to celebrate that person and talk to them.

So I realized that I do. not. want. to. be. cremated. Changing the cremation plans that I had in place became a very urgent and immediate goal last week. I had to start the process of finding an inexpensive grave because I can't afford twelve thousand dollars or more for a grave in one of these high-class cemeteries in Portland. Ellen stepped in and started making phone calls for me. I remembered that Skamania County, in southern Washington on the Columbia River, has some Pioneer Cemeteries, potentially a lower-cost option. Ellen called the county, and then she and Karen went to look at the options. They sealed the deal on a grave site at a Pioneer Cemetery right alongside the river. I couldn't make the trip with them, so they showed me pictures of the stunning views from there – the mountains, the water – I couldn't have asked for a more beautiful spot to be buried. It's wonderful to know that instead of being thrown in the river, I'll be beside it.

**Blessing #39**

> *If there's any place in Oregon that represents me, it's the Columbia River Gorge. When I moved back to Oregon from southern California in the 90's, I haunted that place. I hiked more than 60 trails, multiple times; I spent day after day after day exploring that place. It means so much to me to have a final spot on this earth in that particular location. And if people come out to visit me, they'll get to see a really scenic place as well. I'm really grateful for this.*

## DAY 151 – MONDAY AUGUST 19, 2013

Last night I didn't feel up to a walk outside, but I grabbed my trusty walker and went out to walk the length of the hallway a couple of times. When I started out, I got a little burst of energy. I felt like, *It's time for action; I'm gonna get out there and I'm gonna...ha! Whatever!* I walked the length of the hall and back, took a five-minute break, and then worked up the strength to do it again.

This morning I woke up feeling exhausted and didn't have any strength at all, as usual. I did my same routine, got my cereal and worked at my computer. I had some paperwork and checks to write, and my aide was here mid-day. Now I'm having the aides fix my lunch, instead of doing it myself.

I talked with Allen today about the gravesite arrangements, and he was happy with that; he thought it was a good plan. Ellen came over for a while, and we talked for so long that I got really tired. I get exhausted just having a conversation; my brain starts to throb. Just from talking.

**Blessing #40**

> *On the other hand, it's a blessing that I can still talk and converse with people. My doctors believe the tumor spread to my brain so it could have affected me much more, where I wouldn't have been able to have a conversation. Being able to connect with people, in person and through phone calls, is so important to me at this time.*

## DAY 152 – TUESDAY AUGUST 20, 2013

I'm taking my evening walks in the hallway now. It's not much of a walk but it *does* make me feel good. I know that at this stage of the game it can't improve my health – the cancer will win – but it gives me a mental boost that I can still walk a ways. It's just the idea that I'm not completely finished yet. So that was last night.

When I woke up this morning, in addition to fatigue, I was feeling more pressure and some pain in my head. I feel like the proverbial handwriting is on the wall, and there's gonna be more pressure and pain, and something's gonna happen – some kinda brain event. Maybe an aneurysm or a seizure. Now it's just a matter of doing all I can every day, and waiting for that event.

This morning I noticed that readership has dropped way off on my blog. I bet people are thinking, *Well, maybe this guy's not on the verge of dying after all, plus it's the same basic thing every day, so let's move on and find something else!* Ha! But I'm not doing it for anybody else. I wanna post the beautiful book of John on the internet and I'm enjoying doing it. It gets me outta bed every morning!

**Blessing #42**

*Actually three things get me outta bed – the blog, and sending a text to Karen and a text to Allen, so they know I'm still alive and I'm up and doing something. Every morning is a huge struggle. Without those three things, I seriously believe I'd just be lying in bed all day long. Susan says there are people who just stay in bed; they don't get up, they don't do anything. I feel very blessed that I have the incentive to get up, even if I end up taking a lot of breaks throughout the day.*

## DAY 153 – WEDNESDAY AUGUST 21, 2013

Last night I couldn't muster the energy to go and walk up and down the hall even once. I feel as though one thing after another just gets taken away from me and it's discouraging. I just couldn't get out and walk.

This morning around 10 am, the day started to fall apart because I started receiving one telephone call after another. Once again I felt like if the phone rang one more time, my head would explode. To me it's stunning how many decisions you have to make when you need to have people helping you. I have to decide what the aides should do when they're here. It took three phone calls to arrange a time for Susan's next visit. Building management made me some extra keys and called to ask when they could deliver them. Nobody else will make decisions for you if you can still make them! Even the little decisions pile up and wear me out; I feel absolutely pulverized. On top of that, there are the pleasant phone calls, the friends whom I *want* to talk to, and those conversations get tiring as well.

My advice to anyone who's young is to start saving money right away because if you ever end up in similar circumstances, you'll wanna have the money to hire a personal assistant to handle all the phone calls and decisions so that you don't have to. It's hard for anybody else to understand how a hospice patient feels when all these people need pieces of their time to make decisions.

## DAY 154 – THURSDAY AUGUST 22, 2013

Today I saw Susan, who's been on vacation so I haven't seen her for at least a couple weeks. When she arrived, she readily saw that I had really deteriorated quite a bit since the last time she saw me. She can tell; she knows what she's looking for. She doesn't bother measuring my muscles anymore. I don't want her to anyway; it would be too scary since it feels like they're all wasting away. She checks my blood oxygen level and listens to my lungs to see what's going on.

Based on her assessment, within a couple weeks I'll probably be bedridden. The tumors in my liver and brain are getting fat off of whatever I eat, leaving me with no nutrients or energy, and that'll progress until I really can't get up and do anything anymore. She said that at that point I'll be better off with a hospital bed. Hospice will provide that. But at that point I'll also be needing a higher level of personal care, like help with bathing. So within the next few days, hospice will coordinate with the county to figure out whether I can get more help from the aides who already work here, or whether I'll have to go to an adult foster care home. I really wanna stay here where it's nice and peaceful and quiet, so I hope they can work that out. Right now it's just kind of a red tape ball, but we should know for sure by Monday.

I was dreading hearing the word "bedridden". I knew it was coming but I didn't wanna ask; I did the ostrich thing and stuck my head in the sand to wait it out. Susan said that once I'm bedridden, I probably won't wanna eat anymore. Then it's maybe another two to three weeks to end the whole thing, because my caregivers can not force me to eat or drink if I refuse to. There could be more pain through this whole process but they have plenty of medications for that. So it looks like it'll be at most four weeks, and this whole thing will finally be over.

## DAY 155 – FRIDAY AUGUST 23, 2013

I did another hallway walk last night. I'm finding that some nights I can't even get out there, while other nights I can make it down the hall and back a couple times as long as I take a break at each end. You can find interesting things everywhere you go, if you just pay attention. For instance, that hallway has a life of its own! People often go in and out of their apartments and the elevators. Most of the time they don't even see me sitting at the end of the hall. Last night, a guy came out of his apartment, talking on his cell phone. He went up to one window where you can see into the courtyard of a neighboring apartment building. I overheard his half of his wacko conversation with his friend who was in the courtyard down below, talking about a woman who was also hanging out down there. It sounded like they both got quite a laugh at someone's expense. After a while he hung up and turned around, which was when he finally saw me sitting thirty feet away. Woops! I wasn't trying to eavesdrop, but he didn't bother to check whether anyone was listening, either. People are not very observant.

This morning – well, getting out of bed in the morning is going to be more and more of a battle for me. The whole question of whether I'll be staying in my apartment 'til the end has weighed on my mind all day. That has me very, very upset; it's causing a lot of anxiety. The thought of moving to a new place, when it's just a matter of a few weeks, the idea of turning my life over to somebody who's gonna take care of me – having somebody tell me when I'm gonna eat or sleep – facing those possibilities doesn't give me a good feeling.

## DAY 156 – SATURDAY AUGUST 24, 2013

I woke up with quite a bit of energy this morning got my breakfast and finished my blog post by about 10:30. Then all of a sudden I was just overwhelmed with fatigue. I laid down on my bed, and I was knocked out until my aide knocked on the door around noon. When I got up at that point, I had *nothing* in the tank. I could barely walk! I just let her in and I went back to bed. It was a kind of a waker-upper, how serious the fatigue was and how quickly it came on. I'll have to be prepared for it in the future, knowing it can hit hard at any time.

I wear my tennis shoes when I take my hallway walks; seems like it takes me about ten minutes to tie them nowadays. I can't get the strings straightened out and they get all wadded up. But once I get out there, I feel better – I don't know why. Maybe it's a sense of potential accomplishment.

There's one disturbing thing that bothers me out in the hallway. In one apartment there's a married couple, a man and woman who are probably in their early 60's. The wife had a stroke about four or five months ago. I've known people who worked to recover from a stroke, and I've never seen anybody try harder than she does. She does her exercises, takes walks, goes up and down the stairs. I have the greatest admiration for her, because she's doing everything in her power to get well. It's a joy to see her, and her level of commitment. We don't communicate because she doesn't speak much English but, every time I see her, I give her a thumbs-up. She has a very devoted person in her life, maybe her daughter or a friend, who is skilled in physical therapy. This person comes over daily to help her with the exercises, and I have the biggest admiration for her too. It's an amazing thing to try to help somebody recover from a stroke; I know because I went down that road with my mother.

The problem is the man in the house. I understand, these things happen. One person has a stroke and suddenly the other has to take care of the house and the meals and everything. The care-taker ends up with a bunch of stuff that maybe they've never done, and they definitely don't wanna do. But this particular guy yells at his wife all the time. Sometimes I just wanna knock on his door and tell him to stop! She doesn't need that; she's under so much stress as it is. In my estimation, it's really cruel. I wish I could intervene but I doubt it would do any good. Anyway I heard a little bit of that this afternoon, and it was very disturbing.

## DAY 157 – SUNDAY AUGUST 25, 2013

This morning I woke up feeling exhausted. It's not like the old days, where I woke up and had some energy for at least a little while. But I got my cereal and started to work on the blog. Suddenly the program developed a glitch, and I couldn't get the type to set up in the right size. I tried *everything*. Finally I just cancelled the whole post and started all over again. I definitely didn't need that to happen. I reposted the whole thing and it worked the second time around, but it took tremendous mental energy. This kinda stuff would-a been a piece of cake a year ago! After that I just went back to bed for a couple hours.

Early this afternoon, Emma stopped by after church. We had a terrific conversation. I've found that I get exhausted speaking with *some* people, but not with others. I enjoy talking with Emma. But there are others with whom the conversation doesn't feel connected and I lose interest quickly. I get frustrated and I want it to end. I tell them, "Sorry, I can't talk any more." Emma *isn't* one of those people.

Later on Karen came over. She and I have been trying to figure out how to write a eulogy for my memorial service. She came up with the idea of making a recording of me giving an overview of my life, and then building a eulogy around that. So we did the recording, and I think we got all the key points in. Well, I left out about three or four volumes, but unfortunately we can't fit *everything* into a eulogy. Ha! Karen agreed to write it, and I feel tremendously relieved and peaceful about that.

## DAY 158 – MONDAY AUGUST 26, 2013

If it weren't for my blog, I would probably stay in bed until noon. The blog sets up a timetable; I have to get certain things done within a certain period of time, including eating my breakfast. I woke up this morning and put my feet on the floor, and I wasn't goin' anywhere. I didn't want to. But after about five minutes I thought, *OK, I have someplace to go, I'd better get to it*. So I got outta bed, and went over to the computer. Once I made it that far, I started to feel a little bit better – mentally if not physically – because it was something to focus on.

The big aggravation today was that my aide didn't show up. Nobody told me this would happen. I called the aide station downstairs and they said I wasn't scheduled today. A schedule glitch or something. It was extremely upsetting. I made two or three telephone calls to the head office, the big headquarters of the aide station place, and I couldn't get anything outta them. They didn't know what to say or do; I felt like I was dealing with a bunch of amateurs.

Then I started re-thinking my idea of staying here in the apartment. I won't be able to deal with people like that as I get worse, making telephone calls and having to find people to come over. The situation brought up so many doubts, regarding how to handle my final care. It went on all day, being passed from one person to another to another. Finally they called back and apologized and reassured me that someone would be here tomorrow at twelve for sure. But I'm still re-thinking my whole situation. What happened today was a huge red flag. If I go to adult foster care, I won't have to worry about somebody coming in because they're *always* gonna be there. I have to give this some serious thought – maybe I'll have to sacrifice my independence here, for the sake of more peace of mind. I don't wanna have to call people all day long to get help. It was a frustrating and extremely tiring day.

**DAY 159 – TUESDAY AUGUST 27, 2013**

Last night I went out in the hallway for my walk. First I spun my walker around at my end of the hallway and sat there a few minutes conducting an analysis of the whole situation. Finally I decided to take off. I went about slug-speed, just one step after another, but I felt OK. Then I sat at the far end of the hallway and spent five minutes staring back down *this* way until I worked up enough energy to return. When I got back home, I felt good. Every day it feels good to pound that disease with a good punch in the mouth. It's like saying, "You haven't completely knocked me out yet!" I've still got a couple punches left in me!

This morning was tough; I wake up feeling like I wanna get up but I nearly can't. I finally decided I had to get my breakfast put together, which turned into a really huge mess because I had run outta milk. I didn't know what to do. I had some frozen yogurt, which I tried to thaw out in the blender and the microwave so that I could pour it over my cereal. But frozen yogurt doesn't turn into *milk* when it thaws. When I combined the two, the cereal didn't soak up the thawed yogurt so I had a crunchy, gooey, not-very-tasty mess in a bowl. It was so frustrating that I almost threw the bowl off the deck. I mean, you can't just eat a bowl of dry Rice Chex!

My aide came by at noon and fixed a nice breakfast of scrambled eggs and pancakes with butter and syrup, and that tasted wonderful. She also picked up groceries for me, so I'm all set for tomorrow morning.

Today there was more discussion with my healthcare providers and organizers about whether I'm gonna stay here or go to foster care for my final days. Karen thinks that the people who are pushing for foster care may be worried about incidents like yesterday, where the aide didn't show up due to a schedule glitch, so they're being protective. I don't know what they're trying to protect me from – having to eat my cereal with ice cream? I mean, I'm gonna die soon anyway!

Meanwhile, starting in a few days, I'll have more coverage here in the building. The aides will come up whenever I need them instead of just being scheduled for two hours a day. That makes a who-o-o-ole bunch of difference right there, so I wanna try it and see how it goes. Can we all work and play together right here in this building, with that arrangement? If not, I can always change my mind and go to a foster facility later on; that is my choice.

## 41
# THE HANDWRITING ON THE WALL

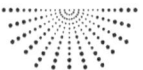

**DAY 160 – WEDNESDAY AUGUST 28, 2013**

*L*ast night when it got to be time for my little hallway walk, I realized that I just didn't have it in me. I didn't even bother to go out the door.

This morning it was really tough to get out of bed, and as I worked on my blog, I had trouble getting my fingers to work properly on the keyboard. I was exhausted but I got the blog post up. Then I wanted to go back to bed, but first I had to sit there for a coupl-a three minutes more to work up the energy to walk back to my bed. I m having more and more difficulty moving around, and I have to accept that now I need to use my walker even just walking around my own apartment.

Close to noon – I'm not saying I had enough energy – but I got enough of *something* to get out of bed and get dressed for the day. I always wear one of my Nike shirts that say "Run" on them. Every time I see myself in the bathroom mirror, it gives me a lift and kinda makes me laugh. *Run*. Just do it, get out there, make it happen... I went through the gyrations of getting my clothes on and fixing the bed, and my aide showed up right at noon on the dot.

A new aide came here today, Cherise. While she was here, I was listening to the speeches from the Mall in Washington, DC. It was the 50th anniversary of Dr. Martin Luther King, Jr.'s "I Have a Dream" speech. Cherise got interested in the speeches as well, and we ended up having a very interesting conversation. She's black and she has lived in Portland her whole life. Her parents were from the deep south and she still has other extended family in Birmingham, Alabama, so she has heard a lot about the history there. I told her about my visit to the Birmingham Civil Rights Institute a few years ago, and I enjoyed hearing her thoughts about the speeches today.

At some point this afternoon the hospice pastor called me. We've never met in person! We've tried and it hasn't worked out. But he calls me every week.

I'm gonna take my regular bath tonight, to soak and relax. It still gives me a feeling of well-being, and helps to dissipate pain. Some people tell me it's not a good idea for me to still take baths when I hardly have the energy to get out of a chair. I say that even if I have to get a pulley system to pull me out of the tub, I'm still gonna take a bath every night!

**DAY 161 – THURSDAY AUGUST 29, 2013**

### A LAST TIME FOR EVERYTHING

*Last night I contemplated going outside and doing the hallway thing, but just getting up and going over to my walker and starting out the door, I was too wiped out and I had to scrap the idea. It's another one of those situations where I've lost something for the last time. Walking is good for you – it decreases pain and swelling – but I barely have the energy to walk around the apartment, let alone get up and down the hall. I may give it a shot one of these nights, just to see, but my guess is no.*

Today I just couldn't get a blog post done. I didn't get enough done yesterday to prepare for today's post, and I ran into glitches and I couldn't figure it out. I just finished my breakfast and didn't get *anything* done, and went back to bed.

Throughout the day I had the most difficult routine I've had in quite a while; several people were scheduled to come by. First my aide came in and fixed me lunch. Then I had something very exciting scheduled; I was getting my hair cut. It was getting a little long and I like it short. My usual hair-cutter came to my apartment and set up shop. She brought a few tools and a barber cloth to wrap around me.

Oh, when she started cutting my hair, I felt *so* good. It was really wonderful. The thing I liked most was that she knows my situation, and she handled it just great. I've gone to her every few weeks for the past several years, and we reminisced just like the old days. It was a delightful experience! When she was finished, my head felt *so* good. I asked her to cut it a little shorter than usual, and she did a great job.

Later Susan came by for a meeting with Corinne, a nurse from the healthcare organization that manages the aides. They discussed how my coverage with the aides is gonna change. Not only will I have more coverage, but they'll have specific days to do certain tasks: laundry one day, cleaning another day, and so on. So I won't have to figure out what I need them to do each time they're here, which is mentally exhausting. In the end we were all on the same page that I *will* stay in this apartment until the end, unless I need skilled nursing care for pain or for handling some bodily function, like dealing with a catheter. In that case I'd go to the hospital. Susan is an absolutely awesome lady.

Overall it was an extremely productive and worthwhile day. There was a bit of a failure in that I didn't get my blog post done, but I've reconciled myself to the fact that it might not happen every day. I was amazed again by how much energy the brain gobbles up, how you can be completely exhausted just sitting still. I think we take it for granted, the work that our brains do all day long. Dealing with stress, working the intellect, running all the body's mechanisms and stuff that we're not even conscious of. So even though I rested a bunch of times today, now I feel like a melted-down M&M candy, just kinda "eh."

**Blessing #42**

*It was a very blessed day, and I'm happy that I have so many people around me who really, really care about what's going on in my life here. They really care! Even the healthcare people, I can tell. My hospice nurse – I've been so fortunate to have one of the most professional and kind nurses that I've ever run into my life.*

## DAY 162 – FRIDAY AUGUST 30, 2013

When I woke up this morning, I felt as exhausted as I did yesterday, only worse. Ha! It just keeps getting *worse!* I got my feet on the floor and sat there 'til I had the energy to stand up. I started on my usual morning routine but it was a struggle. I went back and forth from the computer and the cereal bowl, to my bed, then back to the computer and the cereal bowl. It took me two hours to eat the whole bowl of cereal. I just couldn't do it all at one time. I got that blog post done, but I made a determination today, that I can't do a post every day anymore. It's too much for me.

Other than that, my aide was here, and I saw Ellen, and one of her daughters, and later Karen came by. It was almost as busy as yesterday! And I spoke with a former coworker; we'd been phone-tagging for a while but now he's planning to visit next week, along with some other people whom I'd really love to see at least one more time.

## DAY 163 – SATURDAY AUGUST 31, 2013

Last night I thought about going for a walk in the hallway but no, there ain't gonna be no more walking. That's the, I don't know, umpteenth thing that I can't look forward to anymore right now. It's really sad to lose something for what you know is the final time, something that you care about. Based on how I feel, and my inability to walk nearly anywhere without Johnnie Walker, I would say I'm headed into the last days of this – this *thing*.

I've been thinking about how some people hang on to life a little longer, like they're waiting for something. When my son first went to the University of Oregon, my mother was living with Catherine and me. She'd had a stroke and we had 24-hour in-home care for her. While I was away to see Allen get settled at college my mother had been hospitalized for a few days with a heart problem, but since she didn't seem to be in imminent danger, she was sent home before I got back. She was waiting for me to come home and tell her about the trip, and about Allen. She could no longer speak, but I knew she could hear me and understand me. We could also communicate with our eyes, and write short notes.

I got home around six o'clock and told her that if she felt like it, I would tell her about the whole trip after dinner. I could tell she was really tired, and she said she would wait 'til the next day. So I kissed her good night and said, "Tomorrow after breakfast, we'll sit down and talk." She had this big smile on her face, and she went to sleep. My mom died that night, but I really believe that she had been waiting for me to come home and confirm that all had gone well with Allen.

I spoke with Susan about this subject a few days ago. She said that yes, people hang on. For *something*. Their brother whom they haven't seen for 25 years, or a child they haven't seen for a while. She said it's very common. In this process I've discovered that three things have been incredibly helpful to keep me going: my blog, my recordings with Karen, and my final preparations. Nobody wants to leave a lotta chaos and confusion at the end. For instance I had to make the decision about burial or cremation. Janine has said that her husband, my friend Ronald, was obsessed with getting things in order, for *her*, and that that definitely kept him going. He wanted to have everything sorted out before the end.

I really like the story of General Ulysses S. Grant, the commanding officer of the Union forces in the Civil War. He was also, of course, president of the United States. Despite his career, he ended up almost broke, and he developed a terminal illness. He still had a family and he wanted to provide for them, so he became obsessed with writing his autobiography. The autobiography of a president and General of the army in the Civil War would obviously be well sought after. So he sat on his front porch with a big blanket wrapped around him, and wrote and wrote and wrote and wrote. He wrote two volumes, and not long after he finished, he died. The autobiography was a huge success, and it provided for his family. I admire that kind of courage. People will do *anything* in their power to hang on to get something done!

**DAY 164 – SUNDAY SEPTEMBER 1, 2013**

When I woke up this morning, I realized things had deteriorated even more last night than the previous night. I put my feet on the floor and I didn't wanna go anywhere. Just flat out didn't wanna go anywhere. I find that kinda scary because the nurse said that within two weeks I'd probably be bedridden. I've already gone through a little over a week since she said that, so within one *more* week I could be bedridden.

**Blessing #43**

*It was really, really difficult to do anything this morning. Fortunately, my new arrangements have started with the caregivers from the second floor; all I have to do is call, and they will come up and take care of whatever I need. That's a huge relief. The timing on that is a miracle because I don't think it would've been possible to get through the coming week without the extra care. I feel very blessed because that takes away a lot of anguish regarding what will happen to me.*

I don't really get hungry anymore, aside from when I get up in the morning. I almost have to force myself to eat, after breakfast. And I can no longer prepare my food. Several days ago I made a bowl of cereal. It took four trips to the kitchen to put it together. Just a bowl of cereal! Get out the bowl, go back and lie down for five minutes. Get out the cereal and milk, go back and lie down. And so on. Even making a smoothie, I thought, *I gotta put these ingredients in, and stand here and blend it up,* and I was totally overwhelmed! It's another big turning point in this entire situation.

Then there's the inability to get around, never mind using the walker. Once I'm bedridden, I won't be able to get up. At that point, life will have taken a serious turn for the worse, because I'll be stuck there. Without my phone, I think I'd go crazy in that situation. I've been reflecting on this today. I'll have to wait for someone to come help me to get outta bed. That's gonna be very difficult to take!

For now, although it's a *real* struggle, I'm still able to use my walker to get around the apartment and out onto the deck. I had a really wonderful time sitting outdoors in the sunshine today. So invigorating. It's funny; when I'm sitting there with sunshine covering my whole body, I feel so relaxed and it's the only time of day when I feel normal and healthy. I actually feel like I'm sitting out on the beach out there.

But I see the handwriting on the wall with this whole thing. It's hard to give up all these things along the way and I've been doing all I can to fight it. A lotta people don't bother to fight; they're dying and they just give up and hang around watching TV. To them, it wouldn't be a big issue to give up biking or walking because they wouldn't even realize they were giving something up! I'm still willing to fight, but when you don't have any strength, you can't fight anymore. This day had a lot of plusses – I spoke with some people whom I really love – but I have to get ready for the next episode in the saga. Things are gonna change rapidly here soon.

## DAY 165 – MONDAY SEPTEMBER 2, 2013

What can I say, it's been a tough day. Hey, that rhymes!

The day started out with a whole bunch of communication snafus. I have to send out text messages to two or three people every night. Last night's messages didn't go through, so those people were all upset. Same thing happened this morning. I didn't know that it wasn't working! Karen is on a business trip to the east coast so she made a call to the aide station downstairs, and someone came up and fixed my phone so that it all got straightened out.

We all realized that we cannot rely solely on my cell phone to get emergency help; I need a backup system. I've been working on that today with help from Ellen, Karen, Allen and so on. The thing is, it seems like every day there's another communication nightmare. Who's gonna do this? Who's gonna handle that? Not just with the phone. The medical providers: "Do you need a hospital bed?", "Do you *not* need a hospital bed?", "When should we bring in the hospital bed?" I just want it to end! I wanna relax and just go to sleep.

On the good side, I had a visit from Karen's friends and mine, June and Irving. That was very nice; I really enjoyed their company. At this point, when people visit, it's gonna be the last time I ever see them. Karen helped me make a list of everyone who's been calling and when they can come by, and that's a life-saver because I just can't remember anything anymore.

On the negative side, today felt like another huge loss for me. I didn't have the energy to go near my blog, let alone put up a post. I just can't get over there. It's too perplexing and it just drives me nuts. I've got one post ready to go, and hopefully I can put that up tomorrow. But I don't know. I'm considering just posting, "Don is no longer able to post at this time," or maybe "Stay tuned," so that people know I'm still gonna try.

## DAY 166 – TUESDAY SEPTEMBER 3, 2013

When I woke up this morning, I realized that my goose is cooked. Ha! I felt much worse than yesterday. Well, it's to be expected.

---

### A LAST TIME FOR EVERYTHING

*For three days I had a blog post ready but I hadn't posted it. I went out to my desk and it took an awful long time just to get into a comfortable position at the computer. I got the blog post done, and when I finished, I just kinda leaned back in my chair and realized that I'm not gonna do any more posts. I just do not have the energy. I can't do it anymore. Along with that realization came all the sadness because I felt that I had been doing a good thing. That's been kinda hurtful today.*

---

Today the chaos continued over getting a backup phone line in case my cell phone isn't working again. People were making phone calls and trying to put all kinds of things together, and I didn't even ask them to do it. Then I remembered that my internet connection includes a landline. So I already actually have a backup; I just haven't used it since I've lived here. Fortunately Frank was planning to visit this afternoon, and I knew he would be able to handle it. He had said last week that he was feeling somewhat left out of the loop, so I was glad I had a chance to ask for his help with something really important. Sure enough, one phone call to my internet provider took care of it. Later Ellen brought me a cordless phone. That was a relief but dealing with these issues and logistics day after day after day is just really, really taxing. I keep thinking, *When are these difficult days gonna end?*

## DAY 167 – WEDNESDAY SEPTEMBER 4, 2013

Wednesday was a big fat nightmare. Around noontime, the building fire alarm went off. I figured it was a false alarm since it happens frequently. People burn something while they're cooking and that sets off the alarm, so I never really pay any attention. I usually check for smoke in the hall and if I were to see any, I would leave the building. But I didn't see or smell anything, so I waited to see what would happen. I can't get myself outside anyway: my aides downstairs would have to come and get me outta here.

After about five minutes, two of the aides knocked on the door. One of them said, "Don, I've got really bad news; everyone has to evacuate the building. We'll wheel you out on your walker chair and then find some way to get you comfortable outside."

I replied, "I can't do it, I don't have the strength to go out there."

They said, "We have to. The fire department has ordered us to evacuate the building." So they got me on the walker and pushed me out. It's not a wheelchair, so I had to hold my feet up.

We got outside and everybody was lined up along the front sidewalk. A lotta people hadn't seen me for a while because I haven't been out, and they wanted to say hello but I was too tired. The aides took me aside and tried to find a more comfortable spot for me. They had all sorts of ideas like going to another building or dragging a chair out from our building. Finally after an hour, when I felt like I could no longer sit up straight, one of the aides arrived to go to work, driving a minivan. She got a parking space right in front and said I could rest in the vehicle. I put the seat back, rolled up some clothing under my head for a pillow, and it felt amazing, because I just couldn't sit outside any longer.

About an hour after that, they let everyone back in the building. The aides got me upstairs and into bed, but we heard that the power wouldn't be back on until two a.m. Lanterns were delivered to everyone. I was worried for about a minute and then I figured I'd just sleep through it all until tomorrow. After that, a couple of the aides came up and checked on me a few times. I think the lights were back on by midnight, so I really wasn't in the dark for very long. I was just thankful to be able to relax and rest in my bed.

### Blessing #44

> *That was a terrifying experience, but I started thinking about how amazing it is to be living here. Think about war zones or disaster areas, and people like me, in a rickety little hospital. I can't imagine how terrifying that would be, compared to having the people and the care that I have here. I am really so blessed.*

## DAY 168 – THURSDAY SEPTEMBER 5, 2013

My big appointment for the day was with Susan. We were gonna talk about whether I need a hospital bed and when to make that decision. She also evaluated my mobility and what I'm capable of physically. She said she could see that my illness has progressed a tremendous amount in just the past week since she last saw me. She ordered a wheelchair for me, in case of another power outage or whatever, because sitting outside on my walker is too much. Also that way, if I'm up for it, somebody could take me outside for a walk.

We had a real heart-to-heart talk about my condition. Susan has always been straight with me, which I've asked her to do. She told me, "The way you're progressing right now, I would say that you have three to four weeks." I asked her what to expect from here on out. She said that I'll get weaker and weaker, and won't want food, and I'll basically lie in my bed all the time, sleeping. At some point my body will just shut down. As a hospice nurse, Susan has seen this happen to a lot of people.

But I still see a lot of positives. I haven't had any pain. If I do end up having pain, it'll be in the final stages, at which point we'll add morphine to the situation. With morphine, you don't know what you're doing but you're pain-free. And at that point you don't want food anymore. Which is fine because the digestion process can cause a lot of discomfort. It probably sounds crazy but I actually feel better now that I have a real timeframe, instead of just guessing.

## DAY 169 – FRIDAY SEPTEMBER 6, 2013

The big event today was that I said good-bye to one of my very best friends. Pastor Phillip has been a support to me in Portland for over 20 years, and it was marvelous to see him because our conversation was very uplifting. He's going to handle my funeral, including delivering the eulogy.

Other than that, I think a few people called me but I don't remember their names right now.

### DAY 170 – SATURDAY SEPTEMBER 7, 2013

Today I had the opportunity to go sit outside in the sun on the deck a few times. Also, my aides have been really helpful. They're here several times a day. Those two things are huge blessings.

The other big things today were that Karen was back from her trip, and my son finally arrived in town. He came by late in the evening for a little while, then went to stay at Ellen's house.

I also got through my bath routine last night, which is easier now that I have a nice bath chair in there. Taking a bath is still really invigorating. My aide waits outside while I take my bath, in case I need help.

Other than that, Frank called me today, and I was able to eat.

So overall I accomplished everything that I had hoped to do today. On any day that I manage to finish the day and then get back into bed on my own at night, I rate that as a huge day and I thank God for it.

### DAY 171 – SUNDAY SEPTEMBER 8, 2013

It's Sunday, Sept. the 8th, and it's the 171st day of my journey.

Waking up this morning was even worse than yesterday, considering my lack of energy. But I was able to get up, get my clothes on and get ready for the day. I always wear my street clothes – running gear, Nike tennis shoes, all of that. It's good to look the part! I don't want to look like some guy who's just lying around in bed all day.

I had a good morning, after having a wonderful night's sleep last night. But even when I sleep really well, if I lie in one place for too long, I get a cramped muscle and I wake up with pain. My muscles are all just right next to the skin, with no protection or cushioning.

I had breakfast around noontime. Then Emma called and said she was coming over, and my son Allen was scheduled to come over around the same time. Emma and I had a really wonderful conversation, and she got to meet Allen. She didn't stay all that long, and I had a longer conversation with Allen after that. My son and I have a really good relationship right now, but I'd like it to get a little deeper at this point. I'm sure that'll happen in the coming week. Anyway I was really happy to see him.

Later in the afternoon Karen came over and we got my stereo system rearranged in my bedroom so that I could just turn it on with the remote without having to get out of bed and walk to the living room. That was a big accomplishment today. I'm mainly gonna listen to music; it'll be great to have that, and I'm really excited about it.

**Blessing #45**

*That's pretty much it for today. I feel blessed that I got through the day. I certainly would like to have more energy, but getting through the day is a big thing. I'll quit there.*

# EPILOGUE

**DAYS 172 – 175, and somewhat beyond**

After September 8th, 2013, Don no longer had the energy to continue making recordings. The last time he and I had a coherent conversation was when I saw him on Wednesday, September 12th. He said he was "seeing" people he'd known long ago who had already died. On September 13th, Don's son called me close to noontime. I was working in an office not far from downtown Portland. One of Don's home health aides had reported that Don had had an unusual burst of energy and really wanted to get up and have breakfast that morning. Apparently it's not unusual for someone to behave that way just hours before death. I don't recall much else about that phone call; afterwards I headed over to Don's apartment right away. By the time I arrived, he was only marginally conscious. I believe he realized that I was there, but it was impossible to have a conversation with him.

Around four hours later Don died, surrounded by people who loved him. Besides me, Ellen was there with her son Allen and daughter Renee, and Emma was there. We had all been gathered around him for a while, maybe an hour, and at some point we realized he had stopped breathing. I am so glad that he got his wish: when the time came to leave this life, he was at home.

On Friday the following week, there was a graveside memorial service, conducted by Pastor Phillip and attended by family and friends. It was a gorgeous September day, at a stunning location in the Columbia Gorge. I'm so glad that Don got his other wish: burial in the scenic region that had so inspired him through countless hikes.

A few days later there was an informal gathering of Don's former neighbors, who had no way to get to the memorial service. I led them in singing Don's favorite hymn, *Amazing Grace*. The Russian guy (from Day 90, who was so insensitive to Don in the elevator) seemed baffled by the gathering. He had seen me with Don several times so he tried to ask what was going on. I speak no Russian so I didn't know how to tell him that Don had died. I finally drew my finger horizontally across my throat to indicate death; that he understood, and he was suddenly very surprised and saddened.

**Beyond the Transcriptions: Potential Lessons**

As much as I hope Don's story is interesting and enjoyable, I hope it can serve a practical purpose too. Often people feel awkward around someone who's seriously ill or dying. It's understandable. Close to death, a person may not look healthy or happy and perhaps it's obvious that they're suffering. Maybe they don't seem like the person you remember. They may be facing fears and decisions that a healthy person has never considered, and that's what they want to talk about. They can no longer do many things that they enjoyed, which healthy individuals may take for granted – eating a fabulous meal, taking a scenic hike or a tropical cruise, driving a car, patenting a new invention, seeing the New England Patriots win or lose a game, starting a tribute band, holding their first grandchild, flying a helicopter, whatever it is. Instead they're more concerned about who's going to feed or bathe them when they can't take care of themselves anymore.

Take the person's wishes into account when making plans – they may not actually want one last trip to Vegas or a family reunion or whatever. They might not have the energy, or won't want others to see them tired or weakened by disease. Also, I'd advise against telling lengthy stories about how you beat the disease from which the person is now dying.

Friends and family of a dying person are sometimes afraid to reach out, or they turn away and slam a door, because they *don't know what to say*. What questions are OK to ask? How can they express their terrible sadness, knowing they're going to lose someone they love? Is it OK to laugh with your uncle who's in hospice care, who has suddenly developed a morbid sense of humor to cope with what's happening?

Don talked about how he wanted to be treated, as well as describing many conversations that went awry and upset him. He was one among the millions who die on this planet every year, but I'm willing to believe his advice would apply to many: reach out. Contact or visit the dying person. Spend quality time with her or him (silence your phone!) but don't talk or visit for too long, especially if that person gets tired easily. It takes effort to host visitors, more so if you're exhausted by disease. Ask, "How are you?," but don't ask for extensive medical details. Cry or express your sadness, but don't act so distraught that the dying individual has to make the effort to comfort *you*. Be willing to say, "I love you and I will miss you," but don't burden them with guilt for *leaving* you.

Help with tasks that the person can no longer do, once you're fairly sure they want and need help. Don always wanted to have a plan and have control over his situation, and he felt great about his daily accomplishments as he became less and less capable. But he was tremendously thankful to have help when he truly could no longer put clothing in a front-loading wash machine or pick up a couple items at the grocery store.

I believe it truly benefited Don to have several daily objectives – his blog, our recordings, his walks around the neighborhood. Without his John in Cyberspace blog, he felt he'd be tempted to stay in bed all morning instead of getting up. One evening he was sure he didn't have the energy to take an evening walk, but he convinced himself that he couldn't be absolutely certain unless he actually tried to go. These things gave him a daily sense of accomplishment, and distracted him from a constant focus on declining health. Blogging, recording, and walking may not be every dying person's idea of time well spent, but some other project might be beneficial, if the individual is self-motivated to do it.

Don't launch into detailed conversations about future events that you know a dying person would love to witness – but probably won't be around for – unless you're sure they want to discuss those things. For Don, those future events included the last few weeks of *Breaking Bad* and the college football season. *(Go Ducks!)* He didn't want to spend a lot of time discussing and speculating on subjects that he figured he wouldn't be alive to witness.

Listen with an open, relaxed frame of mind, whether you're in the same room or chatting on the phone. Medical realities can truly be frightening: "Uncle Frank was always so strong and healthy and *now* look at him – will that happen to *me?*" Put those thoughts out of your mind if you can, until *after* your visit or phone call. Don't project yourself into their situation. If you're sitting there thinking, "I sure hope I never end up like Grandma, forgetting which of her siblings are still alive," you're not really listening or being present to Grandma when she needs you. Take the time later on, by yourself or in conversation with a (healthy) friend, to express your thoughts and fears.

If someone you love is slowly headed toward the end, meaning you'll be facing that person's death with them for weeks, months or more, take care of *yourself* as well. I was extremely fortunate (as Don was) that Don had access to experienced home health aides when he began to need them. So I won't address the topic of finding and relying on people to help with a dying person's physical needs so that family and friends can take a break. But the situation did take its toll on me.

It drained my energy without replenishing it, and I had moments of intense sadness and hopelessness. I sought out a therapist with whom to discuss my emotions and how I was dealing with them. I also had a couple avenues of temporary escape: multiple business trips as part of my job in 2013, and weekly rehearsals, playing trombone in a jazz band (*Thank you NoPo Big Band!*).

In the end, this is what I feel most fortunate about: five months is a good, long stretch of time to say good-bye to someone and express things such as "I love you; you're so very important to me." I was seven years old when my father died of cancer. I was too young to understand that he was terminally ill, and I wasn't taken to see him in the hospital during the last couple days of his life, so I didn't have a chance to say good-bye. I wouldn't have understood what that meant at that time anyway. I couldn't comprehend that he was on his way out.

With Don, I believe I felt most of the pain of losing him before he was even gone. We said what we needed to say to each other, and I didn't end up with the pain of "things left unsaid." I was seated beside him – with others whom he loved – when he breathed his last breath. I had the honor of helping to organize his memorial service, including contributing the eulogy, for which he'd given his approval several weeks earlier. I'll be forever grateful to have known Don and been part of his life at a point when I could really make a difference to him, and grateful that he was so willing to talk about his experiences during those last five months.

Years after Don's career in publishing ended, he thought his John in Cyberspace blog was his last publication. Through reporting daily on his journey, I'd have to disagree and say that *this story* is his last publication.

Rest in peace, Don McCall.

## ACKNOWLEDGMENTS IN ALPHABETICAL ORDER

I want to express gratitude to some people who were in my life when Don was, and also to those whom I met later on, who encouraged and supported my efforts to create this book. This list includes many people who appear in the book under different names, so I'm *mostly* only listing individuals by their first names below. If the vagueness of my list leads you to question whether I included you or not, please err on the optimistic side and accept my thanks!

Anne and Scott
Barry Shatzman
Chris and Diane
Dana and Gerald
Denise
Don
Eva-Maria
Jean and Jim
Laura
Maggie and Jim
Margaret
Marian and Matt

My immediate and extended family
Pam and her family
Steve Jackson
The 2013 NoPo Big Band Social Committee
Todd L. Palmer
Wilson Construction, Inc.

<u>All</u> with whom I rehearsed and performed music when
I lived in Oregon

When I read a book I'm always curious about the author's appearance, so I'm including a photo of Don and me. (Photo credit: Gemma, with PSU Family Photo Day at Fieldwork, Portland, OR, 5/12/2013)

Here are links to Don's blogs, still available for reading:
http://johnincyberspace.blogspot.com/
http://squarepeople.blogspot.com/

My Question-of-the-Week Recording Project
https://www.reverbnation.com/questionoftheweek

www.ingramcontent.com/pod-product-compliance
Lightning Source LLC
Chambersburg PA
CBHW030315100526
44592CB00010B/439